ISBN- 13: 978-1523275281

CreateSpace Independent Publishing Platform

Nara Japan, 758-763: A Study and Translation of

Shoku Nihongi, Tenpyō Hōji 2 -- Tenpyō Hōji 7

By Ross Bender

For William Theodore de Bary

Acknowledgments

Thanks are due to many people for assistance in a variety of ways in this ongoing project. Sakaehara Towao originally inspired me to undertake a translation of the full text of *Shoku Nihongi*. Alexander Vovin has given invaluable advice on my translation of the Old Japanese *senmyō*, and has been an unflagging and enthusiastic supporter of the project from the beginning. Terufumi and Mayumi Futaba in Kyoto have, in addition to being long-time friends, helped to make arrangements for my stays in Nara. Hirabayashi Akihito and Kimoto Yoshinobu have generously shared time from their busy schedules to answer my questions. Peter Nosco, John Bentley and Bryan Lowe read the introduction and made helpful suggestions. Bentley and Lowe aided with various parts of the translation, as did Victor Mair, Fangyi Cheng and Haiqing Wen. Molly Des Jardin, Michael Williams, and Brian Vivier of the East Asian collection at Van Pelt Library, University of Pennsylvania provided answers to several queries. Other assistance over the years has come from Deborah Co, Karl Friday, Drew Gerstle, Cynthea Bogel, Matthew Stavros, Alexander Mescheryakov, and Ekaterina Komova. However, while this volume of translations will necessarily contain many flaws, they are all of my own making.

My wife of over thirty years, Sylvia, has been extraordinarily patient with and supportive of my rather esoteric interests, and my son Julian aided me greatly with the formatting and publication of the text. Although the old proverb warns to "Never trust an editor," both Michael Cooper and Paul Swanson have in the past been both trustworthy and extremely helpful.

This translation is dedicated to William Theodore de Bary of Columbia University, who introduced me to ancient Japanese thought and also served on my dissertation committee.

Abbreviations

JGKU	*Jingo Keiun*
MNZ	*Motoori Norinaga Zenshū*
NR	*Nihon Ryōiki*
NS	*Nihon Shoki*
OCOJ	*Oxford Corpus of Old Japanese*
RR	*Ritsuryō*
SKT	*Shinshaku Kanbun Taikei*
SN	*Shoku Nihongi (SNKBT)*
TPHJ	*Tenpyō Hōji*
TPJG	*Tenpyō Jingo*
TPKP	*Tenpyō Kanpō*
TPSH	*Tenpyō Shōhō*

Table of Contents

About The Translation

Shoku Nihongi 続日本紀 (Chronicles of Japan, Continued) is the much
neglected official court record of the eighth century, covering roughly the years
697-791. It was presented to the court of Emperor Kanmu in two recensions,
794 and 797. Fujiwara no Tsugutada 藤原継縄 (727-796) and Sugano no
Mamichi 菅野 真道 (741-811), the chief compilers, made the initial presentation
of thirty-four volumes in 794. In 797 Sugano no Mamichi and others presented
the final work in forty volumes after the death of Tsugutada. Sakamoto Tarō
outlines three stages in the compilation of the work. Stage One was compiled at
the court of Emperor Junnin and comprised thirty volumes covering 697-757.
Stage Two, at the court of Emperor Kōnin, consisted of a revision of these thirty
volumes, although Volume 20 covering the critical year of 757 was apparently
lost in the process. Also at Kōnin's court, twenty volumes were compiled
covering the years 758-770. Stage Three, at the court of Emperor Kanmu,
involved editing the material up to 758 into twenty volumes, then revising and
adding twenty further volumes to take the history up to the year 791.[1]

---

[1] Sakamoto, tr. Brownlee 1990, 90-96. Sakamoto 1970, pp. 167-219 and especially pp. 358-360
has a useful overview of *Shoku Nihongi*'s compilation, as does SNKBT SNI 1989 pp. 494 -505,
with a compact chart on p. 501. See Nakanishi 2002, pp. 1-18 for a more recent overview of
scholarship on *Shoku Nihongi* and analysis of the process of compilation. Nakanishi's entire
book is an intensive textual analysis of *Shoku Nihongi*.

The chronicle has a long textual and manuscript history [2], yet was not as popular as its predecessor *Nihon Shoki*, or *Nihongi*, which was regularly lectured upon at the imperial court from early Heian times onward. At the end of the 18th century the great philologist Motoori Norinaga published his study of the sixty-two imperial edicts, or *senmyō*, inscribed in Old Japanese in the chronicle. Norinaga, however, had no use for the bulk of the document, written in classical Chinese of the variety current at the early Tang court.

Not until the postwar period was there was a resurgence in Japanese scholarship on the document, with a group in Osaka founding the journal *Shoku Nihongi Kenkyū* in 1954. In fact it was not until the very end of the twentieth century that the first major critical collated edition was published. This was the Iwanami edition in five volumes, comprising volumes 12-16 of *Shin Nihon Koten Bungaku Taikei* (SNKBT), published from 1989-1998, with a sixth *bekkan* index and *nenpyō* published in the year 2000. Edited by a team headed by Aoki Kazuo, this monumental edition presents the *kanbun* text and a *yomikudashi* on facing pages, with copious headnotes citing divergent editions and a plethora of footnotes and supplementary endnotes. The *Kanazawabunkobon*,[3] comprising *Maki* 巻 11-40, dates from the Kamakura period and is now located in the Hōsa Library in Nagoya city.[4] Supplemented by

---

[2] SNKBT SNI 1989 pp. 523-563 has the most comprehensive treatment of this history.

[3] 金沢文庫本

[4] 名古屋市蓬左文庫

Maki 1-10 dating from the *Keichō* era[5] the forty-volume collection known as the *Hōsabunkobon*[6] is the primary basis for the SNKBT text. Facsimile editions have been published by Yagi Shoten (1990-93) and Rinkawa Shoten (1999-2000). Each comprises five volumes. The Waseda University website has a printed edition from 1657 (*Meireki* 明暦 3)[7] published by (the school of) Tateno Harutoki 立野春節[校]; this edition is held by many Japanese university libraries.

Along with the publication of the Iwanami edition came translations into modern Japanese, by Hayashi Rokurō (1985-89), Naoki Kōjirō (1986-92), and Ujitani Tsutomu (1992-95). While a *kanbun Kokushi Taikei* edition was first published in 1898, and a *kundoku* version in 1938, it was thus only at the very end of the twentieth century that the chronicle became available to a wider literate and non-specialist audience in Japan.

The SNKBT edition comprises five volumes, of forty *maki* 巻, or "rolls", distributed as follows:

I	*Maki* 1-6
II	*Maki* 7-15
III	*Maki* 16-24
IV	*Maki* 25-33
V	*Maki* 34-40

---

[5] *Keichō* era (1596-1620) text 慶長補写本
[6] 蓬左文庫本
[7] http://www.wul.waseda.ac.jp/kotenseki/html/ri05/ri05_02450_0016/index.html. Listed among the printed editions in the SNKBT SN1, p. 20.

The average length of a *maki* is roughly fifty-two pages (facing pages of *kanbun* and *yomikudashi*), although the later volumes tend to be longer. This translation covers the years *Tenpyō Hōji* 2 (roughly the year 758) through *Tenpyō Hōji* 7 (roughly the year 763). It begins roughly four-fifths of the way through *Maki* 20 and concludes at the end of *Maki* 24.

Scholars in the West have paid very little scholarly attention to *Shoku Nihongi*. Sir George Sansom's pioneering effort to translate the *senmyō* in 1924 was left unfinished. He acknowledged that the translation was "a painful process" and went on to more interesting projects. J.B.Snellen pronounced the chronicle "dry as dust" and his English translation covers only the years 697-715. There is a Russian translation of the years 697-707 (Meshcheryakov 2006-12) and a German translation of the years 780-91 (Lewin 1962).

The digitized text of *Shoku Nihongi* is in the public domain and now freely available on a number of Japanese websites. Readers should note that the text I provide with the translation (http://www.j-texts.com/jodai/shokuall.html) differs in points with the SNKBT edition, which is now the authoritative text but not yet available in digital format. However, it is close enough as to be useful for readers wishing to identify terms and particularly names. In the translation I provide kanji in the text for the most significant names, measures, political offices and names of Buddhist texts when they are first mentioned. Obviously the serious student should consult the SNKBT text. Footnotes from that edition when mentioned in my footnotes are given in the form "SNIII page number, note number."

While I try to follow the SNKBT readings for personal and place names, I sometimes simplify to readings which are common in Japanese secondary literature. Thus e.g. "Chikuzen" for *Tsukushi no michi no kuchi*. Court ranks are reduced to the formula e.g. "Jr 5 Upper", rather than "Junior Fifth Rank, Upper Grade." For weights and measures, whose precise value in 8th century Japan is unclear, I have used gross approximations: "bushel", "ounce", "hectare." The Appendix provides a kanji reference list and glossary.

Jean and Robert Karl Reischauer's *Early Japanese History*, first published in 1937 and reissued in 1967, is the indispensable guide to translations of Japanese court titles and political institutions. Although some of their translations may seem antiquated, they have the virtue of providing the greatest consistent number of translations of court titles available, and this coverage and consistency is still valuable. Richard J. Miller's Japan's *First Bureaucracy: A Study of Eighth-Century Government* (1979), largely based on the ninth-century *Ryō no Shuge*, is sometimes useful as a reference, although his translations of court titles often differ from the Reischauers'. The *Online Glossary of Japanese Historical Terms* and other resources in the University of Tokyo's Historiographical Institute website are sometimes of use. [8] The *Glossary*'s coverage is spotty, although especially good for German translations. For

---

[8] http://wwwap.hi.u-tokyo.ac.jp/ships/db-e.html

Chinese titles, Charles O. Hucker's 1985 *A Dictionary of Official Titles in Imperial China* is still the standard. *The Princeton Dictionary of Buddhism* (2014) is immensely useful. Among the many Japanese dictionaries and encyclopedias available I found *Nihon Kodaishi Dajiten* 日本古代史大辞典 (2006) edited by Ueda Masaaki to be especially helpful. A. Charles Muller's online *Digital Dictionary of Buddhism*, along with the *CJKV-English Dictionary* and many associated resources is a superb work, constantly being updated.[9] A work in progress is The *Oxford Corpus of Old Japanese.* [10]

Each date is given in the following format: ***Tenpyō Hōji* 2.1.5** 戊寅 ***tsuchinoe-tora* [February 17, 758]**. Thus: year, month, day, calendrical designation (*kanshi* 干支), transliteration of *kanshi*, corresponding date in the Julian calendar. Intercalary months are given as for example "INT8." [11] Conversion to dates in the Julian calendar was made possible by *Nengo-Calc,* by Matthias Schemm, Seminar für Japanologie Universität Tübingen.[12] The dates for each entry frequently do not correspond exactly to the Western years: "758" actually begins on February 13, 758 and ends on February 2, 759 in the Julian calendar.

---

[9] http://www.buddhism-dict.net/ddb/
[10] http://vsarpj.orinst.ox.ac.uk/corpus/texts.html
[11] See Tsumura 2012 for an overview in English on how the intercalations were calculated.
[12] http://www.yukikurete.de/nengo_calc.htm

Introduction

With the suppression of the Tachibana no Naramaro conspiracy of 757 (TPHJ 1) Fujiwara no Nakamaro became the most powerful man in Japan. The narrative of the years 758-763 (TPHJ 2-7) is the story of his consolidation of almost supreme power.[13] In July of 758 the Empress Kōken abdicated and the puppet Emperor Junnin took the throne; Junnin was Nakamaro's son-in-law and had resided in Nakamaro's Tamura Mansion in the Left Capital, south of the *Hokkeji*. Junnin's installation as Emperor resulted in a new configuration of the complex imperial institution, which included the Retired Empress Kōken, Nakamaro, and his patron the Empress Dowager Kōmyō, Kōken's mother. By the end of 763 Nakamaro had been named Grand Preceptor, or *Daishi*, an office understood as equivalent to *Daijōdaijin*, First Minister of the Great Council of State, the supreme head of the *Ritsuryō* bureaucracy and a role normally assigned only posthumously.[14]

---

[13] Kishi 1969, 218 termed his rule a "dictatorship" (*dokusai* 独裁).
[14] *Daishi* 太師; *Daijōdaijin* 太政大臣

In foreign relations these years are notable for a close relationship with the kingdom of Parhae[15] and chilly relationships with the Korean kingdom of Silla.[16] In fact Nakamaro's aim in the latter years was to invade Silla, a grandiose ambition that never came to fruition. Parhae, in present-day northeast China and northern Korea, served not only as a trading partner and ally but as a gateway to Tang China. Envoys from Parhae reported to the Japanese court on the extremely troubled situation on the continent following the 756 rebellion of An Lushan [17] and the consequent disorders.

Rampant inflation led to the issuance of several new types of coins in 760, as well as new measures to stabilize prices, especially those of rice. The government instituted ever-normal granaries to even out the cost of grain and appointed a variety of new regional inspectors to investigate and remedy suffering in the provinces. From 761 to 763 an abnormal number of major disasters, including drought, famine and epidemic plagued the realm and contributed to political instability. In late 759 construction began on a new Northern Capital at Hora[18] in Ōmi province, an area where Nakamaro and his family were particularly influential. Both Junnin and Retired Empress Kōken moved to the new capital temporarily in 761, where they soon experienced a major falling-out. The reason is not specified in the annals of the time, although

---

[15] J. Bokkai 渤海
[16] J. Shiragi 新羅
[17] J. An Rokushan 安禄山
[18] 保良京

it may have been due to the appearance of the monk Dōkyō[19] as an influence on the Retired Empress; Dōkyō's obituary in *Shoku Nihongi* records that it was at Hora that he treated Kōken for illness.[20] Both sovereigns returned to Nara in 762, Junnin to the Heijō Palace and Kōken to the *Hokkeji*, a temple built on the grounds of her grandfather Fujiwara no Fuhito's mansion. In June of 762 the Retired Empress issued her famous edict, *Senmyō 27*, excoriating Junnin and proclaiming that henceforth he would handle only minor affairs of state, while she would deal with fundamental policy.

In July of 760 the Dowager Empress Kōmyō passed away; she had been ailing at least since the summer of 758. Both Buddhist and Shinto prayers were undertaken on her behalf during this time. Kōken ordered in an edict of 758 that killing be prohibited throughout the realm for the year, and that in future the meat of deer and wild boar not be served at the imperial table.[21] Junnin's edict of TPHJ 4.3.13 ordered prayers for her healing to the *kami* of heaven and earth throughout the realm, and awarded promotions in rank to Shinto priests beginning with those at Ise *Daijingū*. As she had been the chief benefactor and sponsor of Fujiwara no Nakamaro, her death, together with the subsequent events at the Hora Capital, signified increasing disruption of the Nakamaro supremacy. Upon Kōken's abdication in 758, a remarkable series of lengthy memorials from both the high civil officialdom and the Buddhist clergy

---

[19] 道鏡
[20] *Hōki* 3.4.7 (772).
[21] TPHJ 2.7.4

reflected on the divine legitimacy of both Kōken's and Kōmyō's rule. These materials comprised summaries of Buddhist, Shinto and Confucian motifs in the political theology of the day.

Institutional developments are reflected in a burgeoning of new types of petitions to the throne, reports from the theoretically (from the standpoint of the Japanese court) subordinate kingdoms of Parhae and Silla, and pronouncements of the various organs of government. All three forms of imperial edicts, the *shō*, *choku* and *senmyō* are evidenced in the *Shoku Nihongi* record. Particularly because of the unsettled relationship between Retired Empress Kōken and the titular Emperor Junnin, it is sometimes difficult to know which monarch was issuing these diktats. In addition there is evidence that Nakamaro was exercising certain prerogatives traditionally belonging to the imperial sovereigns, as Junnin granted him the right to mint coins and use the seal "House of Emi."[22] Also, when Junnin gave an edict (TPHJ 2.8.25) changing the names of bureaucratic offices, the Dowager Empress' Househould Office (*Shibi Chūdai*)[23] was changed to "Earthly Palace Council:"[24]

> "The Dowager Empress' Household Office is in the palace, receives edicts and executes all governmental matters. This is because earth is entrusted by heaven to nourish the ten thousand things. Thus it is changed to Earthly Palace Council. The Ministry of Central Affairs, since it proclaims and transmits the edicts, must be reliable. Thus it is changed to Ministry of Fidelity."

---

[22] TPHJ 2.8.25.
[23] 紫微中台
[24] *Kongūkan* 坤宮官

Although this underscores the importance of the role played by the Earthly Palace Council in the Nakamaro supremacy, it was still subordinate to the "Heavenly Council of State"[25], the new name for the *Daijōkan*, Great Council of State, as before.

The Junnin Interregnum and the Nakamaro Supremacy

Junnin *Haitei*,[26] the "Deposed Emperor Junnin," is notorious as the puppet[27] of Fujiwara no Nakamaro, who married his daughter-in-law, the widow of Mayori[28] to the Prince Ōi.[29] The Prince was the son of Imperial Prince Toneri and a grandson of Emperor Tenmu; after his marriage he resided in Nakamaro's Tamura Mansion. After Crown Prince Funado, designated posthumously by Emperor Shōmu, was stripped of his rank by Kōken in early 757, Ōi was chosen to replace him by a conclave of nobles advising the Empress.[30] In 758 he ascended the throne and was titular Emperor until Retired Empress Kōken deposed him in 764, after Nakamaro rebelled and was defeated. Kōken sent him he is also known by his nickname "the Awaji Duke."

Upon Junnin's accession there was no change of the era name; the *nengō* remained *Tenpyō Hōji*. This is one more indication of the Deposed Emperor's

---

[25] *Genjōkan* 乾政官

[26] 淳仁廃帝 (733-765).

[27] *Kairai* 傀儡. This is the commonly accepted designation. See for example Dobashi 2005 and Katsuura 2014, ii.
[28] 真従
[29] 大炊
[30] TPHJ 1.3.29; TPHJ 1.4.4.

questionable status. In fact he was not added to the official list of titular monarchs until 1870, in an act of the newly reconstituted *Daijōkan* and an edict of the Emperor Meiji.[31] Thus Junnin's "interregnum" might better be termed an "interruption" in the reign of the Last Empress. Takinami Sadako goes so far as to designate this period Kōken's *insei*.[32]

Table 1 shows the list of imperial edicts issued by both Kōken and Junnin during this period. Note that Kōken issued a number of edicts shortly after she abdicated, then *Senmyō* 26 in 760, and finally *Senmyō* 27 in 762. In 760 she was designated the Takano *Tennō*,[33] a usage which was common through the end of her reign in the *Shoku Nihongi* text. The table reflects the somewhat byzantine nature of the imperial institution at this time. After Kōken's formal declaration of power in *Senmyō* 27,[34] it is sometimes difficult to discern who precisely was issuing the imperial edicts, although by default I have assigned them to Junnin. This list of edicts does not of course provide direct evidence of the role of Dowager Empress Kōmyō or Fujiwara no Nakamaro in the extracodal *Shibi Chūdai*, an iteration of Kōmyō's household office that had been growing in power since its institution in 749. As noted above, the name of this office was changed to "Earthly Palace Council" on TPHJ 2.8.25.

---

[31] *Hōrei zensho-Meiji 3*, Frames 166-7. *Rekidai shōchoku zenshū*, Frame 74.
[32] 院政 Takinami 2004, 171 and ff.

[33] 高野天皇

[34] This declaration is referred to in the secondary literature as the *bunri sengen* 分離宣言. See Kimoto 2011, 251 and ff. for a detailed analysis of the effects of this edict.

TABLE 1: Edicts *Tenpyō Hōji 2-7*

Edict	Tennō	Date	Year	Summary
Shō	Kōken	TPHJ 2.1.5	758	Orders rebels to reform selves
Shō	Kōken	TPHJ 2.1.5	758	Sends couriers to investigate suffering
Shō	Kōken	TPHJ 2.2.20	758	Prohibits drunken gatherings
Choku	Kōken	TPHJ 2.2.27	758	Receives silkworm cocoon oracle
Shō	Kōken	TPHJ 2.3.10	758	Cancels 5-5 festival
Choku	Kōken	TPHJ 2.7.3	758	Sets ages for elderly
Choku	Kōken	TPHJ 2.7.4	758	Forbids killing in realm
Choku	Kōken	TPHJ 2.7.4	758	Liberates government slaves
Senmyō 23	Kōken	TPHJ 2.8.1	758	Abdication
Senmyō 24	Junnin	TPHJ 2.8.1	758	Accession
Shō	Kōken (Ret.)	TPHJ 2.8.1	758	Accepts honorific names
Choku	Kōken (Ret.)	TPHJ 2.8.1	758	Orders honorifics for Nakamaro
Shō	Junnin	TPHJ 2.8.2	758	Permits priest Enkyō to resign rank
Choku	Kōken (Ret.)	TPHJ 2.8.9	758	Orders honorific name for Shōmu
Choku	Kōken (Ret.)	TPHJ 2.8.9	758	Orders honorific name for Kusakabe
Choku	Junnin	TPHJ 2.8.18	758	Orders Perfection of Wisdom Sutra chanted
Choku	Junnin	TPHJ 2.8.25	758	Names Nakamaro *Daiho*; retitles bureaucracy
Choku	Junnin	TPHJ 2.10.25	758	Regulates governors' terms, sends *Junsatsushi*
Choku	Junnin	TPHJ 2.10.25	758	Regulates low level officials' terms
Choku	Junnin	TPHJ 3.1.27	759	Summons dancing girls to Parhae banquet
Choku	Junnin	TPHJ 3.5.9	759	Orders memorials from officials, B clergy
Choku	Junnin	TPHJ 3.5.9	759	Establishes ever-normal granaries, aid to hungry
Senmyō 25	Junnin	TPHJ 3.6.16	759	Raises family's status to imperial
Choku	Junnin	TPHJ 3.6.22	759	Promotes *Ritsuryō, Kyuku, Shiki*
Choku	Junnin	TPHJ 3.7.3	759	Raises rank of Head Censor
Choku	Junnin	TPHJ 3.9.26	759	Remits taxes for Michinooku laborers
Shō	Junnin	TPHJ 3.11.2	759	Remits taxes for typhoon sufferers
Shō	Junnin	TPHJ 3.11.4	759	Gifts to typhoon sufferers
Choku	Junnin	TPHJ 3.11.30	759	Increases Oshikatsu's guards
Senmyō 26	Takano *	TPHJ 4.1.4	760	Appoints Oshikatsu Grand Preceptor
Choku	Takano *	TPHJ 4.1.4	760	Rewards for construction of NE forts
Shō	Junnin	TPHJ 4.15	760	Accepts report of Parhae envoys
Shō	Junnin	TPHJ 4.1.7	760	Awards Parhae envoy Jr 3 rank
Shō	Junnin	TPHJ 4.3.13	760	Shinto prayers for Kōmyō's health
Choku	Junnin	TPHJ 4.3.16	760	Issues new coins
Choku	Junnin	TPHJ 4.5.19	760	Orders relief aid for epidemics
Choku	Junnin	TPHJ 4.8.7	760	Posthumous honors for Oshikatsu's relatives
Choku	Junnin	TPHJ 4.8.7	760	Raises income for Kyushu governors
Choku	Junnin	TPHJ 4.11.6	760	Great amnesty
Choku	Junnin	TPHJ 4.12.12	761	Raises rank, income for Rear Palace officials
Choku	Junnin	TPHJ 4.12.12	761	Dowager Empress' graves named imperial tombs
Choku	Junnin	TPHJ 5.2.1	761	Raises status of the four Cap Ranks
Choku	Junnin	TPHJ 5.2.1	761	Names officials to administer Capital
Shō	Junnin	TPHJ 5.6.28	761	Awards rank on Kōmyō's death anniversary
Choku	Junnin	TPHJ 5.8.1	761	Orders reforms for provincial governors
Shō	Junnin	TPHJ 5.10.28	761	Rewards Ōmi officials – Hora Palace construction
Choku	Junnin	TPHJ 5.10.28	761	Names Inner Districts for Hora Capital
Choku	Junnin	TPHJ 6.4.23	762	Donates fiefs to *Okadera* in Ōmi
Senmyō 27	Kōken (Ret.)	TPHJ 6.6.3	762	Kōken sets limits to Junnin's power
Shō	Junnin ?	TPHJ 6.7.19	762	Permits Ki Ihimaro to resign
Choku	Junnin ?	TPHJ 6.8.9	762	Orders Kyushu to aid Tang envoys

Shō	Junnin ?	TPHJ 6.8.20	762	Permits Fumuya Jōsamu using cane in palace
Shō	Junnin ?	TPHJ 6.9.30	762	Sends condolences to family of Toshitari
Shō	Junnin ?	TPHJ 7.1.15	763	Forgives public and private debt
Shō	Junnin ?	TPHJ 7.2.4	763	Gifts to Parhae envoy banquet
Choku	Junnin ?	TPHJ 7.8.1	763	Remits rice tax due to drought
Shō	Junnin ?	TPHJ 7.8.19	763	Grants *kabane* to family of Prince Ikeda
Choku	Junnin ?	TPHJ 7.9.1	763	Blames disasters on provincial officials

*Takano Tennō – Retired Empress Kōken

Another indication of Junnin's status is the frequent title of "*Mikado*"[35] assigned to him in the *Shoku Nihongi* text; Kōken is never so labeled.

Empress Kōken first named Nakamaro to the headship of the *Shibi Chūdai* in 749,[36] when he already held Senior Third Rank and the office of Major Counsellor. But with Junnin's accession in 758 he ascended rapidly to unprecedented status both within the *Ritsuryō* bureaucracy and in the *Shibi Chūdai*. In fact it is a major feature of this era that he in effect remade the entire bureaucracy by renaming all the major *Ritsuryō* offices. This has been generally characterized as a "Tangification" of the Japanese bureaucracy, reflecting Chinese influence. However, it is also clear that some of the new titles in fact were inspired by the Parhae kingdom.[37] For historians and translators this is perhaps the most vexing characteristic of the *Tenpyō Hōji* period. See Table 2 below for the major changes; I have given English translations of all the new offices in the text and glossary. The *Shoku Nihongi* text, while largely consistent in utilizing the new terminology, occasionally harks back to the old nomenclature, thus providing a good bit of confusion for the reader.

---

[35] 帝
[36] TPSH 1.8.10.
[37] See especially Enomoto Jun'ichi 2013, 20-43 for a discussion and several detailed charts; also chart in Kishi 1969, 237. See TPHJ 2.8.25 in the translation for the lengthy edict.

18

TABLE 2: Changes in Bureaucratic Nomenclature

Daijōkan 太政官 – Great Council of State	*Genjōkan* 乾政官 – Heavenly Council of State
Shibi Chūdai 紫微中台 - Dowager Empress' Household	*Kongūkan* 坤宮官 – Earthly Palace Council
Nakatsukasashō 中務省 - Ministry of Central Affairs	*Shinbushō* 信部省 – Ministry of Fidelity
Shikibushō 式部省 - Ministry of Ceremonial	*Monbushō* 文部省 – Ministry of Civil Affairs
Jibushō 治部省 - Ministry of Civil Administration	*Reibushō* 礼部省 – Ministry of Rites
Minbushō 民部省 - Ministry of Popular Affairs	*Ninbushō* 仁部省 – Ministry of Benevolence
Hyōbushō 兵部省 - Ministry of War	*Mubushō* 武部省 – Ministry of Military Affairs
Gyōbushō 刑部省 - Ministry of Righteousness	*Gibushō* 義部省 – Ministry of Righteousness
Ōkurashō 大蔵省 - Ministry of the Treasury	*Setsubushō* 節部省 – Ministry of Moderation
Kunaishō 宮内省 - Ministry of the Imperial Household	*Chibushō* 智部省 – Ministry of Wisdom

In broader terms the Nakamaro supremacy can be traced through the awards of new and unique office titles, each of which corresponds to a title in the formal *Ritsuryō* civil service. Thus in 758 Junnin named him *"Daiho"*, [38] or "Grand Guardian." This is an ancient Chinese title supposedly dating back to the Zhou dynasty, when there were "Three Dukes" – sometimes translated as the Grand Preceptor, [39] Grand Mentor, [40] and Grand Guardian. [41] *Daiho* was understood to be the equivalent of *Udaijin*, Grand Minister of the Right. In that edict Junnin also granted him the honorific name of Emi Oshikatsu. [42] "Emi" was to signify his nobility and wisdom; "Oshikatsu" recognized his role in defeating Tachibana no Naramaro. Junnin also granted him sustenance households and

---

[38] 大保

[39] 太師

[40] 太傅
[41] 太保
[42] 恵美押勝

merit lands, and more significantly the right to mint coins, lend rice for interest, and use the seal "House of Emi."[43]

In 760 the Retired Empress Kōken, as *Takano Tennō*, appointed Nakamaro *Daishi* (Grand Preceptor) in *Senmyō* 26;[44] this was specified as the equivalent of *Daijōdaijin*. In the edict she noted that "this office is one which is left vacant when there is no specially qualified person to fill it." The *Shoku Nihongi* entry begins "The Takano *Tennō* (Retired Empress Kōken) and the *Mikado* (Emperor Junnin) went to the Private Palace and conferred the Jr First Rank on the Grand Guardian Jr 2 Fujiwara Emi no Asomi Oshikatsu." Here again is evidence of the joint rulership shared between titular and retired sovereign, as well as the vaunted position granted to Nakamaro. Later that year the Dowager Empress Kōmyō passed away.[45] Although she had been ailing for some time, with her death a critical prop to the Nakamaro supremacy disappeared.[46]

The *Shoku Nihongi* entry for *Hōki* 3.4.7 (772) comprises the obituary of the Buddhist priest and healer monk Dōkyō. According to this account, it was in TPHJ 5 (761) that Dōkyō nursed the ailing Retired Empress Kōken in the Hora Palace. Although this story is not related in the *Shoku Nihongi* annals for TPHJ

---

[43] 恵美家印
[44] TPHJ 4.1.4.
[45] TPHJ 4.6.7.
[46] The classic biography of Nakamaro is Kishi 1969. Kimoto Yoshinobu's new biography appeared in 2011. Kimoto's edited volume *Fujiwara no Nakamaro Seiken to Sono Jidai* (2013) is the most comprehensive treatment, comprising fourteen chapters by specialists on every aspect of his rule.

5, this date is commonly accepted as the beginning point for the priest's influence on the Retired Empress. He first appears in the entry for TPHJ 7.9.4 (763), when Kōken appointed him as Junior Assistant Abbot.

Foreign Relations: Parhae, Tang, and Silla

Remnants of the royal family of Koguryō and Malgal peoples from the east established the kingdom of Parhae in 698 in what is now northeast China and northern Korea. In the *Shoku Nihongi* the kingdom is sometimes labeled "Bokkai" and sometimes "Koma."[47] The two seem to be used interchangeably, the latter emphasizing the Japanese court's understanding that Parhae was founded by aristocrats from the old kingdom of Koguryō. There is still debate about the status of Parhae, some claiming that it was almost a protectorate of Tang and some that it was a completely independent Korean kingdom.[48] Whatever the future consensus, it is clear that the kingdom was a close ally of Japan and that its bureaucratic nomenclature influenced Nakamaro's renaming of the *Ritsuryō* civil service.[49] For the purpose of this translation I have rendered Parhae names with a Chinese pronunciation.

During this era, *Shoku Nihongi* records the visits of three embassies from Parhae, all of which arrived in the company of Japanese diplomats returning

---

[47] 渤海; 高麗. Rather confusingly SNKBT here consistently gives the reading 'Koma' for the latter, although it can also be read 'Kōrai' in referring to the old kingdom of Koguryō.
[48] *A New History of Parhae* (2012) trans. John Duncan, Seoul: Northeast Asian History Foundation (*Parhae ui yoksa wa munwha* 2005) renders all Parhae names as Korean. See p. 14.
[49] Kōchi Haruhito in Kimoto 2013, 89-110, especially chart on p. 98.

from Parhae. The first was headed by the Parhae Ambassador Yang Chengching and stayed in Japan from late 758 to early 759;[50] the second headed by Parhae envoy Gao Nanshen was in Japan from late 759 to early 760;[51] the last headed by Wang Xinfu sojourned in Japan from late 762 to early 763.[52] Parhae embassies always aimed to land on the northern seacoast in Echizen province – that was the entry point for the first and third, although the second was blown off course and arrived at Tsushima, then formally entered Japan at the Kyushu Government Headquarters (*Dazaifu*).[53] Since these embassies all arrived in the winter, Parhae envoys were always honored guests at the Japanese court's New Year ceremonies the following year.

Both the Emperor and the great minister Emi no Oshikatsu treated the Parhae guests lavishly. In addition to serving as occasions for exchanging trade goods (Japan in particular valued Parhae furs),[54] these visits also served as important sources of information concerning the disordered situation in Tang China. The Parhae ambassadors and envoys were given sumptuous banquets, both at court and at Oshikatsu's mansion; they composed poetry in Chinese and took part in archery matches. The Japanese Emperor awarded all three ambassadors Senior 3rd court rank, and conferred distinguished rank on the lesser members of the embassy.

---

[50] TPHJ 2.9.18 and ff.
[51] TPHJ 3.10.18 and ff.
[52] TPHJ 6.10.1 and ff.
[53] See Ueda Takeshi 2004, 229 for a map of Parhae missions to Japan.
[54] Von Verscheuer 2006, 8-21 provides an excellent overview of tributary exchanges with Parhae, Korea and China during the eighth and ninth centuries.

Diplomatic exchanges recorded in *Shoku Nihongi* are particularly important as reflections of northeast Asian international relations of the time, and specifically for the information conveyed to Japan of the situation in Tang China. Japan had sent its Ambassador Fujiwara no Kiyokawa to Tang in 752, and the Parhae embassies reported on their attempts, sometimes successful, to contact him in the Tang capital where he remained for the rest of his life.[55] The entry for TPHJ 2.12.10 comprises a thorough account of the An Lushan uprising of 756, Emperor Xuanzong's flight, and developments in 758. On TPHJ 7.1.17 the envoy Wang Xinfu reported on the death of Emperors Xuanzong and Suzong, and the accession of Daizong in 762. After the first report Emperor Junnin sent special instructions to the Kyushu Headquarters to prepare for any possible Chinese attack on Japan.

Of course the formal diplomatic communiqués in *Shoku Nihongi* reflect the Japanese court's understanding of itself as the "elder brother" of the Parhae king and Parhae's status as intimate yet "barbarian" interlocutor. Thus Yang Chengqing conveyed the Parhae king's condolences on the death of Emperor Shōmu, and Junnin responded "We rejoice at this visit, that the King has not forgotten his heart of old, and has sent an envoy with tribute. We commend the King for his profound loyalty." Junnin responded to Gao Nanshen's conveyance of regards with the statement "We are greatly pleased by the goodwill and

---

[55] *SNKBT* gives the Sinicized reading of his name "Kasei". He was awarded honorary appointments in absentia: Head Ministry of Benevolence; Hitachi Governor. TPHJ 4.2.20; TPHJ 7.1.19.

fidelity of the King." Lastly, the Japanese Emperor responded to Wang Xinfu's report by sending instructions to Kyushu Headquarters to provide special care to the Tang envoy Chen Weiyue who with his embassy was stranded at Dazaifu due to the unsettled conditions in Tang.

Two fascinating incidents occurred in connection with the Japanese embassies to Parhae. In 763 the ship Noto, returning to Japan, met with a violent storm at sea:

> Then the people on the ship prayed:
>
> "If due to the lucky numinous spirit of this ship we reach home without incident, we shall certainly beg the court to grant the ship a braided cap as a reward."
>
> Since the ship reached home without incident, on this day, according to the promise of the prayer, the court granted the ship Jr 5 Lower Rank. The cap was brocade on one side and coarse silk on the other, with purple chin strap.[56]

Later that year appeared the very detailed account of how a Japanese official returning from Parhae ran into heavy weather and reacted by tossing several students, Buddhist priests and women overboard to lighten the load. The official was subsequently arrested and confined in jail in Nara.[57]

Only one Japanese mission actually succeeded in reaching Tang China during this period; two attempts were unsuccessful.[58] Although Parhae acted as

[56] TPHJ 7.8.12.
[57] TPHJ 7.10.6.
[58] See chart in Tōno Haruyuki 2007, 204.

intermediary with Tang and provided narratives of events there, one Tang embassy headed by Chen Weiyue landed at Kyushu Headquarters in the fall of 761. They accompanied Ko Gendo, the Japanese Ambassador to Tang, upon his return. Ko brought with him gifts from the Tang emperor (presumably Suzong) of a suit of armor, a sword, spear and a quiver of arrows. Due to the disorder in China, this embassy was unable to return and stayed in Kyushu at least until early 763. During this period Junnin issued two edicts ordering that the Chinese embassy was to be provided with supplies including food and clothing for the winter.[59] In addition, the court dispatched a messenger in 762 to provide a banquet at *Dazaifu* for the Tang envoys.[60] On TPHJ 6.5.19 the Japanese court received a bizarre communication from the Vice-Envoy denouncing Chen Weiyue and asking that he be appointed in Chen's stead. The court replied that Chen should remain in command.

Ko Gendo also brought a request from the Tang emperor for supplies of cattle horns to make bows for the army. On TPHJ 5.10.10 the Japanese court ordered provinces in six circuits to provide 7,800 head of horned cattle for this purpose. In 763 the court formally discarded the *Yifeng* calendar and adopted the newer *Dayan* calendar;[61] this calendar was mentioned in the Japanese curriculum of 757, and it is unclear why it was not accepted until this time. Further Tang influence is reflected in the frequent performance of Chinese

---

[59] TPHJ 6.8.9; TPHJ 7.1.17.
[60] TPHJ 6.1.6.
[61] TPHJ 7.8.18.

music and dance at the Japanese court, and particularly in military matters. In 760 sword-bearing retainers were sent to Kyushu and ordered to study Chinese military strategies with Kibi no Makibi, a former envoy to Tang. These tactics included the "Nine Earth tactics of Sunzi".[62]

Most intricate and fraught with tension was Japan's relationship with the Korean kingdom of Silla. Despite Japan's close alliance with Parhae, it is not evident that the latter had urged Japan to attack Silla. Nevertheless preparations for an expedition against the peninsula developed rapidly under the Nakamaro supremacy. In mid-759 the Kyushu Headquarters were ordered to begin preparations for an attack on Silla and the Governor-General was sent to the *Kashiibyō*[63] to report the matter.[64] The *Kashii* Shrine in northern Kyushu was believed to entomb the legendary Emperor Chūai and his Empress Jingū, renowned for having undertaken an invasion on Korea in ancient times. That autumn an entry in the annal reported that five hundred ships from all parts of Japan had been constructed for the attack; perplexingly, the report noted that this work had been completed within three years, although 759 is the first *Shoku Nihongi* evidence for such a plan.[65]

---

[62] TPHJ 4.11.10. Often translated as the "Nine Variables."
[63] 香椎廟 also *Kashii* Shrine 香椎宮
[64] TPHJ 3.6.18; 3.8.6.
[65] TPHJ 3.9.19.

In October of 760 a Silla envoy arrived in Kyushu, but he was rebuffed and told to return home.[66] In 761 twenty Japanese youth were ordered to study the Silla language as part of invasion planning, and in late 762 two high officials were sent to present *mitegura* to the *Kashii* Shrine to report military drills practicing for the assault.[67]

But early the next year another Silla embassy arrived in Kyushu, and this time was given permission to enter the capital.[68] This time the Japanese court seems to have been satisfied with the rank of the envoys and the sincerity of their visit. At any rate this piece of diplomacy apparently averted the crisis, since *Shoku Nihongi* records nothing further about invasion plans. In 764 another Silla envoy arrived for a brief call and was well received.[69] Complicating relations with the peninsula was the fact that large numbers of people from Silla had emigrated to Japan over the years, and constituted a tiny but significant part of the population. In 758, roughly a year before invasion planning was noted, immigrants from Silla were settled in Musashi Province, and a Silla District established there. The group comprised thirty-two Buddhist priests, two nuns, nineteen men and twenty-one women; it is not specified when exactly they had come to Japan.[70] Interspersed with warlike intentions were

---

[66] TPHJ 4.9.16.
[67] TPHJ 5.1.9; 6.11.16.
[68] TPHJ 7.2.10.
[69] TPHJ 8.7.19.
[70] TPHJ 2.8.24.

orders to aid Silla immigrants who wished to return home, and the settlement of another one hundred thirty-one migrants in Musashi.[71]

Negotiations between Japanese officials and the first Silla envoy in 760 are recorded in detail. The Japanese complaint was that an envoy to the Silla capital in 753, Ono no Tamori, had been rudely treated.[72] So the Silla envoy was sent home with this message:

> "Since you are of such low rank we cannot accept you as a guest. You should return home and inform your government of the situation. When there is a sufficiently high-ranking person, with the proper protocol, with tribute as of old, with clearly articulated words – when these four conditions are met, then he may proceed to our court."

By contrast, the 763 envoy was permitted to enter the capital for the purpose of bringing tribute. However, he was told that "Henceforth only the King or Prince or high officials of Silla may come to court." Obviously a certain diplomatic frostiness remained between the putative Japanese empire and its Korean subject.[73]

---

[71] TPHJ 3.9.4; 4.4.28.

[72] An entry in the Silla annals of the *Samguk Sagi* 三国史記(12th century) says [King Kyŏngdŏk Year 12 (753)]: "An envoy arrived from Japan. As he was arrogant with no propriety, the King did not receive him so he returned home." Schultz and Kang, 2012, 298. This is the only *Samguk Sagi* reference to Japan for the period under consideration.

[73] For a very brief overview of relations between Silla and Japan in the 7th and 8th centuries see Hon Sunchan in Tamura Enchō 1981, 319-24.

Coinage, Inflation, and Natural Disasters

New coins were minted in 760 in response to rampant inflation and out of control counterfeiting. Counterfeiting had long been considered a serious crime; it was one of the offences specified as not forgiven in the general amnesties. On *TPHJ* 4.3.16 the Emperor gave the following edict:

> "Coins have been circulated and used for a long time. Nothing is more fundamental and convenient than their use for public and private purposes. However recently counterfeiting has become rampant, and counterfeit coins already amount to half of the coins in circulation. We fear that if their use is suddenly suppressed there will be disorder, and so We wish to manufacture new coins and use them together with the old. We desire not to harm the people and to benefit the country. The new coins will be inscribed '*Bannen Tsūhō*'.[74] One new coin will be worth ten of the old.[75] The silver coins inscribed '*Taihei Genhō*'[76] will be worth ten of the new coins. The gold coins inscribed '*Kaiki Shōhō*'[77] will be worth ten of the silver coins."

William Wayne Farris has pointed out that, although coins were struck for the first time in the Wadō era, "Outside the Kinai…coins were not accepted readily, and rice sheaves which served as 'near-money' in the well-known provincial and district financial system *(suiko sei* 出挙制) were the chief unit of

---

[74] 万年通宝 '*Bannen*' meaning 'ten thousand years,' an auspicious phrase. Note the reference to *nengō* (*Wadō, Shōhō*) and 'Great Peace' 大平 and 'Treasure' 宝 in the names of the coins.
[75] *Wadō Kaichin* 和同開珎
[76] 大平元宝
[77] 開基勝宝

account."[78] The new coins were distributed to Buddhist temples, priests and nuns, Shinto priests, and to the Hundred Officials,[79] but Japan did not develop a true money economy in the Nara period.

Late in 759 the Emperor had issued an edict noting that many people were starving near the official markets in the capital, and along the roads to the provinces. Thereupon it was ordered that special granaries[80] should be established: "Rice should be bought at low prices and sold at the high, then the profit gathered. It should then be used to succor those who are suffering from hunger and enable them to return home. This should be done not only to aid the hungry in provinces outside the capital, but likewise to control the price of rice within the capital."[81] Price-Regulators were appointed to head the Right and Left Ever-Normal Granaries. To compound the difficulties an abnormally severe cluster of major disasters afflicted the nation from 761 to 763, including drought, famine and epidemic illness. In spring of 763 after the report of famine in Shinano, the annal notes that "In the capital the price of rice rose. Rice was sold in the Left and Right Capital to stabilize the prices." These disasters, coupled with the short-lived move to the northern capital at Hora, compounded the political instability of the period.

---

[78] Farris 1998b, 309. See also pp. 313-318 for an excellent overview in English of the development of coinage in the Nara period. See Sakaehara 1991, 79-102 for an intensive analysis of currency in the Nara period including pictures of all the coins in use at the time.
[79] TPHJ 4.8.22.
[80] *jōheisō* 常平倉
[81] TPHJ 3.5.9.

Political Theology: A Dialog Between Throne and Officialdom

The account of the abdication of the Empress Kōken and the accession of Emperor Junnin on TPHJ 2.8.1 is notable as one of the longest single entries in *Shoku Nihongi*. On this occasion the two imperial edicts in Old Japanese, *Senmyō* 23 and 24, are followed by a list of promotions in rank, then memorials from the Hundred Officials and the Office of Buddhist Priestly Affairs. Then in response the newly retired Kōken issued two edicts inscribed in classical Chinese.

TABLE 3: Edicts and Memorials, *Tenpyō Hōji* 2.8.1

1	*Senmyō* 宣命 23 – Edict of Abdication by Empress Kōken
2	*Senmyō* 宣命 24 – Edict of Accession by Emperor Junnin
3	Awards of Promotion in Rank (*Joi* 叙位) by the New Emperor
4	Memorial 表 from the High Officials (*Hyakkan* 百官)
5	Memorial 表 from the Office of Buddhist Priestly Affairs (*Sōgō* 僧綱)
6	*Shō* 詔 from Retired Empress Kōken
7	*Choku* 勅 from Retired Empress Kōken

Senmyō 23 and 24

These two edicts are specimens of the most flowery type of Old Japanese edict. They comprise language describing the divine imperium, a concept that had begun to be codified for example in the myths of *Tenson Kōrin*, the accounts of the descent of the grandchild of *Amaterasu* from the High Plain of

31

Heaven in *Kojiki* and *Nihon Shoki*.[82] They also employ language appearing in the *Man'yōshū*.[83] Kōken's abdication edict, *Senmyō 23*, begins thus:

> "Let all hearken to the edict which is proclaimed as the command of the Empress who rules the land as a manifest deity ... who in the body of a god rules the land from the High Throne of Heaven, from which for generations the Emperors have ruled, beginning with the distant Imperial ancestors, just as the distant Imperial ancestors, the male and female *kami* in the High Plain of Heaven, decreed that their descendants should rule All Under Heaven."

Senmyō 24, Junnin's accession edict, contains similar language, and also includes the epithet "the Emperor who rules the great land of the Eight Islands as a manifest deity."

This language is quite obviously nativist as opposed to Buddhist or classical Chinese verbiage. It may be described as Shinto, in that it is beginning to clearly articulate doctrine concerning the divinity of the Emperors. Not all of the *senmyō* employ such powerfully Shinto wording; less than a third of the prefaces to the sixty-two Old Japanese edicts in *Shoku Nihongi* utilize this language. Most of the *senmyō* were issued in much more mundane contexts than

---

[82] 天孫降臨. Hirabayashi Akihito 2015, 248-53 traces the development of this foundational myth in the *Kiki* 記紀 in the context of imperial acceptance of Buddhism. He concludes that this harmonization of Buddhism with *Tenson Kōrin* was established by the time of Tenmu *Tennō*.

[83] Torquil Duthie 2014, pp. 412-15 discusses "ritualized texts", comparing and contrasting the *senmyō* briefly to "ritual poems" in *Man'yōshū*. Bentley 2001, pp. 27-31, analyzes types of ancient liturgies (including *senmyō*). His focus on two liturgies from *Kojiki* and *Nihon Shoki* addresses the question of whether these were poetry, song, or 'verse-prose.' His conclusion in brief is that religious functions gave rise to liturgies, which then evolved into song/poetry. But while poetry settled into a regular pattern (the basic *waka* 5-7), liturgies (*norito* and *senmyō*) did not.

abdications or accessions. Although I have suggested that for imperial edicts, whether *senmyō*, *choku* or *shō*, the medium is the message in that the former embodied most fully the nativist ideology, it must also be noted that even these edicts contained classical Chinese literary tropes.[84] Thus both of these edicts contain references to the heavy burden of office and the clumsiness and weakness of the sovereign.[85] Also, Junnin's edict uses the phrase "knowing not whether to advance or retreat", a trope similar to one found inter alia in the *Yijing*.[86] In summary, while the Old Japanese *senmyō* are the locus classicus for such terminology as "Manifest Deity", they employ references to the Chinese classics as well.

Memorial from the Hundred Officials

In contrast to the *senmyō*, the memorial from the high civic officials is laced with explicit references to the Chinese classics, omens and Buddhism. Here the emphasis is on the cosmology supporting the imperial reign, with repeated allusions to the stars, sun and moon, Heaven, the Sage, and the Yellow

---

[84] Bender 2010, p. 240.

[85] See Knechtges 2005, pp. 27-29 for a third-century Chinese example of the "Three Refusals," a declaration by Cao Pi of his unworthiness to take the throne. Knechtges discusses Cao Pi's memorials as in the tradition of the "three refusals," here an extreme example of rhetorical humility and self-abnegation. Note however that while Junnin, in his accession edict, declares himself to be "clumsy, weak and foolish", he does not refuse the throne even one time.

[86] 進[母]不知[爾]、退[母]不知[爾]. Similar phrases are quite common, found also in *Senmyō* 5, 13, 14, 24, 25, 48, 49, 61. Cf. 知進而不知退, found inter alia in the *Yijing* and the *Shiji*. However, in the Chinese case there is only one negation, translated by Victor Mair as "knowing only to go forward but not to retreat". Mair points out that the Japanese version seems to be "inspired by or a transformation of the Chinese." (Personal communication, 5/20/2014). Note that in the translation below, the *Shoku Nihongi* editors frequently attempt to find loci for various terms in the Chinese classics, although these are often in garbled or incomplete form. Vovin 2005, p. 61, identifies the compound 進退 in *Senmyō* 62 as a loanword from Early Middle Chinese.

Emperor. The *Shoku Nihongi* editors have identified numerous quotations, some direct but many quite garbled, from classics such as the *Lunyu, Yijing, Zuozhuan* and *Shiji*.[87] The memorial is a pastiche of such material, but also of quite specific Buddhist terminology. The Dowager Empress, says the memorial, possesses a profound Buddhist faith which resulted in her establishment of medical facilities for the common people.

What precisely did the scribes who composed this memorial know of the classics? One very specific answer may be found in the curriculum for the imperial academy spelled out in a 757 entry in *Shoku Nihongi*. [88] The course of study for students in the Chinese classics included *Shujing, Shijing, Yijing*, and *Zuozhuan*, in addition to the *Lunyu* and *Xiaojing*. [89] History specialists were expected to study the *Shiji, Hanshu* and *Hou Hanshu*. [90] Students of medicine, acupuncture, astronomy, *yinyang* and calendar were faced with a large smorgasbord of lesser-known works. Although not listed in the 757 curriculum, the *Wenxuan*,[91] a medieval Chinese anthology of literature, was also apparently well-known in Nara Japan.

The thrust of the memorial was to confer honorific names on the Retired Empress and Dowager Emperor. It states that "the meaning of honorific names is clearly explained as arising from virtuous actions," and that the tradition of

---

[87] 論語, 易経, 左伝, 史記.
[88] TPHJ 1.11.9. See Bender and Zhao 2009 for a translation.
[89] 書経, 詩経, 易経, 左伝, 論語, 孝経.
[90] 史記, 漢書, 後漢書.
[91] 文選

awarding honorifics has a long history. The name bestowed on Kōken was "*Hōji Shōtoku Kōken Kōtei* 宝字称徳孝謙皇帝." Here we see a reference to the current era name, *Tenpyō Hōji*, and to the names by which the Empress is commonly known – Shōtoku and Kōken. Kōmyō is awarded the honorific name of "*Tenpyō Ōshin Ninshō Kōtaigō* 天平応真仁正皇太后." The era name referenced is that of her late husband Shōmu, namely *Tenpyō*. "*Kōtaigō*" is the title for a retired Empress. The terms "*Ōshin*" and "*Ninshō*" are more obscure, but the former is an old translation of the Buddhist term "Arhat", meaning "worthy true one." "*Ninshō*" is a combination of the graphs for "benevolent" and "correct."

Finally, the memorial's attention to omens is noteworthy, as it cites *shōzui*[92] and *kichijō*,[93] both terms for auspicious omens. Two specific examples of fortunate omens during the reign of Kōken are cited. As I have demonstrated elsewhere[94] the appearance and interpretation of lucky signs was an important motif in the political theology of her reign.

Memorial from the Council of Buddhist Priestly Affairs

The spokesman for the *Sōgō* here is the highest ranking priest in the bureaucracy, the *Sōjō Sharamon Sō Bodaisena*.[95] This was the Indian monk

---

[92] 祥瑞
[93] 吉祥
[94] Bender 2013.
[95] 僧正沙羅門僧菩提僊那

known in Japan as Bodai, the "Brahmin priest" who arrived in Japan in 736 and performed the eye-opening ceremony for the *Daibutsu* in 752. As one would expect, the memorial is replete with Buddhist doctrine and a depiction of the sovereign ruling with sympathy and compassion for all living things. Perhaps more surprising are the many specific comparisons of the Japanese ruler to ancient classical Chinese culture heroes, such as the Emperor Shun who sought for wise men, and Emperor Wu, who discovered the River Chart in the tides of the Yellow River.

In fact this memorial is as much of a hodge-podge of Buddhist theology and Chinese lore as that from the civil officials. The Empress is compared to Kings Cheng and Kang of the Zhou, the Yellow Emperor, and the ancient Three Sovereigns and Five Emperors. Again, specific auspicious omens during the reign of Kōken are cited. Perhaps most striking is a passage which is redolent of the *Shanhaijing*,[96] the mythical geography dating back to Han times: "The villages where grow the winding trees and the borderlands where dwell the creatures with men's faces and serpents' bodies, inquire about honorific names, hear the voices of the Sovereign and wish to bask in his light." This text also emphasizes the search for distant precedents for the bestowal of honorific names, and concludes with the same titles as the previous memorial.

---

[96] 山海經

Two Edicts from Retired Empress Kōken

Concluding the lengthy *Shoku Nihongi* entry for TPHJ 2.8.1 are two brief edicts from the Retired Empress, inscribed in Chinese. The first, a *shō*, emphasizes the Sovereign's unworthiness, but accepts the honorific titles on her own and on the Dowager Empress's behalf. Again, the text emphasizes auspicious omens received in the past. The Retired Empress announces a great amnesty; she also proclaims promotions in rank to shrine priests at Ise *Daijingū* and to students at the imperial academy, and special boons for Buddhist priests who have committed offenses. In addition the Retired Empress awards the Senior Assistant Ganjin the title of Great Esteemed Monk[97] and releases him from his duties at the *Sōgō*.

In a final brief edict, a *choku*, the Retired Empress commands the heads of the various bureaucracies to search ancient precedents to discover an appropriate honorific for Fujiwara no Nakamaro and then to submit it to the throne.

Toward an Imperial Political Theology

The series of edicts and memorials describe an elaborate ceremony of controlled and fastidious cession of the imperial throne. Shōmu *Tennō*'s death in 756 resulted in a quarrel over his posthumous will designating Prince Funado as the successor to Kōken, a dispute that was resolved in favor of Prince Ōi, future

---

[97] *Daiwajō* 大和上

Emperor Junnin, the son-in-law of Fujiwara no Nakamaro. In 757 Tachibana no Naramaro's dangerous but seriously bungled conspiracy to overthrow the Empress was nipped in the bud by the imperial court armies with the support of Nakamaro. Now in 758, we witness Emperor Kōken being firmly and politely ushered out of office and designated Retired Empress with great fanfare, while Nakamaro's son-in-law is installed on the throne. Notable also is the retirement of the eminent priest Ganjin, the Senior Assistant Abbott, who is eased out of the Council of Buddhist Priestly Affairs with the honorary title of Great Esteemed Monk. This left Bodai as Chief Abbot, in firm control of the *Sōgō*. It is not evident from these passages whether there had been conflict between the two immigrant monks, Bodai from India and Ganjin from China, but if so it has now been resolved.

I have shown here that in a rare dialog between throne and high officialdom we find an abundance of theological material. The examples here of edicts and memorials are inscribed in *Shoku Nihongi* and although this entry may in fact evidence oral decrees and petitions being delivered in real time, that is not clear from the chronicle. Imperial edicts, replied to by memorials of high officialdom, are responded to in turn by a now Retired Empress. They demonstrate not a complete and systematic political theology, but rather prove that in the Nara period the best minds of a generation were striving towards articulation of a theology of imperial legitimacy, of supernatural support for political rule. Issuing from three powerful constituents of imperial government in Nara – the throne, the civil bureaucracy, and the Buddhist bureaucracy -- the language and concepts in these rich, lengthy and ponderous texts present a marvelous conglomeration of doctrine whose precise derivation is not always necessarily clear. While the Old Japanese *senmyō* emphasize powerful nativist Shinto concepts like "manifest deity" and the "High Throne of Heavenly Sun Succession," even these documents contain language reminiscent of classical Chinese diction. References to both archaic Chinese culture heroes and Buddhist enlightenment are stirred together in the two memorials. Thus we find allusions to omenology, filial piety, virtuous ancient Chinese kings, compassionate rule, cosmic symbolism, the Eight-fold Path, rites and music, veneration of ancestors, the "Profound Doctrine of Three Empties",[98] the ruler as Sage, and on and on.

These elegant texts may strike us at first glance as a conceptual and inchoate hodge-podge, but they provide vivid evidence of developing moves toward a political theology of legitimacy in mid- to late-eighth century Japan. The microscopic focus here on very specific passages from a single entry in *Shoku Nihongi* does not reveal a fully articulated statement of how the gods, Buddhas, and other higher powers such as archaic Chinese culture heroes together provide a conceptual legitimatization for the Japanese ruler. But as similar texts from the yet understudied *Shoku Nihongi* and other eighth-century material are examined and read closely in conjunction with one another, we can

---

[98] 三空之玄宗

be confident that a clearer focus will emerge of the official ideology of this critical period in the history of Japan.

Conclusion

The *Tenpyō Hōji* years covered in this translation saw Fujiwara no Nakamaro's rise to supremacy with the honorific name of Emi no Oshikatsu and appointments to novel court offices corresponding to Great Minister of the Right (*Udaijin*) and First Minister of the Great Council of State (*Daijōdaijin*). Nakamaro/Oshikatsu completely renamed the old *Ritsuryō* bureaucracy with nomenclature suggested by Tang and Parhae. Dowager Empress Kōmyō, his aunt, was his major backer while the new Emperor Junnin was his puppet. Retired Empress Kōken faded from the scene only temporarily, and reemerged especially after 762 as a major figure in the multifaceted imperial institution.

Nakamaro's bizarre plan to invade the Korean kingdom of Silla was apparently put aside after resumption of diplomatic relations. Japan's major trading partner and ally in this era was the kingdom of Parhae. Inflation and counterfeiting in the Japanese realm led to the minting of new copper, silver and gold coins in 760. Attempts were made to stabilize the price of rice by the establishment of ever-normal granaries and officers to administer them.

Finally, an unusual series of imperial edicts and memorials to the sovereigns by the high civil officials and Buddhist clergy revealed in remarkable detail motifs in a theology of legitimacy that began to be better articulated during this period. Although not a completely systematic ideology, the strands of Shinto, Buddhist, and Confucian thought were woven together in imperial decrees and memorials to the throne, giving evidence of sophisticated attempts by the intellectuals of the day to provide a basis for imperial rule.

Translation: Tenpyō Hōji 2 – Tenpyō Hōji 7

[The year begins toward the end of *Shoku Nihongi Maki* 20]

Tenpyō Hōji 2

天平宝字二年（七五八）正月戊寅【甲戌朔五】二年春正月戊寅。詔曰。朕以庸虚。忝承大位。母臨区宇。子育黎元。思与賢良。共清風化。長固宝暦。久安兆民。豈意、很戻近臣。潜懐不軌。同悪相済。終起乱階。頼宗社威霊。遽従殱殄。既是逆人・親党。私懐並不自安。雖犯深愆。尚加微貶。使其坦然無懼。息其反側之心。如聞。百僚在位。仍有憂惶。宜悉朕懐。不労疑慮。昔者。張敞負釁。更致朱軒。安国免徒。重紆青組。咸能洗心励節。輸款尽忠。事美一時。誉流千載。今之志士。豈謝前賢。改滌過咎。勉己自新。方冀、瑕不掩徳。要待良治。用靡棄材。以成大廈。凡百列位。宜鏡斯言。夙夜無怠。務脩爾職。」又詔曰。朕聞。則天施化。聖主遺章。順月宣風。先王嘉令。故能二儀無愆。四時和協。休気布於率土。仁寿致於群生。今者、三陽既建。万物初萌。和景惟新。人宜納慶。是以別使八道。巡問民苦。務恤貧病。矜救飢寒。所冀、撫字之道。将神合仁。亭育之慈。与天通事。疾疫咸却。年穀必成。家無寒寠之憂。国有来蘇之楽。所司宜知差清平使。勉加賑恤。称朕意焉。」以従五位下石川朝臣豊成為京畿内使。録事一人。正六位下藤原朝臣浄弁為東海。東山道使。判官一人。録事二人。正六位上紀朝臣広純為北陸道使。正六位上大伴宿禰潔足為山陰道使。正六位上藤原朝臣倉下麻呂為山陽道使。従六位下阿倍朝臣広人為南海道使。正六位上藤原朝臣楓麻呂為西海道使。道別録事一人。

Tenpyō Hōji 2.1.5 戊寅 *tsuchinoe-tora*

[February 17, 758]

The Empress gave an edict:

"Although We are mediocre and Our body is weak, We have gratefully received the imperial rank. We reign over the world like a mother and nurture the people as Our children. We consider that, along with wise and virtuous retainers We purify the mores, and over the ages strengthen the imperial position, and bring peace to the myriad people. However, suddenly some close retainers with perverse and twisted hearts secretly harbored immoral malice in their hearts, and with the aid of likewise evil companions finally sparked a revolt. Thanks to the authoritative spirit of the ancestral temples, they were immediately destroyed. Now as We consider the wicked bandits and their intimate companions there is still a feeling of unease. Although they committed a very great evil, We punished them lightly, so that they now may feel tranquil with nothing more to fear, and their rebellious hearts may be at rest. We have heard that the hundred officials who possess rank may have emotions of sadness or fear. But let them know Our inner feelings, and have no anxiety or fear.

"In ancient times Zhang Chang[99] of Han was given the death penalty for a crime, but later he was pardoned and and again became a high official. Han Anguo[100] suffered defeat, but later attained high rank. All reformed themselves and restored their honor. All renewed their sincerity and served loyally, and their glory has lasted for a thousand years. Why should not those today with the same

---

[99] 張敞
[100] 安国

42

aspirations not aim for the wisdom of those of old? Those who have committed offenses should change and diligently reform themselves. What We now desire is that they repair their flaws and restore their virtue. By polishing the flaws they can be restored to former beauty. A great mansion can be reconstructed without discarding the material but by using it skillfully. Let the hundred officials, taking these words as mirror and example, strive night and day without laziness, and accomplish their duties."

The Empress gave a further edict:

"We have heard thus: 'As for carrying out virtuous government according to the law of heaven, there are precedents left by the sage kings. Advancing civilization in accordance with the motions of the moon is the excellent law left by the former kings." Thus the *yin* and *yang* without fail harmonize the four seasons. Propitious pneuma[101] fills the land and the people receive blessings and are able to achieve long life. Now is the beginning of spring,[102] and the ten thousand crops are beginning to sprout. It is a good time when the mellow weather renews itself day by day, and the people too receive auspicious events. Thus We have dispatched messengers to circulate over the eight roads[103] to inquire about the suffering of the people, to provide relief to the sick and poor,

---

[101] *qi* 気

[102] SNIII, p 245, n. 17. The quotation is from the *Li ji* (Book of Rites). "Spring" is literally the "third *yang*". Entering winter is the first *yang*, leaving winter is the second *yang*, entering spring is the third *yang*.

[103] The *Kinai* and the seven circuits: 東海道, 東山道, 北陸道, 山陰道, 山陽道, 南海道, 西海道

43

and to give alms to those who suffer from famine and cold. We desire to caressingly nourish the people, to bring together the *kami* and the heart of benevolence, to bring compassionate cultivation throughout heaven and all things, to end all illness and disease, that the annual grains flourish without fail, that in households there is not the grief of cold and hunger, that the joy of seasonal renewal is experienced among the people of the nation. Let the officials of the bureaucracy bear this in mind, select persons of integrity and fairness, and strive as my envoys to spread compassion. Let it be as We wish."

Jr 5 Lower Ishikawa no Asomi Toyonari appointed envoy to the capital and *Kinai* with the aid of one Recording Officer. Sr 6 Lower Fujiwara no Asomi Jōben appointed envoy to *Tōkaidō* and *Tōsandō*, with one Secretary and two Recording Officers. Sr 6 Upper Ki no Asomi Hirosumi appointed envoy to *Hokurikudō*. Sr 6 Upper Ōtomo no Sukune Kiyotari appointed envoy to *San'indō*. Sr 6 Upper Fujiwara no Asomi Kurajimaro appointed envoy to *San'yōdō*. Jr 6 Lower Abe no Asomi Hirohito appointed envoy to *Sankaidō*. Sr 6 Upper Fujiwara no Asomi Kaerudemaro appointed envoy to *Saikaidō*. One Recording Officer appointed to each circuit.

天平宝字二年（七五八）二月辛亥【癸卯朔九】○二月辛亥。左大舎人広野王賜池上真人姓。

Tenpyō Hōji* 2.2.9** 辛亥 ***kanoto-i

[March 22, 758]

The Left Imperial Attendant Prince Hirono granted the *kabane* of Ikenoue no Mahito.

天平宝字二年（七五八）二月壬戌【二十】○壬戌。詔曰。随時立制。有国通規。議代行権。昔王彝訓。頃者。民間宴集。動有違愆。或同悪相聚。濫非聖化。或酔乱無節。便致闘争。拠理論之。甚乖道理。自今已後。王公已下。除供祭療患以外。不得飲酒。其朋友・寮属。内外親情。至於暇景。応相追訪者。先申官司。然後聴集。如有犯者。五位已上停一年封禄。六位已下解見任。已外決杖八十。冀将淳風俗。能成人善。習礼於未識。防乱於未然也。

Tenpyō Hōji 2.2.20 壬戌 *mizunoe-inu*

[April 2, 758]

The Empress gave an edict:

"To consider the times and carry out the laws, decisions have been taken since ancient times to protect the nation and to regulate institutions – these are teachings handed down by the ancient sage kings. Recently people gathering for banquets have erred recklessly. In some cases evil companions have gathered and outrageously slandered sage governance. In some cases all decorum has been lost, leading to drunken brawls. This is an exceeding affront to propriety and reason. Hereafter everyone, from members of the imperial family and the noble houses on down, is prohibited from drinking alcohol except on ceremonial occasions or in times of illness. When friends or near and distant relatives and acquaintances visit, on that day they shall first request permission from the appropriate offices, and only then shall gatherings be allowed. If there are offenders, in the case of fifth rank and up, they will be penalized one year's stipend. In the case of sixth rank and lower, they will lose their present office. Other people will be punished with eighty lashes of the cane. We desire to purify the customs and encourage the good, to instill ritual etiquette and prevent any tendency to disorder."

天平宝字二年（七五八）二月己巳【廿七】○己巳。勅曰。得大和国守従四位下大伴宿禰稲公等奏称。部下城下郡大和神山生奇藤。其根虫彫成文十六字。王大則并天下人此内任大平臣守昊命。即下博士議之。咸云。臣守天下。王大則并。内任此人。昊命大平。此知。群臣尽忠。共守天下。王大覆載。無不兼并。聖上挙賢。内任此人。昊天報徳。命其大平者也。加以。地即大和神山。藤此当今宰輔。事已有効。更亦何疑。朕恭受天＝［貝＋兄］。還恐不徳。吁哉、卿士。戒之。慎之。敬順神教。各修爾職。勤存撫育。共致良治。其大和国者、宜免今年調。当郡司者、加位一級。貢瑞人大和雑物者、特叙従六位下。賜＝［糸＋施の旁］廿疋。綿＝屯。布六十端。正税二千束。

Tenpyō Hōji 2.2.27 己巳 *tsuchinoto-mi*

[April 9, 758]

The Empress gave an edict:

"The Governor of Yamato Province Jr 4 Lower Ōtomo no Sukune Inakimi made the following report:

'In the district of Shikinoshimo, on Yamato Kamuyama, a marvelous wisteria tree grew. On its roots insects carved the following 16 characters: 王大則并天下人此内任太平臣守昊命.[104] These characters were then submitted to the

---

[104] *Ōtaisokuhei tenkanin shinainin taiheishinshu kōmei*

46

Learned Scholars and after discussion they all agreed on the following interpretation:

"The subjects guard the realm and are united in the great law of the king. If these people are appointed to the inner government, then heaven will command great peace."

'More fully interpreted, it is understood:

"When the subjects serve loyally, together they protect the realm. The sovereign rules over the land, and there is no discord. If sage rulers employ wise ministers, and appoint them to the inner government, then heaven repays their virtue and mandates that the land will be at peace." Not only that, but the wisteria on Yamato Kamuyama refers to the present Inner Minister Fujiwara Nakamaro.[105] Can there be any doubt that this is definitely a sign?'

The Empress said:

"We gratefully accept the gift of heaven, and upon reflection fear that we lack virtue. Ah nobles, We humbly reproach Ourselves. We revere the teaching of the *kami*, and striving at Our various duties, diligently attempt to nourish the people and bestow good government. Taxes in kind are remitted for Yamato Province for this year. We award one degree of rank to the district official. Yamato no Saimotsu who presented the omen is specially awarded Jr 6 Lower

---

[105] Nakamaro is here referred to as *Saiho* 宰輔. *Fuji* 藤 is taken to signify "Fujiwara."

47

Rank, twenty rolls of plain weave silk, forty hanks of silk floss, sixty lengths of hemp cloth, and two thousand sheaves of stored rice."

天平宝字二年（七五八）三月辛巳【壬申朔十】○三月辛巳。詔曰。朕聞。孝子思親。終身罔極。言編竹帛。千古不刊。去天平勝宝八歳五月。先帝登遐。朕自遘凶閔。雖懷感傷。為礼所防。俯従吉事。但每臨端五。風樹驚心。設席行觴。所不忍為也。自今已後。率土公私。一准重陽。永停此節焉。

Tenpyō Hōji* 2.3.10** 辛巳 ***kanoto-mi

[April 21, 758]

The Empress gave an edict:

"A filial child's consideration of her parents should not end with death. These words are written in ancient books and left down from distant times. On the fifth of the eighth month in *Tenpyō Shōhō* 8 the late Emperor Shōmu passed away. Since We have encountered this penetrating, futile, and sad event, We have had a heart of distress in Our breast, but because of the demands of rites, we have followed protocol for auspicious events, though we were under stress. But now that the ceremony of the fifth day of the fifth month[106] approaches, with its fresh spring winds, my heart is pained and I cannot bear to attend the feast and partake of the food. Thus hereafter, as in the case of the festival of the ninth day of the ninth month[107] the ceremony of the fifth month will not be held.

---

[106] *Tango* 端五

[107] *Chōyō* 重陽 -- formerly a festival day, but the death date of Emperor Tenmu.

天平宝字二年（七五八）三月壬午【十一】○壬午。伊予国神野郡人少初位上賀茂直馬主等賜賀茂伊予朝臣姓。

Tenpyō Hōji 2.3.11 壬午 *mizunoe-uma*

[April 22, 758]

Persons of Iyo Province, Kamuno district *Shōso*[108] Upper Kamo no Atai Umanushi were granted the *kabane* of Kamo Iyo no Asomi.

天平宝字二年（七五八）三月丁亥【十六】○丁亥。舶名播磨。速鳥並叙従五位下。其冠者。各以錦造。入唐使所乗者也。

Tenpyō Hōji 2.3.16 丁亥 *hinoto-i*

[April 27, 758]

The ships named Harima and Hayatori were each granted Jr 5 Lower rank. The caps were made of brocade. The ships were those that the envoys to Tang were to sail in.

天平宝字二年（七五八）四月乙卯【壬寅朔十四】○夏四月乙卯。従五位上藤原朝臣魚名為備中守。

Tenpyō Hōji 2.4.14 乙卯 Summer *unoto-u*

[May 25, 758]

Jr 5 Upper Fujiwara no Asomi Uona appointed Governor of Bitchū[109] Province.

天平宝字二年（七五八）四月庚申【十九】○庚申。初尾張連馬身以壬申年功。先朝叙小錦下。未被賜姓。其身早亡。於是。馬身子孫並賜宿禰姓。

Tenpyō Hōji 2.4.19 庚申 *kanoe-saru*

---

[108] 少初 – a pre-*Ritsuryō* title
[109] *Kibinomichinonaka*

[May 30, 758]

Previously Owari Muraji Mami was granted the rank of Smaller Brocade Lower[110] by the previous court for his meritorious efforts in the Jinshin War, but before his *kabane* could be awarded he died. Therefore his descendants are granted the *kabane* of Sukune.

天平宝字二年（七五八）四月辛酉【二十】○辛酉。中務卿正四位下阿倍朝臣佐美麻呂卒。

Tenpyō Hōji **2.4.20** 辛酉 *kanoto-tori*

[May 31, 758]

The Head of the Ministry of Central Affairs[111] Sr 4 Lower Ahe no Asomi Samimaro died.

天平宝字二年（七五八）四月己巳【廿八】○己巳。内薬司佑兼出雲国員外掾正六位上難波薬師奈良等一十一人言。奈良等遠祖徳来。本高麗人。帰百済国。昔泊瀬朝倉朝廷詔百済国。訪求才人。爰以、徳来貢進聖朝。徳来五世孫恵日。小治田朝廷御世。被遣大唐。学得医術。因号薬師。遂以為姓。今愚闇子孫。不論男女。共蒙薬師之姓。窃恐名実錯乱。伏願。改薬師字。蒙難波連。許之。

Tenpyō Hōji **2.4.28** 己巳 *tsuchinoto-mi*

[June 8, 758]

---

[110] *Shōkinge* 小錦下
[111] *Nakatsukasa Kyō* 中務卿. Note that the SNKBT consistently uses "*Chūmu*" for "*Nakatsukasa*".

50

The Assistant Head of the Palace Medical Office[112] and concurrently Izumo Assistant Irregular Governor[113] Sr 6 Upper Naniwa no Kusushi Nara and others (eleven people in all) stated:

"The distant ancestor of Tokurai of Nara and the others was originally a person of Koguryō but migrated to Paekche. In ancient times Emperor Yūryaku[114] sent an edict to Paeckche seeking talented people. Then Paekche presented Tokurai to the sagely Japanese court. Tokurai's fifth-generation descendant Enichi in the time of the Oharida Court[115] was dispatched to Tang China to study medicine. Thus he was named Kusushi and granted that *kabane*. Now his humble descendants are not physicians, neither male nor female and yet they bear the *kabane* of Kusushi. Thus we fear that the true meaning of the *kabane* has become confused. We humbly petition that the kabane be changed to Naniwa no Muraji."

This was granted.

天平宝字二年（七五八）五月丙戌【辛未朔十六】○夏五月丙戌。大宰府言。承前公廨稲、合一百万束。然中間、官人任意費用。今但遺一十余万束。官人数多。所給甚少。離家既遠。生活尚難。於是、以所遺公廨。悉合正税。更割諸国正税。国別遍置。不失其本。毎年出挙。以所得利。依式班給。其諸国地子稲者。一依先符。任為公廨。以充府中雑事。

Tenpyō Hōji* 2.5.16** 丙戌 ***hinoe-inu

---

[112] *Naiyakushi Suke* 内薬司佑
[113] *Ingaijō* 員外掾
[114] 雄略天皇 – *Hatsuseasakara no Mikado* 泊瀬朝倉朝廷

[115] 小治田朝廷 – Suiko *Tennō*

51

[June 25, 758]

The Kyushu Government Headquarters stated:

"We formerly received one million sheaves of loaned government rice.[116] However later the officials spent lavishly and now we receive only one hundred thousand sheaves. The officials are many, and the amount they are paid is extremely small. They serve at a great distance removed from their families, and their life is difficult. Therefore we should like to reorganize the tax system, combining the stored rice[117] with what is left of the loaned government rice and dividing it among the provinces. Each year the interest from the loan rice[118] is to be distributed according to the regulation of the previous year.[119] Rice from the official provincial land may be freely used for general expenses of the Kyushu Headquarters, according to the previous pronouncement of the Great Council of State.[120]

天平宝字二年（七五八）五月乙未【廿五】○乙未。正六位上大和宿禰弟守授従五位下。

Tenpyō Hōji **2.5.25**　乙未　*kinoto-hitsuji*

[July 4, 758]

Sr 6 Upper Yamato no Sukune Otomori awarded Jr 5 Lower Rank.

---

[116] *Kugetō* 公廨稲. SNIII p 252 n 1 summarizes this complex passage. Notes 2-8 (pp. 252-3) provide details of the reorganization of the tax system in Kyushu, and notes that portions of the text are unclear.
[117] *Shōzei* 正税.
[118] *Suiko* 出挙
[119] *Shiki* 式. SNIII p 252 n 6.
[120] *Fu* 符. SNIII p 253 n 8.

天平宝字二年（七五八）六月甲辰【辛丑朔四】〇六月甲辰。大宰陰陽師
従六位下余益人。造法華寺判官従六位下余東人等四人、賜百済朝臣姓。
越後目正七位上高麗使主馬養。内侍典侍従五位下高麗使主浄日等五人、
多可連。散位大属正六位上狛広足。散位正八位下狛浄成等四人、長背連。

Tenpyō Hōji 2.6.4 甲辰 *kinoe-tatsu*

[July 13, 758]

The Kyushu Headquarters Diviner[121] Jr 6 Lower Yo no Masuhito and the
Secretary for *Hokkeji* Construction Jr 6 Lower Yo no Azumahito and others
(four people in all) were granted the *kabane* Kudara no Asomi. The Echigo
Province Special Assistant Governor Sr 7 Upper Koma no Shishu Umakai and
the Inner Palace Assistant Head[122] Jr 5 Lower Koma no Shishu Kiyohi and
others (five people in all) were granted the *kabune* Taka no Muraji. Scattered-
rank *Daizoku*[123] Sr 6 Upper Koma no Muraji Hirotari and Scattered Rank Sr 8
Lower Koma no Kiyonari and others (four people in all) were granted the
kabane Nagase no Muraji.

天平宝字二年（七五八）六月辛亥【十一】〇辛亥。陸奥国言。去年八月
以来。帰降夷俘。男女惣一千六百九十余人。或去離本土。帰慕皇化。或
身渉戦場。与賊結怨。惣是新来。良未安堵。亦夷性狼心。猶予多疑。望
請。准天平十年閏七月十四日勅。量給種子。令得佃田。永為王民。以充
辺軍。許之。

Tenpyō Hōji 2.6.11 辛亥 *kanoto-i*

---

[121] *Onmyōji* 陰陽師
[122] *Naishi Suke* 内侍典侍
[123] 大属 – pre-*Ritsuryō* rank

[July 20, 758]

Michinooku Province stated:

"Since the eighth month of last year over one thousand six hundred ninety *Emishi* both male and female have migrated to Michinooku. Some have come from distant hometowns hoping to submit to the imperial reign. Some have been injured by robbers while crossing the battlefield. These are all people who have newly submitted and they are not yet settled. Furthermore the *Emishi* have the hearts of wolves, and it is doubtful that they have already been pacified. We petition that, in accordance with the edict of *Tenpyō* 10.Int7.14, they be given seed and land to cultivate. Thus they will become imperial subjects forever, and help to constitute troops to defend our borders."

This was granted.

天平宝字二年（七五八）六月丙辰【十六】○丙辰。以従四位上佐伯宿禰毛人為常陸守。参議従三位文室真人智努為出雲守。従五位上大伴宿禰家持為因幡守。

Tenpyō Hōji **2.6.16** 丙辰 *hinoe-tatsu*

[July 25, 758]

Jr 4 Upper Saeki no Sukune Emishi appointed Hitachi Governor. The Imperial Adviser Jr 3 Fun'ya no Mahito Chino appointed Izumo Governor. Jr 5 Upper Saeki no Ōtomo Sukune Yakamochi appointed Governor of Inaba.

天平宝字二年（七五八）六月乙丑【廿五】○乙丑。大和国葛上郡人従八位上桑原史年足等男女九十六人。近江国神埼郡人正八位下桑原史人勝等男女一千一百五十五人同言曰。伏奉去天平勝宝九歳五月廿六日勅書称。内大臣。太政大臣之名不得称者。今年足・人勝等先祖、後漢苗裔＝言興并帝利等。於難波高津宮御宇天皇之世。転自高麗。帰化聖境。本是同祖。今分数姓。望請。依勅、一改史字。因蒙同姓。於是。桑原史。大友桑原史。大友史。大友部史。桑原史戸。史戸六氏、同賜桑原直姓。船史船直姓。

Tenpyō Hōji 2.6.25 乙丑 *unoto-ushi*

[August 3, 758]

Ninety-six people, men and women, of Yamato Province Kazurakinokami district including Jr 8 Upper Kuwahara no Fuhito Toshitari, and one thousand one hundred fifty-five people, men and women of Ōmi Province Kanzaki District including Sr 8 Lower Kuwahara no Fuhito Hitokatsu together stated:

"According to an edict of *Tenpyō Shōhō* 9.5.26 the names of the late Great Minister of the Middle[124] and the late First Minister, Council of State[125] were not to be used. The ancestors of Toshitari and Hitokatsu, descendants of the Later Han, Suetōgenkō and Teiri, in the reign of the Emperor who reigned from *Naniwatakatsunomiya* [126], immigrated from Koguryō to within the boundaries of the sagely reign of Japan. At first they had the same ancestors, but now their numbers have multiplied and divided into numerous clans. What we ask, in accordance with the edict is that the character *fuhito* 史 be changed and that we be given different *kabane*."

---

[124] Fujiwara no Kamatari.
[125] Fujiwara no Fuhito.
[126] Nintoku *Tennō* 仁徳天皇

Therefore the six clans Kuwahara no Fuhito, Ōtomo no Kuwahara Fuhito, Ōtomo no Fuhito, Ōtomobe no Fuhito, and Kuwahara no Fuhitobe, were granted the *kabane* of Kuwahara no Atai. The Funafuhito clan was granted the *kabane* of Funa no Atai.

天平宝字二年（七五八）七月癸酉【辛未朔三】○秋七月癸酉。勅。東海。東山道問民苦使正六位下藤原朝臣浄弁等奏称。両道百姓尽頭言曰。依去天平勝宝九歳四月四日恩詔。中男正丁、並加一歳。老丁・耆老、倶脱恩私。望請。一准中男・正丁。欲霑非常洪沢者。所請当理。仍須憫矜。宜告天下諸国。自今以後。以六十為老丁。以六十五為耆老。

Tenpyō Hōji 2.7.3 癸酉　**Autumn *mizunoto-tori***
[August 11, 758]

The Empress gave an edict:

"The Special Inspector[127] for *Tōkaidō* and *Tōsandō* Sr 6 Upper Fujiwara no Asomi Jōben reported:

"The people of both circuits all agreed, saying:

'Although according to the edict of *Tenpyō Shōhō* 9.4.4 the ages of middle adulthood[128] and full adulthood[129] were raised by one year each,

---

[127] *Monminkushi* 問民苦使. SNIII p 255 n 24 – this is the first appearance of the term. On TPHJ 2.1.5 the Empress had sent out messengers to inquire about the suffering of the people.
[128] *chūnan* 中男
[129] *shōchō* 正丁

the age of seniors[130] and elderly[131] were not addressed in the edict. We beg for this special compassionate dispensation.' "

"We find this petition to be reasonable. It shall be granted. Let it be announced in all provinces of the realm that from now on age 60 shall be designated "senior" and age 65 shall be "elderly".[132]

天平宝字二年（七五八）七月甲戌【四】○甲戌。勅。比来、皇太后寝膳不安。稍経旬日。朕思。延年済疾。莫若仁慈。宜令天下諸国。始自今日。迄今年十二月卅日。禁断殺生。又以猪鹿之類。永不得進御。又勅。縁有所思。免官奴婢并紫微中台奴婢。皆悉従良。」従七位上葛井連恵文。正六位上味淳竜丘。難波連奈良並授外従五位下。

Tenpyō Hōji 2.7.4 甲戌 kinoe-inu

[August 12, 758]

The Empress gave an edict:

"Recently the condition of the Dowager Empress Kōmyō has not been good, and this has continued for over ten days. We consider that for extending life and healing disease, there is nothing better than carrying out benevolence and compassion. Therefore throughout all the provinces of the realm, from now until the thirtieth day of the twelfth month, killing is forbidden. Also the meat of wild boar and deer is forever forbidden to be served at Court."

The Empress gave another edict:

---

[130] *rōchō* 老丁
[131] *kirō* 耆老
[132] SNIII p 256 n2 – this lowers the ages designated in *Toryō* 戸令 6 of *Ritsuryō*.

"We further consider that all government male and female slaves, including those of the *Shibi Chūdai* shall be freed and made free people. [133] Jr 7 Upper Fujii no Muraji Efumi and Sr 6 Upper Umezake no Tatsuoka and Naniwa no Muraji Nara all awarded Outer Jr 5 Lower Rank.

天平宝字二年（七五八）七月丙子【六】○丙子。正六位上阿倍朝臣乙加志授従五位下。正六位上額田部宿禰三富。戸憶志。根連鞁韜。生江臣智麻呂。調連牛養。山田史銀並外従五位下。三富本姓額田部川田連也。是日。以額田部宿禰姓、便書位記賜之。

Tenpyō Hōji 2.7.6 丙子

[August 14, 758]

Sr 6 Upper Ahe Asomi Otokashi awarded Jr 5 Lower Rank.

Sr 6 Upper Nukatabe no Sukune Mimasa, He no Okushi, Ne no Muraji Matsukatsu, Ikue no Ōmi Tomomaro, Tsuki no Muraji Ushikai, Yamada no Fuhito Shirogane, all awarded Jr 5 Lower Rank. Mimasa's original *kabane* was Nukatabe Kawata no Muraji. On this day his *kabane* was written in the Register of Ranks as Nukatabe no Sukune.

天平宝字二年（七五八）七月戊戌【廿八】○戊戌。勅。為令朝廷安寧、天下太平。国別奉写金剛般若経卅巻。安置国分僧寺廿巻。尼寺十巻。恒副金光明最勝王経。並令転読焉。

Tenpyō Hōji 2.7.28 戊戌 *tsuchinoe-inu*

---

[133] *ryō* 良

[September 5, 758]

The Empress gave a *choku*:

"For the stability of the court and peace in the realm, thirty rolls[134] of the *Diamond Sutra* [135] shall be copied in every province. Twenty rolls shall be placed in the official provincial monasteries, and ten in the official provincial nunneries. It is ordered that these be read in perpetuity along with the *Golden Light Sutra of the Most Victorious Kings.*[136]

《卷尾続日本紀　巻第廿

[End of *Shoku Nihongi Maki* 20]

《卷首続日本紀　巻第廿一〈起天平宝字二年八月、尽十二月。〉
右大臣従二位兼行皇太子傅中衛大将臣藤原朝臣継縄等奉勅撰」
廃帝
《淳仁天皇即位前紀廃帝。諱大炊王。天渟中原瀛真人天皇之孫。一品舎人親王之第七子也。母当麻氏。名曰山背。上総守従五位上老之女也。帝受禅之日。授正三位。後尊曰大夫人。天平勝宝八歳。皇太子道祖王。諒闇之中。心不在＝。九歳三月廿九日辛丑。高野天皇。皇太后、与右大臣従二位藤原朝臣豊成。大納言従二位藤原朝臣仲麻呂。中納言従三位紀朝臣麻路。多治比真人広足。摂津大夫従三位文屋真人智努等。定策禁中。廃皇太子。以王還第。先是。大納言藤原仲麻呂。妻大炊王。以亡男真従婦粟田諸姉。居於私第。四月四日乙巳。遂迎大炊王於仲麻呂田村第。立為皇太子。時年廿五。

Shoku Nihongi Maki 22 (*Tenpyō Hōji* 2.8 – 2.12)

---

[134] *Maki* 巻
[135] 金剛般若経 *Kongōkyō* (C. *Jingang jing*) - Abbreviation of 金剛般若波羅蜜經. (Skt. *Vajracchedikā-prajñāpāramitā-sūtra*.)

[136] 金光明最勝王経 *Konkōmyō Saishōōkyō.*

Compiled and presented by imperial order by Great Minister of the Right Jr 2 and concurrently Tutor to the Crown Prince and General of the Middle Imperial Guards Fujiwara no Asomi Tsugutada. [Fujiwara Toyonari's second son, in *Enryaku* 13.8, (794)]

The *Haitei* 廃帝 ["Deposed Emperor"]

[Preface upon Junnin *Tennō*'s Enthronement]

The Deposed Emperor's given name was Prince Ōi.[137] He was a grandson of Emperor *Ama no Nunahara Oki no Mahito no Sumera Mikoto* [138], and the seventh son of First Cap Rank Imperial Prince Toneri.[139] His mother was of the Tagima clan, named Yamashiro. She was the daughter of the Governor of Kazusa, Jr 5 Upper Oyu. On the day that the Empress Kōken abdicated, his mother was granted Sr 3rd rank, and respectfully called "Great Consort".

In TPSH 8, the Crown Prince Funado[140] was disrespectful during the mourning period for Retired Emperor Shōmu. On TPSH 9.3.29 Takano *Tennō* (Kōken), and the Dowager Empress Kōmyō together with the Great Minister of the Right Jr 2 Fujiwara no Asomi Toyonari, the Major Counsellor Jr 2 Fujiwara no Asomi Nakamaro, the Middle Counsellor Jr 3 Ki Asomi Maro, Middle Counsellor Tajihi no Mahito Hirotari, Middle Counsellor and Settsu Province Commissioner Jr 3 Funya no Mahito Chino, discussed policy in the palace. They

---

[137] 大炊
[138] 天淳中原瀛真人天皇 – Tenmu *Tennō*.
[139] 舍人親王
[140] 皇太子道祖王

removed the Crown Prince and sent him home to his private mansion with just the title of Prince. Previously the Major Counsellor Nakamaro had married Prince Ōi to the widow of his deceased son Mayori (her name was Awata no Morone) and Ōi resided in the private residence of Nakamaro, the Tamura Mansion.[141] On the fourth day of the fourth month Ōi returned from Tamura Mansion and took his position as Crown Prince. At the time he was 25 years old.

天平宝字二年（七五八）八月庚子朔天平宝字二年八月庚子朔。高野天皇禅位於皇太子。詔曰。【Ｓ２３】現神御宇天皇詔旨〈良麻止〉詔勅〈乎〉、親王・諸王・諸臣・百官人等、衆聞食宣。高天原神積坐皇親神魯棄神魯美命吾孫知食国天下〈止〉、事依奉〈乃〉任〈爾〉、遠皇祖御世始〈弖〉天皇御世御世聞看来天日嗣高御座〈乃〉業〈止奈母〉随神所念行〈久止〉宣天皇勅、衆聞食宣。加久聞看来天日嗣高御座〈乃〉業〈波〉、天坐神・地坐祇〈乃〉相宇豆奈〈比〉奉相扶奉事〈爾〉依〈弖之〉此座平安御座〈弖〉、天下者所知物〈爾〉在〈良自止奈母〉随神所念行〈須〉。然皇〈止〉坐〈弖〉天下政〈乎〉聞看事者、労〈岐〉重〈棄〉事〈爾〉在〈家利〉。年長〈久〉日多〈久〉此座坐〈波〉、荷重力弱〈之弖〉不堪負荷。加以、掛畏朕婆婆皇太后朝〈爾母〉人子之理〈爾〉不得定省〈波〉、朕情〈母〉日夜不安。是以、此位避〈弖〉間〈乃〉人〈爾〉在〈弖之〉如理婆婆〈爾波〉仕奉〈倍自止〉所念行〈弖奈母〉日嗣〈止〉定賜〈弊流〉皇太子〈爾〉授賜〈久止〉宣天皇御命、衆聞食宣。

***Tenpyō Hōji* 2.8.1** 庚子 *kanoe-ne* [note – this extremely long entry is subdivided into sections]

[September 7, 758]

Takano *Tennō* (Kōken) abdicated in favor of the Crown Prince. She gave the following edict [*Senmyō* 23]:

---

[141] *Tamuratei* 田村第

"Let all – imperial princes, princes, ministers, and the hundred officials – hearken to the edict which is proclaimed as the command of the Empress who rules the land as a manifest deity. Let all hearken to the imperial edict issued by the Empress, who in the body of a god rules the land from the High Throne from which for generations the Emperors have ruled, beginning with the reign of the distant Imperial ancestors, just as the distant Imperial ancestors, the male and female *kami* in the High Plain of Heaven[142], decreed that their descendants should rule the Realm of All Under Heaven. We consider that in the body of a god We should rule the Realm, assisted in maintaining the peace and stability of the imperial rank by the gods who are in heaven and the gods who are on earth, in wondrous unity, in the task of the High Throne of Heavenly Sun Succession.

"However, ruling over the Realm as Empress is a weighty matter and cause of suffering. Serving in this rank the years are long and the days are many, and to Us this is a burden – Our strength is weak and We cannot bear it. And not this only, but day and night Our heart is uneasy, since as a child We have not time to devote the care that is expected of a daughter toward Our Mother, the Dowager Empress, whose name is invoked with awe and fear. Thus, thinking to have time to devote Ourselves to the care of Our Revered Mother, We decree that We shall

---

[142] 高天原神積坐皇親神[魯棄]神[魯美] *takamanohara ni kamuzumarimasu sumeraga mutsukamuroki mutsukamuroki.* Norinaga p. 100 states that the phrase *mutsukamuroki mutsukamuroki* may refer explicitly to *Izanagi* 伊邪那岐 and *Izanami* 伊邪那美, or perhaps to all the male and female imperial ancestral deities down to *Amaterasu Ōmikami.*

leave our Rank, and that the Sun Succession shall pass to the designated Crown Prince[143] – let all hearken to these words of the Empress."

是日。皇太子受禅、即天皇位於大極殿。詔曰。【Ｓ２４】明神大八洲所知天皇詔旨〈良麻止〉宣勅、親王・諸王・諸臣・百官人等、天下公民、衆聞食宣。掛畏現神坐倭根子天皇我皇、此天日嗣高御座之業〈乎〉拙劣朕〈爾〉被賜〈弖〉仕奉〈止〉仰賜〈比〉授賜〈閉波〉、頂〈爾〉受賜〈利〉恐〈美〉、受賜〈利〉懼、進〈母〉不知〈爾〉、退〈母〉不知〈爾〉、恐〈美〉坐〈久止〉宣天皇勅、衆聞食宣。然皇坐〈弖〉天下治賜君者、賢人〈乃〉能臣〈乎〉得〈弖之〉天下〈乎婆〉平〈久〉安〈久〉治物〈爾〉在〈良之止奈母〉聞行〈須〉。故是以、大命坐、宣〈久〉。朕雖拙弱。親王始〈弖〉王臣等〈乃〉相穴〈奈比〉奉〈利〉相扶奉〈牟〉事依〈弖之〉此之仰賜〈比〉授賜〈夫〉食国天下之政者、平〈久〉安〈久〉仕奉〈倍之止奈母〉所念行〈須〉。是以、無＝欺之心、以忠赤之誠、食国天下之政者衆助仕奉〈止〉宣天皇勅、衆聞食宣。辞別〈＝［氏十一］〉宣〈久〉。仕奉人等中〈爾〉自〈何〉仕奉状随〈弖〉一二人等冠位上賜〈比〉治賜〈夫〉。百官職事已上及太神宮〈乎〉始〈弖〉諸社禰宜・祝〈爾〉大御物賜〈夫〉。僧綱始〈弖〉諸寺師位僧尼等〈爾〉物布施賜〈夫〉。又百官司〈乃〉人等、諸国兵上・鎮兵・伝駅戸等、今年田租免賜〈久止〉宣天皇勅、衆聞食宣。」

Tenpyō Hōji 2.8.1 庚子 *kanoe-ne* [continued]

[September 7, 758]

On this day the Crown Prince received the abdication and ascended to the imperial throne in the Imperial Council Hall. The Emperor Junnin gave an edict

[*Senmyō* 24]:

"Let all – imperial princes, princes, ministers, the hundred officials, and all the people under heaven – hearken to the words which are proclaimed as the edict of the Emperor, who rules the great land of the Eight Islands as a manifest deity.

---

[143] 皇太子 *Kōtaishi* – the Prince Ōi.

The Empress, our Sovereign, who is the Beloved Child of Yamato, a manifest deity whose name is invoked with awe and fear, has conferred on Us the High Throne of Heavenly Sun Succession, though We are clumsy and weak. Thus let all hearken to the edict of the Emperor, as We have received the duty of rule with awe and trepidation, knowing neither whether to advance or retreat[144].

"Now We have heard that the Lord who pacifies the realm as the Sovereign is one who with the aid of wise and able subjects shall govern all under heaven. Thus We now declare as your Ruler that, though We be weak and foolish, with the aid of the imperial princes first, and also the princes and ministers, We shall be able to govern in peace and stability the Realm of All Under Heaven which has been bequeathed to Us. Thus without flattery or deceit, but with bright and loyal hearts, and with all assisting in the government of the Realm of All Under Heaven, let all hearken to the edict which the Emperor now decrees.

"To speak on another matter, among those working to serve there are some who due to their devotion should be rewarded with official rank. In addition to those bureaucrats among the hundred officials, the *negi* [145] and *hafuri*[146] of the various shrines beginning with Ise *Daijingū* shall receive gifts. Beginning with the Council of Priestly Affairs, the monks and nuns of high rank of the various temples shall receive donations. Also the hundred officials, soldiers and guard

---

[144]進[母]不知[爾] 退[母]不知[爾] -- A similar phrase 知進而不知退 is found *inter alia* in *Yijing* and *Shiji*.
[145] 禰宜
[146] 祝

units of the provinces, and those supplying the post stations shall have their field rice tax remitted for this year -- let all hearken to the edict of the Emperor."

授従三位石川朝臣年足正三位。正四位上船王。他田王。氷上真人塩焼並従三位。正四位下諱〈平城宮御宇高紹天皇〉正四位上。無位菅生王従五位下。従四位下藤原朝臣巨勢麻呂。佐伯宿禰毛人並従四位上。正五位上藤原朝臣御楯従四位下。正五位下粟田朝臣奈世麻呂正五位上。従五位下阿倍朝臣子嶋。紀朝臣伊保。石川朝臣豊成。藤原朝臣真光。当麻真人浄成並従五位上。外従五位上文忌寸馬養。正六位下菅生朝臣嶋足。佐伯宿禰御方。笠朝臣真足。穂積朝臣小東人。阿倍朝臣意宇麻呂。中臣朝臣毛人。県犬養宿禰吉男。紀朝臣牛養。大伴宿禰東人。藤原朝臣楓麻呂。大野朝臣広言。正六位下藤原朝臣久須麻呂。従六位上石川朝臣広成並従五位下。正六位上山辺県主男笠。宍人朝臣倭麻呂。辛小床。大和宿禰斐大麻呂。宇自賀臣山道。忌部首黒麻呂並外従五位下。」又授正四位上河内女王従三位。正五位上当麻真人山背正三位。無位奈貴女王従四位下。無位伊刀女王。垂水女王。正六位上内真人糸井。無位粟田朝臣諸姉。藤原朝臣影並従五位下。外大初位上黄文連真白女。上道臣広羽女。従六位上爪工宿禰飯足並外従五位下。

Tenpyō Hōji 2.8.1 庚子 *kanoe-ne* [continued]

[September 7, 758]

Jr 3 Ishikawa no Asomi Toshitari awarded Sr 3 Rank.

Sr 4 Upper Prince Fune, Prince Ikeda, and Hikami no Mahito Shioyaki all awarded Jr 3 Rank.

Sr 4 Lower Prince Shirakabe (note – *Takatsugi Sumera Mikoto* who ruled the empire from Heijō Palace)[147] Sr 4 Upper Rank.

No-rank Prince Sugafu awarded Jr 5 Lower Rank.

---

[147] imina 諱 – taboo name for the future Emperor Kōnin (光仁天皇) – *Takatsugi Sumera Mikoto* who ruled the realm from Heijō Palace 平城宮御宇高紹天皇

Jr 4 Lower Fujiwara no Asomi Kosemaro and Saeki no Sukune Emishi both awarded Jr 4 Upper Rank.

Sr 5 Upper Fujiwara no Asomi Mitate awarded Jr 4 Lower Rank.

Sr 5 Lower Awata no Asomi Nasemaro awarded Sr 5 Upper Rank.

Jr 5 Lower Ahe no Asomi Koshima, Ki no Asomi Iho, Ishikawa no Asomi Toyonari, Fujiwara no Asomi Masaki, and Tagima no Mahito Kiyonari all awarded Jr 5 Upper Rank.

Outer Jr 5 Upper Fumi no Imiki Umakai, Sr 6 Upper Sugafu no Asomi Shimatari, Saeki no Sukune Mikata, Kasa no Asomi Matari, Hozumi no Asomi Oazumahito, Ahe no Asomi Oumaro, Nakatomi no Asomi Emishi, Agata Inukai no Sukune Yoshio, Ki no Asomi Ushikai, Ōtomo no Sukune Azumahito, Fujiwara no Asomi Kaerutemaro, Ōno no Asomi Hirotate, Sr 6 Lower Fujiwara no Asomi Kusumaro, Jr 6 Upper Ishikawa no Asomi Hironari all awarded Jr 5 Lower Rank.

Sr 6 Upper Yamanohe no Agatanushi Okasa, Shishihito no Asomi Yamatomaro, Kara no Otoko, Yamato no Sukune Hidamaro, Ujika no Omi Yamaji, Imbe no Obito Kuromaro, all awarded Outer Jr 5 Lower Rank.

Also Sr 4 Upper Princess Kawachi awarded Jr 3 Rank.

Sr 5 Upper Tagima no Mahito Yamashiro awarded Sr 3 Rank.

No-rank Princess Naki awarded Jr 4 Lower Rank.

No-rank Princess Ito, Princess Tarumi, Sr 6 Upper Uchi no Mahito Itoi, No-rank Awata no Asomi Morone, and Fujiwara no Asomi Kage all awarded Jr 5 Lower Rank.

Outer *Daisho* [148] Upper Kibumi no Muraji Mashirome, Kamitsumichi no Omi Hirohame, and Jr 6 Upper Hatakumi no Sukune Iitari all awarded Outer Jr 5 Lower Rank.

是日。百官及僧綱詣朝堂上表。上台・中台尊号。其百官表曰。臣仲麻呂
等言。臣聞。星廻日薄。懸象著明。之謂天。出震登乾。乘時首出。之謂
聖。天以不言為徳。非言無以暢其神。聖以無名体道。非名安可詮其用。
冬穴夏巣之世。猶昧典章。雲官火紀之君。方崇徽号。寔乃発揮功業。闡
揚尊名。名之為義。其来尚矣。伏惟。皇帝陛下。臨馭天下。十有余年。
海内清平。朝廷無事。祥瑞頻至。宝字荐臻。乃聖乃神。允文允武。諒無
得而称。暨乎国絶皇嗣。人懐彼此。降天尊於人願。鳴謙克光。損乾徳於
坤儀。鴻基遂固。展誠敬而追遠。攀慕惟深。勤温清以承顔。凩心懇至。
故有九服宅心。咸荷望雲之慶。万方傾首。倶承就日之輝。皇太后叡徳上
昇。善穆儷天之位。深仁下済。爰昭法地之猷。日月於是貞明。乾坤以之
交泰。遂乃欽承顧命。議定皇儲。棄親挙疎。心在公正。実在志於天下。
永無私於一己。既而遊神恵苑。体三空之玄宗。降迹禅林。開一真之妙覚。
大慈至深。建薬院而普済。弘願潜運。設悲田而広救。是以煙浮震幄。宝
＝呈祥。虫彫藤枝。禎文告徳。遂使百神恊賛。天平之化不窮。黎元楽推。
地成之徳逾遠。臣等入参帷＝。出廝周行。鳴珮曳綸。綿積年祀。観斯盛
徳。戴斯昌化。臣子之義。何無称賛。人欲而天必従。狂言而聖尚択。謹
拠典策。敢上尊号。伏乞。奉称上台宝字称徳孝謙皇帝。奉称中台天平応
真仁正皇太后。上恊天休。伝鴻名於万歳。下従人望。揚雅称於千秋。不
勝至懇踊躍之甚。謹詣朝堂。奉表以聞。」

Tenpyō Hōji 2.8.1 庚子 *kanoe-ne* [continued]

[September 7, 758]

---

[148]大初 – a pre-*Ritsuryō* rank.

On this day the Hundred Officials and the Council of Buddhist Priestly Affairs came to the Administrative Palace and presented a petition asking that Retired Empress Kōken be named *Jōdai*,[149] and the Dowager Empress Kōmyō be named *Chūdai*.[150] The following was stated in the petition of the Hundred Officials:

"The Minister Nakamaro and all respectfully state:

'Your subjects have heard 'The stars circle around and the sun gives light, showing clearly the pattern of bodies suspended in the sky – this we call Heaven.[151] He who arises in the east and ascends to heaven, rides the times and rises above the masses – this we call the Sage.[152] Though Heaven without speaking creates virtue, words cannot penetrate its divinity. Though the Sage without name embodies the Way, how can the Sage, nameless, reveal his ways? In the time when men dwelt in holes in the winter and in trees in the summer, and documents had not yet developed, then names were given to the Lords Huang Di and Yan Di,[153] and the giving of honorific names accorded with virtuous action.' Truly the accordance of honorific titles for virtuous action thus has a long history.

---

[149] 上台 – "Retired Empress"

[150] 中台 – as in *Shibi Chūdai* 紫微中台, Office of the Dowager Empress' Household.

[151] SNIII p 268, notes 12 and 13 – somewhat garbled references from the *Wenxuan* 文選 and *Yi Jing* 易經.

[152] SNIII p 268, notes 14 and 15 – more garbled references from the Chinese classics.

[153] SNIII p 268 n 19 – literally 雲官火紀之君, meaning Huang Di 黃帝 and Yan Di 炎帝

"We reverently consider that the Empress has ruled the empire for over ten years. Land and sea have been at peace and there have been no major events at court. [154] Good omens [155] have repeatedly appeared, and lucky omens in writing[156] have also appeared. Thus has the Empress been both a Sage and a *Kami*, and words do not suffice to praise the maintenance of both civil and martial virtues. Some have been anxious about the succession to the imperial throne. The people desire that heavenly blessings be dispensed and that the virtue of humility shine forth. The heavenly virtue is dispensed upon the earth, and it greatly strengthens the foundation of the country. With deep emotions of gratitude and reverence we cherish the memory of distant ancestors. We feel the depth of filial love for the mother, so that we cannot turn away from her face. All heads look up with joyful expectancy to the clouds and the people of the whole land are bathed in the brilliance of the sun.

"Also as for Kōmyō the Dowager Empress, her imperial virtue ascends on high and is aligned with Heaven. Her deep benevolent love is dispensed below, and brightens the the earth. The movements of the sun and moon are always correct, and heaven and earth work together to bring tranquility. Finally, we have reverently received the testament of the Retired Emperor Shōmu that the

---

[154] Preposterous, considering the events of the Tachibana Naramaro conspiracy in the previous year.
[155] *Shōzui* 祥瑞
[156] *Hōji* 宝字

successor to the imperial rank be established.[157] The near relatives were cast aside and justice established.[158] Truly we shall in future consider the best interests of the empire and not merely our own wishes.

"Traveling to the Jetavana Park and realizing the profound doctrine of the Three Emptinesses, *satori* has been opened, the sole miraculous *satori* of the teaching of the Buddha. With a profound and compassionate heart, Kōmyō built medical institutions. Earnestly undertaking a profound vow, she established the clinics for compassionate treatment.[159] With these she succored the common people. On the ceiling curtains of the palace there was the auspicious omen. There was the lucky omen of the insects carving characters into the wisteria roots, heralding the auspicious imperial virtue. Finally the hundred *kami* united their power and aided in giving heavenly peace and the virtue of making peaceful and stable the earth below forever.

"The Ministers enter the imperial presence and depart awarded with the ranks of Zhou. Jeweled ornaments hang from our belts and we are decorated with silk cloth as the ritual events are celebrated over time. As we gaze on the imperial virtue, and glory in prosperous rule as righteous subjects, shall we not award these honorific titles? If the people desire it, then Heaven will certainly grant it.

---

[157] The posthumous edict naming Prince successor to Kōken. He was rejected in favor of Prince Ōi, now the Emperor Junnin.

[158] The conspirators in the Naramaro plot were close relatives, many of them nephews, of Kōmyō (see *Senmyō* 17 above).

[159] *Hidenin* 悲田院

If the people say improper things, the Sage will certainly correct them. Based on the teachings of the classics we dare to reverently award these honorific names.

"We name the *Jōdai* the *Hōji Shōtoku Kōken Kōtei*.[160] We name the *Chūdai* the *Tenpyō Ōshin Ninshō Kōtaigō*.[161] Heaven above will confer these magnificent names for ten thousand years. On earth below these honorific names will conform to the peoples' wishes for a thousand autumns. With joyful dancing and pure hearts, we reverently enter the Administrative Palace and submit this memorial."

僧綱表曰。沙門菩提等言。菩提聞。乾坤高大覆載。以之顕功。日月貞明照臨。由其甄用。至於混群有而饒益。撫万物而曲成。独標十号之尊。式崇四大之極。故能徽猷歴前古以不朽。妙迹流後葉而恒新。然則、表徳称功。莫不由於名号。伏惟。皇帝陛下、乃聖継聖。括六合而承基。乃神襲神。環四溟而光宅。期政道於刑措。駆懐生於仁宜。追遠之孝尤重。錫類之徳弥厚。不以逸遊為念。俯以。謙卑在懐。瑞蚕藻文。薦聖寿之遐祉。宝字結象。開皇基之永昌。皇太后、遊心五乗。棲襟八正。化＝応供。道双至真。発揮神化之丹青。抑揚陶甄之鎔範。正慮独断。捜離明於舜浜。深仁幽罩。浮赤文於尭渚。故能遠安近。至治美於成康。治定功成。無為盛於軒昊。固足以垂顕号建嘉名。軼三五而飛英。超八九而騰茂者也。陛下謙譲。推而不居。菩提等窃疑焉。菩提等、逖察前徽。緬鏡遐載。随時立制。権代適宜。皇王雖殊。其揆一也。菩提等、不勝丹款之誠。謹上尊号。陛下称曰宝字称徳孝謙皇帝。皇太后称曰天平応真仁正皇太后。伏願。陛下・皇太后。抑謙光之小節。従梵侶之＝言。庶使蟠木之郷。燭竜之地。問号仰沢。聴声傾光。凡厥在生。誰不幸甚。沙門菩提等、不任下情。謹奉表以聞。」

***Tenpyō Hōji* 2.8.1** 庚子 *kanoe-ne* [continued]

[September 7, 758]

---

[160] 宝字称徳孝謙皇帝-- *Kōken* might be rendered as "Filial and Modest", and *Shōtoku* as "Praiseworthy and Virtuous."
[161] 天平応真仁正皇太后 -- *Ōshin* - "Obedient and True", *Ninshō* - "Benevolent and Correct."

The Council of Buddhist Priestly Affairs presented a petition, saying:

"Bodaisena[162] and all say:

"I, Bodai, have heard:

'Heaven and Earth in their vastness encompass all things without discrimination and so make manifest all meritorious deeds. Sun and moon illuminate all things brightly and so clarify the functions of all things. Together they benefit all living beings. They nourish all creation and cause it to flourish. The Buddha alone possesses the revered Ten-fold name. Thus the four great ultimate elements -- earth, water, fire, wind -- are venerated.' The Buddhist teaching does not decay over time. These mysterious traces are transmitted down to later ages and always renewed. Meritorious names are given to designate accomplishments that express virtue. The Sovereign[163] transmits his saintliness from ancient times as a Sage, and acts as foundation for the six dimensions – earth, heaven, and the four directions. As a *Kami* the Sovereign inherits his divinity, and rules brightly over all the realm. The Sovereign rules without using punishments, with sympathy and compassion for all living things. Honoring the ancestors with the utmost filial piety, he transmits this virtue to his descendants.

"I humbly reflect that the beautiful characters expressed by the auspicious silkworm[164] indicated that the saintly lifespan will be long, and that the shape of

---

[162] *Shamon Bodai* 沙門菩提 - *Sharamon Sō Bodaisena* 沙羅門僧菩提僊那, the Chief Abbott.
[163] 皇帝陛下
[164] SN III TPHJ 1.8.13.

the auspicious characters carved into the roots of the wisteria[165] expressed that the imperial house will long flourish.[166] As for the Dowager Empress Kōmyō, her heart moves among the Five Ways and dwells in the Eight-fold Path like an arhat on the way of perfect truth. Her appearance is like the surface of tiles colored cinnabar and blue, and she governs the people as a Sage.

"Right deliberation and destroying evil, this is like when Emperor Shun[167] on the banks of the river sought for wise men, and when Emperor Yu[168] discovered the river chart in the tides of the Yellow River. Therefore they ameliorated the distant places and pacified the near. In ruling the Sovereign is superior to Kings Cheng and Kang of the Zhou,[169] who stabilized the government and reigned without incident, and more excellent than the Yellow Emperor and his son. Indeed these honorific names being given to Kōken and Kōmyō exceed those of the Three Sovereigns and Five Emperors [170] and that of the seventy-two disciples of Shakyamuni.[171]

"Your Majesties are humble and have not sought these names. I, Bodai, and the Council secretly doubt whether to suggest them. We have searched for distant good precedents, looked into the mirror of distant ages, and established them in

---

[165] TPHJ 2.2.27
[166] 永昌 A reign name during the Zhou Dynasty of Wu Zetian 689.
[167] 舜
[168] 禹
[169] 成王 and 康王 The second and third Zhou emperors.
[170] 皇 and 帝
[171] SNIII pp 273-4, notes 23-26.

accordance with current time, measured the ages then sought appropriate titles. Although the Sovereigns differ, their natures do not change. I Bodai and all cannot restrain our sincerity, and we respectfully present these honorific names. We name Your Majesty *Hōji Shōtoku Kōken Kōtei*, and we name the Dowager Empress *Tenpyō Ōshin Ninshō Kōgū*. What we fervently ask is that Your Majesty and Dowager Empress accept our trivial honor as the humble words of the Council of Buddhist Priestly Affairs.

"The villages where grow the winding trees and the borderlands where dwell the creatures with men's faces and serpents' bodies, inquire about honorific names, hear the voices of the Sovereign and wish to bask in his light. All bow low and pray for great good fortune. Bodai and the Council humbly present this memorial, hoping for it to be heard."

詔報曰。朕覧卿等所請。鴻業良峻。祗畏允深。忝以寡薄。何当休名。而上天降祐。帳字開平。厚地薦祥。蚕文表徳。窃惟此事。天意難違。俯従衆願。敬膺典礼。号曰宝字称徳孝謙皇帝。又見上皇太后之尊号。感喜交懐。日興忘倦。任公卿之所表。従耆緇之所乞。策曰天平応真仁正皇太后。受此推新之号。何無洗旧之令。宜改百官之名。載施寛大之沢。其天下見禁囚徒。罪無軽重、咸従放免。其依先格。放却本土。無故不上之徒。悉還本司。又自天平宝字元年已前監臨自盗。盗所監臨。及官物欠負未納悉免。天下諸国隠於山林清行逸士十年已上。皆令得度。其中臣・忌部。元預神宮常祀。不關供奉久年。宜両氏六位已下加位一級。其大学生。医針生。暦算生。天文生。陰陽生。年廿五已上授位一階。其依犯擯出僧等、戒律無關。移近一国。」其大僧都鑑真和上、戒行転潔、白頭不変。遠渉滄波、帰我聖朝。号曰大和上。恭敬供養。政事躁煩。不敢労老。宜停僧綱之任。集諸寺僧尼。欲学戒律者。皆属令習。」又勅曰。内相於国。功勲已高。然猶報効未行。名字未加。宜下参議・八省卿・博士等。准古正議奏聞。不得空言所。無濫汗聴覧。

74

Tenpyō Hōji **2.8.1** 庚子 *kanoe-ne* **[continued]**

[September 7, 758]

In response to these memorials, the Retired Empress Kōken gave an edict:

"We, seeing what our nobles desire, realize that the profound task of ruling is indeed lofty, a weighty and awesome duty. Since We are of weak virtue, we wonder how we can merit this honorific name. However, heaven has sent down its aid, and inaugurated an age of peace expressed in the characters on the tapestries.[172] The earth has sent forth omens, and the silkworm characters have expressed virtue.[173] As we earnestly ponder these matters, we may not ignore heaven's wishes. In accordance with the wishes of the people we reverently accept. We shall be named *Hōji Shōtoku Kōken Kōtei*. And when we consider the honorific name presented to the Dowager Empress, We also feel joy. This emotion swells up everyday, and we will not tire of it. According to the petition of the nobles, and according to the wishes of the virtuous priests, her name shall be expressed as *Tenpyō Ōshin Ninshō Kōgū*.

"Upon receiving this new title, shall We not also renew the old laws? Changing the names of the hundred officials, we shall magnanimously dispense favor. As for prisoners who are at present in jail, whether their crimes be light or serious, We pardon all. According to the ordinance of TPSH 4.11.10, those being dispossessed as punishment shall be restored to their previous lands and offices.

---

[172] Omen of TPHJ 1.3.20
[173] Omens of TPHJ 1.8.13, 2.2.27

Also those who previous to TPHJ 1 committed theft while supervising underlings, or whose underlings stole official goods, or who appropriated official goods during a shortage, shall all be pardoned.

"Those who have been diligent in practicing austerities for ten years or more in the mountains and forests in provinces of the realm may all enter the priesthood. The Nakatomi and Imbe clans who from former times practiced ceremonies at the Ise *Daijingū*[174] have done this for long years. Thus those of these clans from 6th rank down shall be promoted one step in rank. University students, medical students, calendar students, math students, astronomy students, and *Yin-yang* divination students aged 25 and up shall be promoted one step in rank. Buddhist priests who have committed an offense and been exiled, but have been diligent in guarding the precepts, may move one province nearer the capital."

"The Eminent Monk and Senior Assistant Abbot Ganjin, unchanged but for his white hair, has righteously guarded the precepts. Crossing the distant sea he immigrated to our court. Therefore he shall reverently serve with the title of Great Eminent Monk, though not exerting his enfeebled body with the complexities of government. He is freed of his responsibilities with the Council of Buddhist Priestly Affairs. Those priests and nuns of the various temples who wish to study the precepts may assemble and learn from him."

The Retired Empress gave another edict:

---

[174] SNIII p 276 n 8 – Ise *Daijingū* or *Jingikan*.

"As for the Inner Minister Fujiwara no Nakamaro, his meritorious service to the state has already been superb. However he has not yet been fully rewarded, and an honorific name honoring his service has not yet been given. Thus the Imperial Advisors, Heads of the Eight Bureaus, and the Learned Scholars are commanded to discuss precedents according to ancient practice and to submit an appropriate name to the throne. Let this name be carefully deliberated and the effort not be in vain."

天平宝字二年（七五八）八月辛丑【二】○辛丑。外従五位下僧延慶。以形異於俗。辞其爵位。詔許之。其位禄・位田者、有勅不収。」授外従五位下山口忌寸佐美麻呂従五位下。正六位上茨田宿禰牧野外従五位下。

Tenpyō Hōji 2.8.2 辛丑 *kanoto-ushi*

[September 8, 758]

The Buddhist Priest Enkyō differs from a layperson in holding rank: Outer Jr 5 Lower. He wishes to resign his rank. The Emperor gave an edict permitting this and stipulating that he should no longer receive income from the stipend and lands associated with the rank.

Outer Jr 5 Lower Yamaguchi no Imiki Samimaro awarded Jr 5 Lower Rank.

Sr 6 Upper Mamuta no Sukune Hirano awarded Outer Jr 5 Lower Rank.

天平宝字二年（七五八）八月癸卯【四】○癸卯。以従五位下笠朝臣真足為伊勢介。正五位下大伴宿禰犬養為右衛士督。

Tenpyō Hōji 2.8.4 癸卯 *mizunoto-u*

[September 10, 758]

Jr 5 Lower Kasa no Asomi Matari appointed Ise Assistant Governor.

Sr 5 Lower Ōtomo no Sukune Inukai appointed Commander of Right Palace Guards.

天平宝字二年（七五八）八月丙午【七】○丙午。増宮人職員。事在別式。

Tenpyō Hōji 2.8.7 丙午 *hinoe-uma*

[September 13, 758]

The number of women serving in the rear palace was increased. The particulars are in a special regulation.

天平宝字二年（七五八）八月戊申【九】○戊申。勅曰。子尊其考。礼家所称。策書鴻名。古人所貴。昔者。先帝敬発洪誓。奉造盧舍那金銅大像。若有朕時不得造了。願於来世。改身猶作。既而鎔銅已成。塗金不足。天感至心之信、終出勝宝之金。我国家、於是、初有奇珍。開闢已来。未聞若斯盛徳者也。加以。賊臣懐悪。潜結逆徒。謀危社稷。良日久矣。而畏威武。欽仰仁風。不敢競鋒。咸自馴服。可謂、聖武之徳。比古有余也。其不奉揚洪業。何以示於後世。敬依旧典。追上尊号。策称勝宝感神聖武皇帝。諡称天璽国押開豊桜彦尊。欲使伝休名於万代。与乾坤而長施。揚茂実於千秋。共日月而久照。普告遐邇。知朕意焉。」又勅。日並知皇子命。天下未称天皇。追崇尊号。古今恒典。自今以後。宜奉称岡宮御宇天皇。

Tenpyō Hōji 2.8.9 戊申 *tsuchinoe-saru*

[September 15, 758]

The Retired Empress Kōken gave an edict:

"That a child reveres her father is the mark of a proper household. The ancients bestowed honorific names and praised the ancestors. The former emperor Shōmu reverently made a great vow and constructed a gilded *Rushana* statue. When it seemed it could not be completed, he vowed that it would be completed in coming reigns. When the statue had already been cast, there was not enough gold to cover it. Heaven sensed the heart-felt faith of the Emperor, and in TPSH 2 sent forth the gold. There was for the first time in our state this marvelous sign. Such wonderful virtue had not been heard of since the creation; such a great virtue had not yet been heard of. The traitorous minister [175] plotted and secretly gathered his evil party. But the sovereign looked up to the benevolent heavens and the rebel submitted completely. Shōmu's virtue is greater than that of the rulers of antiquity. If it had not been so, what would have become of those after him? We reverently search ancient texts and find the practice of posthumous conferral of honorific names. Let him be named "Emperor Shōmu, Victorious Jewel and Divine Resonance",[176] along with the posthumous name *Ameshirushi kunioshiharaki toyosakurahiko no mikoto.*[177] We desire that this beautiful honorific name be handed down to ten thousand generations. Let it be employed for long ages together with heaven and earth, let it announce for a thousand autumns his superior works, let it shine together with the sun and moon. Let Our intention be made known widely to all directions near and far."

The Empress also gave the following edict:

---

[175] SNIII, p 279, n 10-11 identifies him as Tachibana no Naramaro. Other commentators suggest this refers to Fujiwara Hirotsugu's rebellion of 740. See eg Naoki III, p 13.

[176] *Shōhō Kanjin Shōmu Kōtei* 勝宝感神聖武皇帝

[177] 天璽国押開豊桜彦尊

"Prince Kusakabe[178] was not Emperor of all under heaven while he lived. However, it is established custom to bestow posthumous imperial names. From now forth, let him be named *Okanomiya Amenoshitashimeshishi Sumera Mikoto.*"[179]

天平宝字二年（七五八）八月乙卯【十六】○乙卯。遣使大祓天下諸国。欲行大嘗故也。

Tenpyō Hōji 2.8.16 乙卯 *kinoto-u*

[September 22, 758]

Messengers were sent to the various provinces of the realm to carry out the Great Purification.[180] This was to prepare for the Great Thanksgiving Festival and Enthronement Ceremony[181] for the accession of Emperor Junnin.

天平宝字二年（七五八）八月丁巳【十八】○丁巳。勅。大史奏云。案九宮経。来年己亥。当会三合。其経云。三合之歳。有水旱疾疫之災。如聞。摩訶般若波羅密多者。是諸仏之母也。四句偈等、受持読誦。得福徳聚、不可思量。是以、天子念。則兵革災害、不入国裏。庶人念。則疾疫癘鬼、不入家中。断悪獲祥、莫過於此。宜告天下諸国。莫論男女老少。起坐行歩口閑。皆尽念誦摩訶般若波羅密。其文武百官人等。向朝赴司。道路之上。毎日常念。勿空往来。庶使風雨随時。咸無水旱之厄。寒温調気。悉免疾疫之災。普告遐邇。知朕意焉。

Tenpyō Hōji 2.8.18 丁巳 *hinoto-mi*

[September 24, 758]

The Emperor gave an edict:

---

[178] 草壁皇子 was the son of Tenmu and Jitō, and the spouse of Empress Genmei. Although designated Crown Prince, he died before he could be enthroned as Emperor. Also known as *Hinamishinomiko no mikoto* 日並知皇子命

[179] 岡宮御宇天皇

[180] *Ōharae* 大祓

[181] *Ōname* 大嘗, or *Daijōsai* 大嘗祭.

"The Head of the Yin-yang Divination Bureau[182] reported:

'According to the *Kukūkyō*,[183] next year, a *tsuchinotoi* 己亥 year, is a very unlucky year of the Three Confluences. The *Kukūkyō* says "In a Three Confluences year there occur disasters of flooding, drought, and epidemic.'

'We have heard that *The Perfection of Wisdom Sutra*[184] is the mother of all Buddhas. If the verse of four phrases is chanted and the sutra read, then fortunate virtue will be accumulated.[185] When the Son of Heaven prays thus, then military upheavals and natural disasters will not trouble the country, and if the common people pray thus, sickness and evil spirits of evil disease will not enter their houses. Thus evil will be averted and good fortune obtained, and there will be no further danger.'

"Therefore it is proclaimed throughout the various provinces of the empire that the *Perfection of Wisdom Sutra* shall be prayed at all times in the mouths of everyone, man or woman, young or old, traveling or at home, walking or sitting down. The Hundred Officials both civil and military shall when going to court or to their offices while on the way on the roads daily pray this sutra. What we pray is that wind and rain will come in their season, that there shall be no flood or drought, that cold and heat will come in order, that the disaster of epidemic

---

[182] SNIII p 280 n 6 - The *Daishi* 大史 here means the head of the *Onmyōryō*.
[183] SNIII p 280 n 9 - *Kukūkyō*, 九宮教, was perhaps a divination text referred to in the Sui history.
[184] *Makahannya haramitta* (Skt. *Prajñāpāramitā* 摩訶般若波羅蜜多)
[185] The 四句偈 is a summary of the *Prajñāpāramitā* 摩訶般若波羅蜜多 sutra.

disease will be entirely averted. Let this be known widely far and near, and let Our wish be made known."

天平宝字二年（七五八）八月戊午【十九】○戊午。遣摂津大夫従三位池田王。告斎王事于伊勢太神宮。」又遣左大舎人頭従五位下河内王。散位従八位下中臣朝臣池守。大初位上忌部宿禰人成等。奉幣帛於同太神宮。及天下諸国神社等。遣使奉幣。以皇太子即位故也。

Tenpyō Hōji 2.8.19 戊午 *tsuchinoe-uma*

[September 25, 758]

The Settsu Commissioner Jr 3 Prince Ikeda was sent to announce to Ise *Daijingū* that an Ise Princess[186] had been designated. Also the Head of the Left Imperial Attendants Jr 5 Lower Prince Kawachi and Scattered Rank Jr 8 Lower Nakatomi no Asomi Ikemori and *Daisho* Upper Imbe no Sukune Hitonari were sent to present *mitegura* to Ise *Daijingū*. Moreover messengers were sent to present *mitegura* to the Shinto shrines of all provinces of the realm. This was to announce the accession of the Crown Prince Ōi.

天平宝字二年（七五八）八月癸亥【廿四】○癸亥。帰化新羅僧卅二人。尼二人。男十九人。女廿一人。移武蔵国閑地。於是。始置新羅郡焉。

Tenpyō Hōji 2.8.24 癸亥 *mizunoto-i*

[September 30, 758]

Immigrants from Silla – thirty-two Buddhist priests, two nuns, nineteen men and twenty-one women were moved to undeveloped land in Musashi Province. Shiragi District was established there for the first time.

---

[186] *Saiō (Itsuki no Ōkimi* 斎王)

天平宝字二年（七五八）八月甲子【廿五】○甲子。以紫微内相藤原朝臣仲麻呂任大保。勅曰。褒善懲悪。聖主格言。賞績酬労。明主彝則。其藤原朝臣仲麻呂者、晨昏不怠。恪勤守職。事君忠赤。施務無私。愚拙則降其親。賢良則挙其怨。殄逆徒於未戦。黎元獲安。固危基於未然。聖暦終長。国家無乱。略由若人。平章其労。良可嘉賞。其伊尹有＝之勝臣。一佐成湯。遂荷阿衡之号。呂尚渭浜之遺老。且弼文王。終得営丘之封。況自乃祖近江大津宮内大臣已来。世有明徳。翼輔皇室。君歴十帝。年殆一百。朝廷無事。海内清平者哉。因此論之。准古無匹。汎恵之美。莫美於斯。自今以後。宜姓中加恵美二字。禁暴勝強。止戈静乱。故名曰押勝。朕舅之中。汝卿良尚。故字称尚舅。更給功封三千戸。功田一百町。永為伝世之賜。以表不常之勲。別聴鋳銭・挙稲及用恵美家印。是日。大保従二位兼中衛大将藤原恵美朝臣押勝。正三位中納言兼式部卿神祇伯石川朝臣年足。参議従三位出雲守文室真人智努。参議従三位紫微大弼兼兵部卿侍従下総守巨勢朝臣関麻呂。参議紫微大弼正四位下兼左大弁紀朝臣飯麻呂。参議正四位下中務卿藤原朝臣真楯等。奉勅改易官号。太政官、惣持綱紀。掌治邦国。如天施徳生育万物。故改為乾政官。太政大臣曰大師。左大臣曰大傅。右大臣曰大保。大納言曰御史大夫。紫微中台。居中奉勅。頒行諸司。如地承天亭毒庶物。故改為坤宮官。中務省。宣伝勅語。必可有信。故改為信部省。式部省。惣掌文官考賜。故改為文部省。治部省。僧尼賓客。誠応尚礼。故改為礼部省。民部省、施政於民。惟仁為貴。故改為仁部省。兵部省。惣掌武官考賜。故改為武部省。刑部省。窮鞫定罪。要須用義。故改為義部省。大蔵省。出納財物。応有節制。故改為節部省。宮内省。催諸産業。廻聚供御。智水周流。生物相似。故改為智部省。弾正台。糺正内外。粛清風俗。故改為糺政台。図書寮。掌持典籍。供奉内裏。故改為内史局。陰陽寮。陰陽暦数。国家所重。記此大事。故改為大史局。中衛府。鎮国之衛。但此為先。故改為鎮国衛。官重位卑。故大将為正三位官。改曰大尉。少将為従四位上官。曰驍騎将軍。員外少将為正五位下官。曰次将。衛門府。禁衛諸門。監察出入。故改為司門衛。左右衛士府。率諸国勇士。分衛宮掖。故改為左右勇士衛。左右兵衛府。折衝禁暴。虎奔宣威。故改為左右虎賁衛。

Tenpyō Hōji **2.8.25** 甲子 *kinoe-ne*

[October 1, 758]

The Inner Minister of the Dowager Empress's Household[187] Fujiwara no Asomi Nakamaro was appointed Grand Guardian.[188] The Emperor gave an edict:

" 'Praise the good and chastise evil' is a wise saying of a sagely lord. To praise accomplishments and reward toil is the constant policy of the enlightened lord. Now the Fujiwara Grand Guardian, not slacking day or night, diligently pursues his duties. He serves his sovereign with dedication and selflessly carries out his tasks. If subordinates are clumsy and foolish he lowers their rank, even if they are relatives. If they are good and wise, he promotes them, even if they are enemies. Without battling the rebellious traitor Naramaro he subdued him and obtained peace and security. He strengthened the endangered foundation of the state and preserved the steady rule of the imperial house. That the state did not slide into chaos was due to such a person. In recognition of his excellent work, we shall definitely reward him.

"He is like the loyal retainer Yi Yin who served the daughter of the Prince of Yin.[189] Yi Yin aided Chengtang of Yin and received the title of Prime Minister.[190] Lu Chang was a renowned ancient on the Wei River. He served King Wen and was later given a fief.[191]

---

[187] *Shibi Naishō* 紫微内相
[188] *Daiho* 大保 – the equivalent of Great Minister of the Right.
[189] *Yi Yin* 伊尹 SNIII, p 283, n 15-17, gives a reference in the *Wenxuan*.
[190] *Aheng* 阿衡
[191] *Lu Chang* 呂尚 SNIII, p 283, n 20.

"Now since the time of the Fujiwara ancestor the Great Minister of the Middle Kamatari at the Court of Ōmi Ōtsu no Miya, the Fujiwara family has for ten reigns and almost a hundred years assisted the Imperial House with bright virtue, there has been no major incident at the court, and all within the seas has been peaceful.[192] As we assess his contribution, none in the past has been the equal of Nakamaro, and none has been so noble and wise. From now on the two characters '*Emi*'[193] shall be added to the *kabane* of Fujiwara. He has put down the insurrection, suppressed the rebels, halted the battle, and calmed the disorder. Therefore he shall be called *Oshikatsu*.[194] Among Our retainers, this noble is indeed the most precious, and thus his name shall be "Esteemed Father-in-Law."[195] In addition fiefs numbering three thousand households and merit land of one hundred hectares shall be bestowed in perpetuity in eternal recognition of meritorious service. Moreover We grant the right to mint coins and to lend rice for interest, and the use of the seal 'The House of Emi'."

On this day an edict was received by the following high officials: the Grand Guardian Jr 2 and concurrently Major Captain of Middle Imperial Guards Fujiwara Emi no Asomi Oshikatsu; Jr 3 Middle Counsellor and concurrently Head of Ministry of Ceremonial and Department of Deity Affairs Ishikawa no Asomi Toshitari; Imperial Advisor Jr 3 Governor of Izumo Fumuya no Mahito

---

[192] SNIII p 283, n 25 - "Ten reigns" means from Great King Kōtoku to Kōken Tennō, not counting Kobun, although Kōtoku ruled from Naniwa rather than Ōmi.
[193] 恵美
[194] 押勝
[195] *Shōkyū* 尚舅

Chino; Imperial Advisor Jr 3 Senior Assistant, Dowager Empress' Household and concurrently Head of the Ministry of War, Chamberlain, and Shimōsa Governor Kose no Asomi Sekimaro; Imperial Advisor and Senior Assistant, Dowager Empress' Household Sr 4 Lower and concurrently Major Controller of the Left Ki no Asomi Iimaro; and Imperial Advisor Sr 4 Lower Head of the Ministry of Central Affairs Fujiwara no Asomi Matate. [196] They were commanded to change the names of the bureaucracy.

The Great Council of State holds the reins of government and directs the affairs of the state. It dispenses the virtue of heaven and makes the ten thousand things flourish. Thus its name is changed to the Heavenly Council of State. [197] First Minister of the Great Council of State is changed to Grand Preceptor; Great Minister of the Left is changed to Grand Mentor; Great Minister of the Right is changed to Grand Guardian. [198] Major Counsellor is changed to Master of Imperial Scribes. [199]

The Dowager Empress' Household Office is in the palace, receives edicts and executes all governmental matters. This is because earth is entrusted by heaven to nourish the ten thousand things. Thus it is changed to Earthly Palace

---

[196] This group of officials formed the "cabinet" advising the Emperor.
[197] *Genjōkan* 乾政官
[198] *Daishi* 大師; *Daifu* 大傅; *Daiho* 大保. Cf. the Three Dukes of Zhou 三公 or Three Preceptors 三師. During the Zhou period, these were the grand preceptor 大師, grand mentor 大傅, and grand guardian 太保.
[199] *Gyoshi Daibu* 御史大夫.

Council.[200] The Ministry of Central Affairs, since it proclaims and transmits the edicts, must be reliable. Thus it is changed to Ministry of Fidelity. [201] The Ministry of Ceremonial oversees the deliberations and stipends of civil officials. Thus it is changed to Ministry of Civil Affairs. [202] The Ministry of Civil Administration oversees the monks, nuns and overseas visitors and matters of ceremony. Thus it is changed to Ministry of Rites.[203] The Ministry of Popular Affairs administers government for the people and esteems benevolence. Thus it is changed to Ministry of Benevolence.[204] The Ministry of War oversees the deliberations and stipends of the military officials. Thus it is changed to Ministry of Military Affairs.[205] The Ministry of Justice captures and imprisons criminals and decides their punishment, and so carries out righteousness. Thus it is changed to Ministry of Righteousness. [206] The Ministry of the Treasury collects products and limits expenditures. Thus it is changed to Ministry of Moderation.[207] The Ministry of the Imperial Household collects products and

---

[200] *Kongūkan* 坤宮官
[201] *Shinbushō* 信部省 SNIII p 285 n 22 –speculates that the following bureau names -- 仁義礼智信- may have derived from five of the six bureau names of the Palhae bureaucracy. The six bureaus of the Tang bureaucracy differ somewhat – see Kōchi 2013, 98.

[202] *Monbushō* 文部省
[203] *Reibushō* 礼部省
[204] *Ninbushō* 仁部省
[205] *Mubushō* 武部省
[206] *Gibushō* 義部省
[207] *Setsubushō* 節部省

foodstuffs for the table of the Emperor. Wisdom flows like water and nurtures living things. Thus it is changed to Ministry of Wisdom. [208]

The Board of Censors corrects evil behavior within and without and purges impure practices. Thus it is changed to Board of Investigation.[209] The Bureau of Books and Drawings supervises the collection of classics and presents them to the palace. Thus it is changed to Department of Palace Classics.[210] The Bureau of Yinyang Divination oversees *yinyang* and calendrical calculations, and records important events. Thus it is changed to Department of the Great Historian. [211]

The Headquarters of Middle Imperial Guards has as its first duty to guard and protect the state. Thus it is changed to Headquarters of State Protection Guards.[212] But while its importance is crucial for the government, the ranks of its personnel are currently low. Thus the rank of Major Captain shall correspond to Sr 3 and the name changed to Major Commander.[213] The rank of Minor Captain shall correspond to Jr 4 Lower and the name changed to General of Cavalry.[214] The rank of Irregular Minor Captain shall correspond to Sr 5 Lower and the name changed to Vice-Captain.[215] The Headquarters of the Outer Palace

---

[208] *Chibushō* 智部省
[209] *Kyūseidai* 糺政台
[210] *Naishikyoku* 内史局
[211] *Daishikyoku* 大史局
[212] *Chinkokue* 鎮国衛
[213] *Daii* 大尉
[214] *Gyōki Shōgun* 驍騎将軍
[215] *Jishō* 次将

guards protects the palace gates and scrutinizes those who go in and out. Thus its name is changed to Headquarters of the Gatekeepers.[216] The Left and Right Palace Guard recruits brave men from the provinces and allots them to guarding the palace buildings. Thus the name is changed to Left and Right Headquarters of the Brave Warriors.[217] The Left and Right Military Guard defeats the enemies, suppresses boisterous rebels, and has authority like that of a tiger. Thus its name is changed to Headquarters of the Left and Right Elite Tigers. [218]

天平宝字二年（七五八）八月丙寅【廿七】○丙寅。外従五位下津史秋主等卅四人言。船。葛井。津。本是一祖。別為三氏。其二氏者、蒙連姓訖。唯秋主等、未霑改姓。請改史字。於是、賜姓津連。

Tenpyō Hōji 2.8.27 丙寅 *hinoe-tora*

[October 3, 758]

Outer Jr 5 Lower Tsu no Fuhito Akinushi and others (thirty-four in all) said: "The Funa, Fujii, and Tsu all had the same ancestor, but split into three different clans. Among them the Funa and Fujii received the kabane of Muraji, but the Akinushi no Tsu have not had the kabane changed. We are asking that the character 'fuhito' be changed."

Accordingly the *kabane* of Tsu no Muraji was granted.

天平宝字二年（七五八）九月壬申【庚午朔三】○九月壬申。西海道問民苦使従五位下藤原朝臣楓麻呂等採訪民之疾苦廿九件。勅大宰府随事処分。

---

[216] *Shimone* 司門衛
[217] *Yūshie* 勇士衛
[218] *Kohone* 虎賁衛

Tenpyō Hōji 2.9.3 壬申 *mizunoe-saru*

[October 9, 758]

The *Saikaidō* Special Inspector Jr 5 Lower Fujiwara no Asomi Kaerutemaro reported twenty-nine instances of the suffering of the people. An edict was issued to the Kyushu Headquarters ordering them to deal with the situation.

天平宝字二年（七五八）九月丁丑【八】○丁丑。先是。国司交替。未有程期。仍令明法博士論定。明法曹司言。遷任国司。向京期限。依倉庫令。倉蔵及文案孔目。専当官人交替之日。並相分付。然後放還。但今。令条雖立分付之文。律内無科淹滞之罪。因茲。新任国司。不勤受領。得替官人、規延歳月。遂使踰年隔考。還到居官。於事商量。甚乖道理。謹案選叙令云。凡職事官。患経百廿日不愈者、解官者。准是而論。官符到後。百廿日内。付了帰京。若応過限者。申官請裁。違此停留灼然合解。就中。欠負官倉。留連不付者。論実是罪人也。知情許容。限内無領者。准法、是同罪也。何者。職制律云。凡有所請求。主司許者、与同罪。拠此而言。旧人規求延日者。所謂請求也。新司受嘱聴容。所謂主司也。新旧両人。並皆有罪。若此之輩。同合解官。但実無欠負。拘令解官者。原情可責。罪在新人。准律。以故入人罪論者。自茲以後。為例行之。」常陸国鹿嶋神奴二百十八人、便為神戸。

Tenpyō Hōji 2.9.8 丁丑 *hinoto-ushi*

[October 14, 758]

Previously the length of time allowed for provincial governors to proceed to and return from their assignments has not been determined. Therefore the Learned Scholars of the Law[219] were ordered to deliberate and make a judgment. They gave the following report:

---

[219] *Myōbō Hakase* 明法博士

"As to the time limit for governors relinquishing their posts and returning to the capital, the *Sōkoryō*[220] says the following: 'On the day that officials change posts, they must turn over the official records of the amounts in the granaries and other documents to the new governor, and then the former governor may return to the capital.' However, although this process of transfer is written in the codes, the punishment for delay is not spelled out in the criminal code. Thus in certain cases the new appointee does not properly take office on time, the previous officials stay on for an extended period of time, and the evaluation of the situation is thus delayed until the former official finally leaves and returns to the capital. When we discussed this our conclusion was that the situation contradicted the intended principles. When we carefully examined the *Senjoryō*[221], it said 'If an official suffers from disease he has one hundred twenty days of sick leave, and if he is not cured within that time he loses his post.' Reasoning from this article, after a pronouncement from the Great Council of State arrives commanding a change in post, and one hundred twenty days have passed, the former official must return to the capital. In cases where this time limit is exceeded, approval must be sought from the Great Council of State. If the official is clearly in violation and delays he should lose his post. In particular if he has failed to submit taxes from the granary, and continues to delay, he is in fact a criminal offender.

---

[220] 倉庫令 *Ryō* 22. SNIII p 288 n 8 says the text of this particular article (#11) is corrupt, and the reading is based on *Enryaku Kōtai Shiki*. See *Ritsuryō* p 410.
[221] 選叙令 *Ryō* 12. See *Ritsuryō* p 269.

If the incoming official is aware of this, and does not complete his documentation within the time limit, then he is guilty of the same offense. In the *Shikiseirichi*[222] it says: 'In all cases if someone makes a claim in violation of the law and the relevant official is aware of it and allows it, that official is guilty of the same offense.' Reasoning from this, a former official's scheming to lengthen the time of transitions here corresponds making a false claim. If the new official consents to this scheme, both the old and new officials are guilty, and both parties should be relieved of duty. However, if there has been no actual financial loss, then by the provisions of the one hundred twenty day clause the circumstances of the former official shall be investigated and the responsibility made clear. If it seems that the crime is that of the new official, then according to the criminal code, it may be a case of unintentional wrongdoing. Hereafter administration should proceed according to these instances."

Two hundred eighteen shrine slaves at the Kashima Shrine in Hitachi Province were released from their base status and made shrine households[223] for the support of the shrine.

天平宝字二年（七五八）九月己卯【十】○己卯。右京人正六位上辛男床等一十六人賜姓広田連。

Tenpyō Hōji 2.9.10 己卯 tsuchinoto-u

[October 16, 758]

---

[222] 職制律 Article 45. *Ritsuryō* p 79.
[223] *kamube* 神戸

The court granted sixteen people of the Right Capital, Sr 6 Upper Kara no Otoko and others, the *kabane* of Hirota no Muraji.

天平宝字二年（七五八）九月丁亥【十八】○丁亥。小野朝臣田守等至自渤海。渤海大使輔国大将軍兼将軍行木底州刺史兼兵署少正開国公揚承慶已下廿三人。随田守来朝。便於越前国安置。

Tenpyō Hōji 2.9.18 丁亥 *hinoto-i*

[October 24, 758]

Ono no Asomi Tamori and all returned from Parhae. The Parhae Envoy Bulwark Minister and Generalissimo [224] and concurrently Commander of Mude Province,[225] and also Dynasty-founding Duke[226] Yang Chengqing[227] and twenty-three lower officials accompanied Tamori back to Japan. They lodged in Echizen Province.

天平宝字二年（七五八）九月丁酉【廿八】○丁酉。始頒越前。越中。佐渡。出雲。石見。伊予等六国飛駅鈴。国一口。

Tenpyō Hōji 2.9.28 丁酉 *hinoto-tori*

[November 3, 758]

---

[224] 輔国大将軍 A Parhae envoy with this title arrived at the island of Sado on TPSH 4.9.24.

[225] 木底州刺 Official of a province in Parhae. SNIII p 539, note 21.

[226] 兵署少正開国公 SNIII p 290-91, n 13-14 for discussion of these titles and relationship to Tang bureaucratic offices.

[227] 揚承慶 Giving a default *pinyin* pronunciation. See TPSH 4.9.24 above. *A New History of Parhae* (2012) trans. John Duncan, Seoul: Northeast Asian History Foundation (2005) *Parhae ui yoksa wa munwha*) renders all Parhae names as Korean. See p. 14.

For the first time high speed "Flying Stations" bells[228] permitting messengers the use of fast horses were awarded to the six provinces Echizen, Etchū, Sado, Izumo, Iwami and Iyo, one per province.

天平宝字二年（七五八）十月甲子【庚子朔廿五】○冬十月甲子。勅。如聞。吏者民之本也。数遷易。則民不安居。久積習。則民知所従。是以。服其徳而従其化。安其業而信其令。頃年。国司交替。皆以四年為限。斯則、適足労民。未可以化。孔子曰。如有用我。三年有成。夫以大聖之徳。猶須三年。而況中人乎。古者。三載考績。三考黜陟。所以表善簡悪尽臣力者也。自今以後。宜以六歳為限。省送故迎新之費。其毎至三年。遣巡察使。推検政迹。慰問民憂。待満両廻。随状黜陟。庶令移易貪俗。悉変清風。黎元息肩。倉廩有実。普告遐邇。知朕意焉。」又勅。諸国史生遷易。依格。待満六年者。望人既多。任所良少。由此。或有至於白頭不得一任。空帰故郷潜抱怨歎。自今以後。宜以四歳為限。遍及群人。」発陸奥国浮浪人。造桃生城。既而復其調庸。便即占着。又浮宕之徒、貫為柵戸。

Tenpyō Hōji 2.10.25　甲子　**Winter *kinoe-ne***
[November 30, 758]

The Emperor gave an edict:

"We have heard that 'Officials are the foundation for supervision of the people. If these officials are frequently changed, it unsettles the people. If they remain in office for a longer time the people will follow them.' As they continue in office, the people will admire their virtue, follow their guidance, be pacified by their administration, and trust their rule. In recent years provincial governors have changed every four years. But in this time span they can only begin to nurture the people, and not truly educate them. Confucius said 'If I have three years, I can accomplish something.' If for Confucius with his great sagely virtue three

---

[228] *Hiyaku no suzu* 飛駅鈴

years were necessary, how much more so for ordinary people. In ancient China it took three years to evaluate an official's work, but nine years to promote him. This was because it took that long for subjects to demonstrate their ability, being commended for the good and censured for the bad. Henceforth a governor's term of office will be six years, and the cost of sending and having officials return shall be adjusted accordingly. Every three years a regional inspector[229] will be dispatched to investigate the governance and inquire into the peoples' suffering. After the results of two rounds of inspection, the matter of promotion will be decided. What We desire is that the culture of greed among officials be swept away, that the customs will be purified and renewed, that the burdens of the people be alleviated, and that the granaries be filled. Let Our will be widely announced in the Empire."

The Emperor gave a further edict:

"According to a previous ordinance 'The term length of lower level officials[230] in all provinces shall be six years.' However, there are many who wish to be officials, and the openings are few. Thus there are those who wait until their hair is white and return to their native villages in vain without being appointed, and they secretly harbor a grudge. So hereafter the term limit will be four years so that many people will have an opportunity."

---

[229] *Junsatsushi* 巡察使
[230] *Shishō* 史生

Unsettled people[231] were sent to Michinooku Province to build Fort Momonou. These people's taxes in kind and commuted taxes have been remitted to force them to stay in that area. These vagrants were entered in the household registers as "fortress households".[232]

天平宝字二年（七五八）十月丁卯【廿八】○丁卯。授遣渤海大使従五位下小野朝臣田守従五位上。副使正六位下高橋朝臣老麻呂従五位下。其余六十六人各有差。」美濃国席田郡大領外正七位上子人。中衛無位吾志等言。子人等六世祖父乎留和斯知。自賀羅国慕化来朝。当時、未練風俗。不著姓字。望随国号。蒙賜姓字。賜姓賀羅造。

Tenpyō Hōji 2.10.28 丁卯 *hinoto-u*

[December 3, 758]

The ambassador returning from Parhae Jr 5 Lower Ono no Asomi Tamori was awarded Jr 5 Upper Rank. The vice-envoy Sr 6 Lower Takahashi no Asomi Oimaro was awarded Jr 5 Lower Rank. The other sixty-six members of the mission were awarded promotions in rank according to their level.

The chief magistrate[233] of Mushirota district in Mino Province Outer Sr 7 Upper Kohito, and the unranked Middle Imperial Guard Goshi said:

"The sixth-generation ancestor of Kohito and others, Oruwashichi, came to our court from the land of Kara[234]. At that time he had not yet assimilated to the customs of this country and thus was not granted a *kabane*. We beg that we be

---

[231] *Ukarehito* 浮浪人. SNIII p 292 n 8 – also *furō* 浮浪 or *rōnin* 浪人
[232] *kinoe* 柵戸
[233] *Dairyō* 大領
[234] 賀羅 Small ancient kingdom on the southeastern part of Korean peninsula.

96

given a *kabane* in the Japanese language." The petition was accepted and the court granted the *kabane* of Kara no Miyatsuko."

天平宝字二年（七五八）十一月辛卯【己巳朔廿三】〇十一月辛卯。御乾政官院。行大嘗之事。丹波国為由機。播磨国為須岐。

Tenpyō Hōji **2.11.23** 辛卯 *kanoto-u*

[December 27, 758]

The Emperor went to a hall of the Heavenly Council of State and carried out the rites of the Enthronement Ceremony. Tanba Province was designated as *Yuki*, and Harima Province as *Suki*.

天平宝字二年（七五八）十一月癸巳【廿五】〇癸巳。御閤門、宴於五位已上。賜禄有差。

Tenpyō Hōji **2.11.25** 癸巳 *mizunoto-mi*

[December 29, 758]

The Emperor went to the Side Gate[235] and presented a banquet to the officials of fifth rank and up. He gave stipends according to status.

天平宝字二年（七五八）十一月甲午【廿六】〇甲午。饗内外諸司主典已上於朝堂。賜主典已上、番上。及学生等六千六百七十余人布綿有差。其明経・文章・明法・音・算・医・針・陰陽・天文・暦・勤公・勤産・工巧・打射等五十七人、賜糸人十＝［糸＋句］。文人上詩者。更益十＝［糸＋句］。

Tenpyō Hōji **2.11.26** 甲午 *kinoe-uma*

[December 30, 758]

---

[235] *Kōmon* 閤門 – a south gate of the *Daigokuden*.

The Emperor gave a banquet in the Administrative Palace for inner and outer officials of the rank of Clerk and up. The Clerks and other attendants, officials of the guard units, and the students, over six thousand six hundred and seventy people in all, were given hemp cloth and floss silk according to status. Fifty-seven people who were skilled in the classics, letters, law, music, mathematics, medicine, acupuncture, *yinyang*, astronomy and the calendar, public affairs, production, arts and crafts, and martial arts were each awarded a ten-strand silk cord. Literati who had presented poetry[236] were also awarded a ten-strand silk cord.

天平宝字二年（七五八）十一月乙未【廿七】○乙未。神祇官人及由機・須岐両国国郡司等。並加位階。并賜禄有差。授播磨介従五位下上毛野公広浜従五位上。丹波守外従五位下大蔵忌寸麻呂従五位下。

Tenpyō Hōji **2.11.27** 乙未 *kinoto-hitsuji*

[December 31, 758]

Officials of the Department of Deity Affairs and governors of the *Yuki* and *Suki* provinces and districts were all awarded a promotion in rank and stipends according to status. The Assistant Governor of Harima Jr 5 Lower Kamitsukeno no Kimi Hirohama was awarded Jr 5 Upper Rank. Tamba Governor Outer Jr 5 Lower Ōkura no Imiki Maro was awarded Jr 5 Lower Rank.

天平宝字二年（七五八）十二月丙午【己亥朔八】○十二月丙午。徴発坂東騎兵。鎮兵。役夫。及夷俘等。造桃生城・小勝柵。五道倶入。並就功役。毀従四位下矢代女王位記。以被幸先帝而改志也。

Tenpyō Hōji **2.12.8** 丙午 *hinoe-uma*

---

[236] *Shi* 詩

[January 11, 759]

The court requisitioned cavalry, defense troops, laborers and submitted *Emishi* from the eight provinces of Kantō[237] to construct Fort Momonofu and Fort Okachi. Altogether provinces of five circuits participated in this construction effort.

The court removed the rank of Jr 4 Lower Princess Yashiro. Although she had received the favor of the former emperor Shōmu, she later gave her heart to another.[238]

天平宝字二年（七五八）十二月戊申【十】○戊申。遣渤海使小野朝臣田守等奏唐国消息曰。天宝十四載、歳次乙未十一月九日。御史大夫兼范陽節度使安禄山反。挙兵作乱。自称大燕聖武皇帝。改范陽作霊武郡。其宅為潜竜宮。年号聖武。留其子安卿緒。知范陽郡事。自将精兵廿余万騎。啓行南往。十二月。直入洛陽。署置百官。天子遣安西 e 哥舒翰。将卅万衆。守潼津関。使大将軍封常清。将十五万衆。別囲洛陽。天宝十五載。禄山遣将軍孫孝哲等。帥二万騎攻潼津関。哥舒翰壊潼津岸。以墜黄河。絶其通路而還。孝哲鑿山開路。引兵入至于新豊。六月六日。天子遜于剣南。七月甲子。皇太子＝［王＋與］即皇帝位于霊武郡都督府。改元為至徳元載。己卯。天子至于益州。平盧留後事徐帰道。遣果毅都尉行柳城県兼四府経略判官張元澗。来聘渤海。且徴兵馬曰。今載十月。当撃禄山。王須発騎四万。来援平賊。渤海疑其有異心。且留未帰。十二月丙午。徐帰道果鴆劉正臣于北平。潜通禄山。幽州節度使史思明、謀撃天子。安東都護王玄志仍知其謀。帥精兵六千余人。打破柳城、斬徐帰道。自称権知平盧節度。進鎮北平。至徳三載四月。王玄志遣将軍王進義。来聘渤海。且通国故曰。天子帰于西京。迎太上天皇于蜀。居于別宮。弥滅賊徒。故遣下臣来告命矣。渤海王為其事難信。且留進義、遣使詳問。行人未至。事未至可知。其唐王賜渤海国王勅書一巻。亦副状進。於是。勅大宰府曰。安禄山者。是狂胡狡竪也。違天起逆。事必不利。疑、是不能計西。還更掠於海東。古人曰。蜂＝猶毒。何況人乎。其府帥船王。及大弐吉備朝臣

---

[237] *Sakanohimukashi* 坂東
[238] Author of *Man'yōshū* poem 626. Details of the affair not known.

真備。俱是碩学。名顕当代。簡在朕心。委以重任。宜知此状。預設奇謀。縱使不来。儲備無悔。其所謀上策。及応備雑事。一一具録報来。

Tenpyō Hōji 2.12.10 戊申 *tsuchinoe-saru*

[January 13, 759]

The Parhae envoy Ono no Asomi Tamori and all reported on the news from Tang China:

"On *Tianbao* 14.11.9 [239] the Censor-in-Chief [240] and Military Governor of Fanyang[241] An Lushan [242] rebelled, raising troops and causing an insurrection. He named himself the *Dayan Shengwu* Emperor. [243] He renamed Fanyang as Lingwu District, [244] called his mansion Qianlong Palace,[245] and designated the era name as *Shengwu*.[246] His son An Qingxu[247] stayed in Fanyang district, where he raised over two hundred thousand[248] cavalry. He moved south, entering Loyang in the twelfth month, and installed officials of a new government. The Emperor Xuanxong dispatched the Military Governor of Anxi, Geshu Han, [249] leading three hundred thousand troops, to protect the Tongguan Pass[250] and

---

[239] December 755.

[240] *Yushi Dafu* 御史大夫. Corresponding to the head of the Japanese *Danjōdai* 弾正台.

[241] *Fanyang* 范陽. *Jiedushi* 節度使 (J.*Setsudoshi*)

[242] I have relied on the *Cambridge History of China, Vol 3, Sui and T'ang China* (1979), pp 468-84; 561-71, in translating the following.

[243] 大燕聖武皇帝 – *Dayan* was the state established in northeast China by An Lushan in 756; it was destroyed in 763. Note that 聖武 is the Japanese Emperor Shōmu's designation.

[244] 霊武

[245] 潜竜宮

[246] 聖武

[247] 安卿緒

[248] *Cambridge History* p. 473 gives this number; p. 562 says 100,000 – 200,000.

[249] 哥舒翰

[250] 潼津関

General Feng Changqing[251] to surround Loyang with one hundred fity thousand troops. In the next year *Tianbao* 15 (756), An Lushan sent his general Sun Xiaozhe[252] and others with twenty thousand cavalry to attack the TongguanPass. Geshu Han broke through the cliffs at the Tongguan Pass, descended along the Yellow River, intercepted the forces of Sun Xiaozhe and turned them back. Sun Xiaozhe opened a road through the mountains, and leading his troops, arrived at Xinfeng.

On the sixth day of the sixth month, the Emperor fled to Jiannan. On the sixth day of the seventh month the Crown Prince went to Lingwu district and acceded to the throne as Suzong, and changed the year to *Zhide* [253] One.

On the 52nd day the Emperor reached Yi Province. Xu Guidao, staying bchind to handle the business of the Pinglu Military Governor, sent Zhang Yuanjian, the Guoyi Commandant working as the Assistant to the military commissioner of Liucheng County and the Four Prefectures [254] to visit Parhae to attempt to raise troops, saying "This year in the tenth month we will attack An Lushan, so if the King of Parhae will send forty thousand cavalry, we will be able to subdue him." But in Parhe Zhang Yuanjian apparently developed a treacherous heart; for a long time he did not send back any messengers. On the twenty-second day of the

---

[251] 封常清
[252] 孫孝哲
[253] 至德
[254] 平盧留後事徐帰道。遣果毅都尉行柳城県兼四府経略判官張元潤 – special thanks to Victor Mair and his students Fangyi Cheng and Haiqing Wen for the translation of this very difficult passage.

twelfth month Zhang Yuanjian poisoned Guo Liuzhen[255] in the Northern Capital.[256] He made a secret understanding with An Lushan and the Yuchou Military Governor Shi Shiming[257] and plotted to attack the Emperor.

The Governor of Andong district, Wang Xuanzhi[258], learned of this and leading over six thousand troops attacked Liucheng Township[259] and killed Zhang Yuanjian[260]. He styled himself the Pinglu Provisional Military Governor,[261] and leading troops pacified the Northern Capital. In the fourth month of *Zhide* 3 (758), Wang Xuanzhi sent his general Wang Jinyi[262] as a messenger to Parhae. He said "The Emperor Suzong has returned to the western capital and is welcoming the Retired Emperor Xuanzong back to live in a detached palace. The rebels have been completely vanquished. Thus he has dispatched me, his subject, to announce this news." The King of Parhae found it hard to believe Wang Jinyi, and while detaining him, sent a messenger to Tang to inquire about these details. However, his messenger has not yet returned and thus the King of Parhae is uncertain as to the truth.

Tamori, in reporting this, presented an edict in one scroll from the Tang emperor to the king of Parhae.

---

[255] 果鵁劉
[256] 北平. Parhae had five capital cities, the northernmost of which, Shangching 上京, was the main capital from 756.
[257] 史思明
[258] 王玄志
[259] 柳城県
[260] Here referred to by one of his titles, 徐帰道.
[261] 権知平盧節度
[262] 王進義

102

Then the Emperor Junnin sent the following edict to the Kyushu Government Headquarters:

"An Lushan is a raging barbarian, and a cunning man. Turning against heaven, he has raised a rebellion. He must certainly be made to fail. It is not likely that he plans to attack the west, but it may be that he will attack the eastern sea. The ancients said 'A bee is not a scorpion, but is still poisonous. Is this not also true of humans?'

"The Governor-General, Kyushu Headquarters, Prince Fune, and the Senior Assistant Governor-General, Kibi no Asomi Makibi, are both great scholars, and We ask you to consult them and to hear from their illustrious voices. Kindly seek to understand the situation and prepare a policy, and even if An Lushan does not attack make preparations. Write down in detail your deliberations and your strategy proposals and report back to us."

天平宝字二年（七五八）十二月癸丑【十五】○癸丑。左京人広野王賜姓
池上真人。

Tenpyō Hōji 2.12.15 癸丑 *mizunoto-ushi*

[January 18, 759]

A person of the Left Capital, Prince Hiro, was granted the kabane of Ikenoue no Mahito.

天平宝字二年（七五八）十二月壬戌【廿四】○壬戌。渤海使揚承慶等入
京。

Tenpyō Hōji 2.12.24 壬戌 *mizunoe-inu*

[January 27, 759]

The Parhae envoy Yang Chengqing and company entered the capital.

天平宝字二年（七五八）十二月丙寅【廿八】○丙寅。以式部散位四百人。蔭子・位子・留省資人共二百人。兵部散位二百人。為定額与考。自余額外、情願輸銭続労者。一依前格処分。

Tenpyō Hōji **2.12.28** 丙寅 *hinoe-tora*

[January 31, 759]

Stipends were decided upon for four hundred persons of scattered rank in the Ministry of Ceremonial: Shadow rank for children of fifth rank and up;[263] shadow rank for children from sixth rank down to eighth rank;[264] and other miscellaneous dependents -- a total of two hundred people. Also a total of two hundred people of scattered rank from the Ministry of War. Other people without set stipends but who wished to be paid wages for labor were dealt with according to the former ordinance.[265]

《巻尾続日本紀　巻第廿一

[End of *Shoku Nihongi Maki* 21]

---

[263] *Onshi* 蔭子
[264] *Ishi* 位子
[265] SNIII p 301 n 10 -- perhaps a pronouncement of the Great Council of State on Yōrō 5.6.10.

Tenpyō Hōji 3

《卷首続日本紀卷第廿二〈起天平宝字三年正月、尽四年六月。〉
　右大臣従二位兼行皇太子傅中衛大将臣藤原朝臣継縄等奉　勅撰」

Shoku Nihongi Maki 22 (*Tenpyō Hōji* 3.1 to 4.6)

Selected and Presented by imperial command by Great Minister of the Right Jr 2 and concurrently Tutor to the Crown Prince and Major Captain of the Middle Imperial Guard Fujiwara no Asomi Tsugutada et al

廃帝　Haitei (Junnin – the Deposed Emperor)

天平宝字三年（七五九）正月戊辰朔　三年春正月戊辰朔。御大極殿受朝。
文武百官。及高麗蕃客等。各依儀拝賀。

Tenpyō Hōji 3.1.1 戊辰 **Spring** *tsuchinoe-tatsu*

[February 2, 759]

The Emperor went to the Imperial Council Hall to hold an audience. The

hundred civil and military officials and also the barbarian guests from Parhae[266]

carried out the ceremonies and each presented their felicitations.

天平宝字三年（七五九）正月庚午【三】○庚午。帝臨軒。高麗使揚承慶
等貢方物。奏曰。高麗国王大欽茂言。承聞。在於日本照臨八方聖明皇帝。
登遐天宮。攀号感慕。不能黙止。是以。差輔国将軍揚承慶。帰徳将軍揚
泰師等。令齎表文并常貢物入朝。詔曰。高麗国王遥聞先朝登遐天宮。不
能黙止。使揚承慶等来慰。聞之感痛。永慕益深。但歳月既改。海内従吉。
故不以其礼相待也。又不忘旧心。遣使来貢。勤誠之至。深有嘉尚。

---

[266]高麗蕃客. Koma 高麗 is used interchangeably with Parhae in *Shoku Nihongi*, although in the following several entries about the envoys it repeatedly uses the designation "Koma". Read as "Korai", it indicates the Japanese understanding that Parhae was founded by refugees from the Koguryŏ kingdom, destroyed in 668.

Tenpyō Hōji 3.1.3 庚午 *kanoe-uma*

[February 4, 759]

The Emperor[267] approached[268], and the Parhae envoy Yang Chengqing and all presented tribute of the products of their native land and reported:

"The King of the country of Parhae Dai Qinmu[269] says:

'I have heard that in Japan the saintly Emperor Shōmu whose reign illuminated the eight directions of the world, has ascended to rule in the distant palace of heaven. Upon hearing that this Emperor had died I wept and could not remain silent. Thus I have dispatched the Bulwark Minister and Generalissimo Yang Chengqing and the Trustworthy Virtue General Yang Taishi bearing this memorial and the usual tribute to present to the Japanese court.' "

The Emperor in response gave the following edict:

"The King of the country of Parhae, hearing from afar that the former Emperor had ascended to rule in the distant palace of heaven, could not remain silent and has sent Yang Chengqing to express his condolences. Hearing this We are deeply moved, and grieve even more for the former emperor. However the years and months have passed, and the sea and land have returned to their usual peaceful state. Thus we rejoice at this visit, that the King has not forgotten his

---

[267] 帝 *Mikado* - frequently used for Junnin *Haitei* during the years of his rule, while the Retired Empress Kōken is often referred to as "高原天皇 Takano *Tennō*".
[268] That is, left his seat on the throne.
[269] 大欽茂 - King Mun, third king of Parhae.

106

heart of old, and has sent an envoy with tribute. We commend the King for his profound loyalty."

天平宝字三年（七五九）正月甲戌【七】○甲戌。停節宴。雨也

Tenpyō Hōji **3.1.7** 甲戌 *kinoe-inu*

[February 8, 759]

The prescribed banquet was cancelled. This was due to rain.

天平宝字三年（七五九）正月戊寅【十一】○戊寅。以従五位下豊野真人出雲為少納言。従五位下船井王為内史頭。外従五位下宇自可臣山道為画工正。従五位下高橋朝臣人足為上野守。外従五位下生江臣智麻呂為佐渡守。

Tenpyō Hōji **3.1.11** 戊寅 *tsuchinoe-tora*

[February 12, 759]

Jr 5 Lower Toyono no Mahito Izumo appointed Minor Counsellor.

Jr 5 Lower Prince Funai appointed Head of the Bureau of Books and Drawings.

Outer Jr 5 Lower Ujika no Omi Yamaji appointed Head of Office of Pictorials.

Jr 5 Lower Takahashi no Asomi Hitotari appointed Governor of Kozuke.

Outer Jr 5 Lower Ikue no Omi Tomaro appointed Governor of Sado.

天平宝字三年（七五九）正月乙酉【十八】○乙酉。帝臨軒。授高麗大使揚承慶正三位、副使揚泰師従三位。判官馮方礼従五位下。録事已下十九人各有差。賜国王及大使已下禄有差。饗五位已上。及蕃客。并主典已上於朝堂。作女楽於舞台。奏内教坊踏歌於庭。客主典殿已上次之。事畢賜綿各有差。

Tenpyō Hōji **3.1.18** 乙酉 *kinoto-tori*

[February 19, 759]

The Emperor approached and awarded the Parhae ambassador Yang Chengqing the Sr 3rd Rank, and the Vice-Envoy Yang Taishi the Jr 3rd.[270] The Secretary Ping Fangli was awarded Jr 5 Lower. Rank was awarded according to status to the nineteen stipended officials on down. The King of Parhae and the Ambassador on down were given stipends according to status. Parhae envoys of Fifth Rank and up and of the rank of Clerk and up were invited to a banquet in the Administrative Palace. On a stage female dancers performed music, and women of the Office of Female Dancers and Musicians danced to stomping songs in the garden. Envoys the rank of Clerk and up followed them. After this gifts of silk floss were presented.

天平宝字三年（七五九）正月丙戌【十九】○丙戌。内射。喚客。亦令同射。

Tenpyō Hōji **3.1.18** 丙戌 *hinoe-inu*

[February 20, 759]

An archery match was held. The Parhae guests were summoned and also took part.

天平宝字三年（七五九）正月甲午【廿七】○甲午。大保藤原恵美朝臣押勝宴蕃客於田村第。勅賜内裏女楽并綿一万屯。当代文士賦詩送別。副使揚泰師作詩和之。

Tenpyō Hōji **3.1.27** 甲午 *kinoe-uma*

[February 28, 759]

---

[270] Note the extraordinarily high court rank given to the Parhae envoys.

The Grand Guardian Fujiwara Emi no Asomi Oshikatsu invited the Parhae envoys to his Tamura Mansion for a banquet. The Emperor gave an edict summoning dancing girls from the palace and awarded ten thousand hanks of floss silk. Also the literati of the time were summoned to write Chinese poems and present them to the envoys. The Vice-Envoy Yang Taishi also composed a poem and recited it in response.

天平宝字三年（七五九）正月丁酉【三十】○丁酉。授正六位上高元度外従五位下。為迎入唐大使使。

Tenpyō Hōji 3.1.30 丁酉 *hinoto-tori*

[March 3, 759]

Sr 6 Upper Kō Gendo[271] was awarded Outer Jr 5 Lower and was appointed Ambassador to Tang.

天平宝字三年（七五九）二月戊辰朔○二月戊戌朔。賜高麗王書曰。天皇敬問高麗国王。使揚承慶等遠渉滄海。来弔国憂。誠表慇懃。深増酷痛。但随時変礼。聖哲通規。従吉履新。更無余事。兼復所貽信物。依数領之。即因還使。相酬土毛絹卅疋。美濃＝［糸＋施の旁］卅疋。糸二百＝［糸＋句］。綿三百屯。殊嘉爾忠。更加優。賜錦四疋。両面二疋。纈羅四疋。白羅十疋。彩帛＝疋。白綿一百帖。物雖軽尟。寄思良深。至宜並納。国使附来。無船駕去。仍差単使送還本蕃。便従彼郷達於大唐。欲迎前年入唐大使藤原朝臣河清。宜知相資。余寒未退。想王如常。遣書指不多及。」授従五位下当麻真人広名従五位上。

Tenpyō Hōji 3.2.1 戊辰 *tsuchinoe-tatsu*

[March 4, 759]

---

[271] 高元度 From his surname, likely a person of Koguryō descent. His mission was to find the envoy Fujiwara no Asomi Kiyokawa, sent to China in TPSH 4.

The Emperor sent the following document to the King of Parhae:

"The Emperor respectfully greets the King of the country of Parhae. The Envoy Yang Chengqing and his embassy crossed the distant sea and came to our country to express condolences on the death of the late Emperor. They expressed sincere grief and deep mourning. However, time has passed and We have ascended the throne. Fortune has been renewed and a new year has come. Furthermore the exchange of goods has begun again. Thus We send with the returning envoy in return for thirty rolls of fur cloth from Parhae the following: thirty rolls of Mino province plain weave silk; two hundred skeins of silk thread; three hundred hanks of floss silk. Also in deep esteem for your uncommon loyalty, four rolls of brocade; two rolls of double-sided brocade; ten rolls of dyed silk gauze; ten rolls of white silk gauze; forty rolls of multicolored silk; and one hundred hanks of white batting. These are trifling things, but they are sent with truly deep sentiments. We hope you will receive them with pleasure.

"Your envoy traveled with our returning ambassador and thus did not bring ships. We have appointed an envoy and are sending him with your mission back to your country. Our envoy will proceed from your country to Great Tang, in order to search for our ambassador Fujiwara no Asomi Kiyokawa who was sent to Tang in former years. Please aid him. As it is still cold and unsettled, We cannot pay a visit in person, and trust that this written communication shall be sufficient."

On this day Jr 5 Lower Tagima no Mahito Hirona was awarded Jr 5 Upper Rank.

天平宝字三年（七五九）二月癸丑【十六】○癸丑。揚承慶等帰蕃。高元度等亦相随而去。

Tenpyō Hōji 3.2.16　癸丑 *mizunoto-ushi*

[March 19, 759]

Yang Chengqing and his embassy returned to their country. Kō Gendo and his party accompanied them.

天平宝字三年（七五九）三月丁卯朔○三月丁卯朔。日有蝕之。

Tenpyō Hōji 3.3.1 丁卯 *hinoto-u*

[April 2, 759]

Solar eclipse.

天平宝字三年（七五九）三月庚寅【廿四】○庚寅。大宰府言。府官所見。方有不安者四。拠警固式。於博多大津。及壱岐。対馬等要害之処。可置船一百隻以上以備不虞。而今無船可用。交闕機要。不安一也。大宰府者。三面帯海。諸蕃是待。而自罷東国防人。辺戍日以荒散。如不慮之表。万一有変。何以応卒。何以示威。不安二也。管内防人。一停作城。勤赴武芸。習其戦陳。而大弐吉備朝臣真備論曰。且耕且戦、古人称善。乞五十日教習而十日役于築城。所請雖可行。府僚或不同。不安三也。天平四年八月廿二日有勅。所有兵士全免調庸。其白丁者免調輸庸。当時民息兵強。可謂辺鎮。今管内百姓乏絶者衆。不有優復無以自贍。不安四也。勅。船者宜給公糧。以雑徭造。東国防人者衆議不允。仍不依請。管内防人十日役者。依真備之議。優復者。政得其理、民自富強。宜勉所職以副朝委。

Tenpyō Hōji 3.3.24 庚寅 *kanoe-tora*

[April 25, 759]

The Kyushu Government Headquarters said:

"As we survey our territory, there are at present four areas of concern. The regulation for defense of Kyushu[272] states: 'In the essential areas of the great harbor of Hakata, Iki and Tsushima, there should be over one hundred ships, in case of emergency.' Now however the number of ships does not meet this need for a critical point in our defenses. This is the first concern.

"The Headquarters faces the ocean on three sides, and looks toward various barbarian countries. However, the supply of border guards from the eastern provinces has ceased. The defense of our national boundaries is disorganized and neglected. If anything unforeseen should occur, and if there were by chance an incident, how would we be able to react quickly and make a show of force? This is the second concern.

"The border guards within our administration have stopped building forts, and now they train in martial arts and practice battle tactics. However, the Senior Assistant Governor-General Kibi no Asomi Makibi has argued that 'The ancients practiced both agriculture and military tactics; for fifty days they trained in the military arts, and for ten days they built forts.' Even if we were able to carry out what Makibi advocates, some officials in our administration disagree on this matter. This is the third concern.

"In an edict of *Tenpyō* 4.8.22, the soldiers of the *Saikaidō* were completely exempted from taxes in kind and commuted tax, while the ordinary people of the

---

[272] *Keigoshiki* 警固式

forts were subject only to the latter. At that time, the people could rest, the soldiers became stronger, and finally it could be said that the national borders were pacified. Now the people of the jurisdiction are in extreme poverty, and unless the tax system is revised the Headquarters cannot be supported. This is the fourth concern."

In response the Emperor gave a *choku*:

"As for the ships, public rice should be appropriated and the people should build them as part of their general corvee duties. The border guards from the eastern provinces cannot be mobilized and thus the Headquarter's request cannot be fulfilled. For those guards under the Headquarter's jurisdiction, the ten-day labor requirement should be as Makibi suggests. Regarding the exemption of tax and labor duties for the common people, if it can reasonably be carried out as a policy, the people should be enriched and strengthened. The officials should strive hard at their duties with which the court entrusts them."

天平宝字三年（七五九）四月辛亥【丙申朔十六】〇夏四月辛亥。以外従五位下陽胡史玲＝為越後守。

Tenpyō Hōji* 3.4.16 辛亥 *kanoto-i

[May 16, 759]

Outer Jr 5 Lower Yako no Fuhito Ryōgu appointed Governor of Echigo.

天平宝字三年（七五九）五月甲戌【丙寅朔九】〇五月甲戌。勅曰。朕以榮昧。欽承聖烈。母臨六合。子育兆民。見一物之或違。恨尭心之未洽。聞万方之有罪。想湯責而多愧。而今大乱已平。逆臣遠竄。然猶天災屢見。水異頻臻。窃恐。聴易隔於黎元。人含冤枉。鑑難周於宇宙。家懐鬱憂。

庶欲博採嘉言。傍詢妙略。憑衆智而益国。拠群明以利人。宜令百官五位
已上。緇徒師位已上。悉書意見。密封奉表。直言正対。勿有隠諱。朕与
宰相。審簡可否。不須詐称聖徳。苟媚取容。面弗肯陳。退遺後毀。普告
遐邇。知朕意焉。」又勅曰。頃聞。至于三冬間。市辺多餓人。尋問其由。
皆云。諸国調脚不得還郷。或因病憂苦。或無糧飢寒。朕窃念茲。情深矜
愍。宜随国大小。割出公廨。以為常平倉。逐時貴賤。糶糴取利。普救還
脚飢苦。非直霑外国民。兼調京中穀価。其東海。東山。北陸三道。左平
準署掌之。山陰。山陽。南海。西海四道。右平準署掌之。

Tenpyō Hōji 3.5.9 甲戌 *kinoe-inu*

[June 8, 759]

The Emperor[273] gave an edict:

"While We are foolish and sometimes misguided, We have reverently inherited the sagely brilliance of our ancestors. We nurture heaven, earth and the four directions as a mother her children. If there is one thing amiss, it is that We regret not being unable to govern with the heart of the sage king Yao. When We hear of crimes in the many regions, we are ashamed not to have the stature of Tang of Yin.

"Now the great rebellion[274] has been quelled, and the rebels have fled to distant places. However, natural disasters occur constantly, and floods are common. Although We try diligently to hear the voice of the people, it is difficult to look widely into all the corners of the world, and We fear that in some places there may be those who embrace sorrows and melancholy. Thus We desire to receive wise petitions, to widely seek policy suggestions, to improve the country by the

---

[273] Presumably Junnin, although it is odd that he uses the metaphor of a mother nurturing her children.

[274] of Tachibana Naramaro.

peoples' wisdom, and to benefit the people with the knowledge of many. Thus the hundred officials of fifth rank and up, and Buddhist clergy of the level of Master and up, should write their opinions and offer them, and make their declarations directly without fear of concealment. Then We and Our Minister Nakamaro will examine them in detail and decide what can be done. Thus may We be praised for Our sagely virtue without flattery, or criticized openly rather than defamed in the shadows. This should be announced far and wide, and let Our feelings be known."

The Emperor gave another edict:

"Recently, We heard that during the last months of winter there were many starving people near the markets. Upon making inquiries, it seems that these are people who had transported the tax rice from various provinces but were unable to return home. Some suffer from illness, some have no food, and all suffer from hunger and cold. We have reflected on the matter and We grieve deeply. Therefore, a portion of the public tax rice should be taken, in accordance with the size of the province, and ever-normal granaries[275] established. Rice should be bought at low prices and sold at the high, then the profit gathered. It should then be used to succor those who are suffering from hunger and enable them to return home. This should be done not only to aid the hungry in provinces outside the capital, but likewise to control the price of rice within the capital.

---

[275] jōheisō 常平倉

"As for the *Tōkaidō*, *Tōsandō*, and *Hokurikudō*, the Price Regulator[276] of the Left should administer this. In the *San'indō*, *Sanyōdō*, *Nankaidō* and *Saikaidō*, the Price Regulator of the Right should administer this."

天平宝字三年（七五九）五月庚辰【十五】o庚辰。先是。僧善神殉心以縦姦悪。僧専住極口而詈宿徳。並擯佐渡。令其悔過。而戻性不悛。醜声滋彰。至是。還俗従之差科。

Tenpyō Hōji* 3.5.15 庚辰 *kanoe-tatsu

[June 14, 759]

Recently the Buddhist priest Zenshin followed the desires of his heart and indulged in wicked things. The Buddhist priest Senjū has been highly praised for his virtue. Thus they were sent together to a temple in Sado, in an attempt to have Zenshin repent. But he has not amended his ways, and bad reports about him have increased. Therefore he shall be laicized due to his offences.

天平宝字三年（七五九）五月壬午【十七】o壬午。以正五位下大伴宿禰犬養為左中弁。従五位下布勢朝臣人主為右少弁。従五位下阿部朝臣毛人為文部少輔。従五位下大伴宿禰御依為仁部少輔。従五位下石川朝臣人成為節部少輔。外従五位下馬史夷麻呂為典薬頭。正五位上大和宿禰長岡為左京大夫。従五位下佐味朝臣宮守為亮。正五位上粟田朝臣奈勢麻呂為右京大夫。従五位下阿部朝臣三県為亮。外従五位下山辺県主小笠為大和介。従五位上当麻真人広名為河内介。従五位下大野朝臣広主為和泉守。従五位上石上朝臣宅嗣為参河守。従五位下巨曾倍朝臣難波麻呂為近江介。従五位下藤原恵美朝臣久須麻呂為美濃守。従四位上藤原朝臣巨勢麻呂為播磨守。従五位下県犬養宿禰沙弥麻呂為美作介。従五位下阿倍朝臣継人為備前介。外従五位下茨田宿禰牧野為備中介。従五位下穂積朝臣小東人為周防守。従五位上山村王為紀伊守。従五位下県犬養宿禰吉男為肥前守。

Tenpyō Hōji* 3.5.17 壬午 *mizunoe-uma

---

[276] *Hyōjunshō* 平準署 – new office to administer the Ever-Normal granaries.

[June 16, 759]

Sr 5 Lower Ōtomo no Sukune Inukai appointed Middle Controller of the Left.

Jr 5 Lower Fuse no Asomi Hitonushi appointed Middle Controller of the Right.

Jr 5 Lower Abe no Asomi Emishi appointed Junior Assistant, Ministry of Civil Affairs.

Jr 5 Lower Ōtomo no Sukune Miyori appointed Junior Assistant, Ministry of Benevolence.

Jr 5 Lower Ishikawa no Asomi Hitonari appointed Junior Assistant, Ministry of Moderation.

Outer Jr 5 Uma no Fuhito Hinamaro appointed Head of Bureau of Medicine.

Sr 5 Upper Yamato no Sukune Nagaoka appointed Commissioner of the Left Capital.

Jr 5 Lower Sami no Asomi Miyamori appointed Deputy Commissioner of the Left Capital.

Sr 5 Upper Awata no Asomi Nasemaro appointed Commissioner of the Right Capital.

Jr 5 Lower Abe no Asomi Miagata appointed Deputy Commissioner of the Right Capital.

Outer Jr 5 Lower Yamanobe no Agatanushi Okasa appointed Yamato Assistant Governor.

Jr 5 Upper Tagima no Mahito Hirona appointed Kawachi Assistant Governor.

Jr 5 Lower Ōno no Asomi Hirotate appointed Izumi Governor.

Jr 5 Upper Isonokami no Asomi Yakatsugu appointed Mikawa Governor.

Jr 5 Lower Kosobe no Asomi Naniwamaro appointed Ōmi Assistant Governor.

Jr 5 Lower Fujiwara Emi no Asomi Kusumaro appointed Mino Governor.

Jr 4 Lower Fujiwara no Asomi Kosemaro appointed Harima Governor.

Jr 5 Lower Agata Inukai no Sukune Samimaro appointed Mimasaka Assistant Governor.

Jr 5 Lower Abe no Asomi Tsuguhito appointed Bizen Assistant Governor.

Outer Jr 5 Lower Mamuta no Sukune Hirano appointed Bitchū Assistant Governor.

Jr 5 Lower Hozumi no Asomi Oazumahito appointed Suho Governor.

Jr 5 Upper Prince Yamamura appointed Kii Governor.

Jr 5 Lower Agata Inukai no Sukune Yoshio appointed Hizen Governor.

天平宝字三年（七五九）六月庚戌【乙未朔十六】〇六月庚戌。帝御内安殿。喚諸司主典已上。詔曰。【Ｓ２５】現神大八洲所知倭根子天皇詔旨

118

〈止〉宣詔〈乎〉、親王・王・臣・百官人等、天下公民、衆聞食宣。比
来太皇大后御命以〈弖〉朕〈爾〉語宣〈久〉。太政之始〈波〉、人心未
定在〈可波〉、吾子為〈弖〉皇太子〈止〉定〈弖〉先奉昇於君位畢
〈弖〉諸意静了〈奈牟〉後〈爾〉傍上〈乎波〉宣〈牟止〉為〈弖奈母〉
抑〈閇弖〉在〈ツ流〉。然今〈波〉君坐〈弖〉御宇事日月重〈奴〉。是
以、先考追皇〈止〉為。親母大夫人〈止〉為。兄弟姉妹親王〈止〉為
〈与止〉仰給〈夫〉貴〈岐〉御命〈乎〉頂受給〈利〉、歓〈備〉貴
〈美〉懼〈知〉恐〈利弖〉、掛畏我皇聖太上天皇御所〈爾〉奏給〈倍
波〉、奏〈世止〉教宣〈久〉。朕一人〈乎〉昇賜〈比〉治賜〈部流〉厚
恩〈乎母〉、朕世〈爾波〉酬尽奉事難〈之〉。生子〈乃〉八十都岐〈爾
自〉仕奉報〈倍久〉在〈良之止〉、夜昼恐〈麻里〉侍〈乎〉。伊夜益
〈須〉益〈爾〉朕私父母波良何良〈爾〉至〈麻弖爾〉可在状任〈止〉上
賜〈比〉治賜〈夫〉事甚恐〈自〉。受賜事不得〈止〉奏〈世止〉宣
〈夫〉。朕又念〈久〉。前聖武天皇〈乃〉皇太子定賜〈比弖〉天日嗣高
御座〈乃〉坐〈爾〉昇賜物〈乎〉、伊何〈爾可〉恐〈久〉私父母兄弟
〈爾〉及事得〈牟〉、甚恐〈自〉。進〈母〉不知、退〈母〉不知〈止〉
伊奈〈備〉奏。雖然多比重〈弖〉宣〈久〉。吾加久不申成〈奈波〉、敢
〈弖〉申人者不在。凡人子〈乃〉去禍、蒙福〈麻久〉欲為〈流〉事
〈波〉、為親〈爾止奈利〉。此大福〈乎〉取惣持〈弖〉、親王〈爾〉送
奉〈止〉教〈部〉宣〈夫〉御命〈乎〉受給〈利弖奈母〉加久為〈流〉。
故是以、自今以後、追皇舎人親王、宜称崇道尽敬皇帝、当麻夫人称大夫
人、兄弟姉妹悉称親王〈止〉宣天皇御命、衆聞食宣。辞別宣〈久〉。朕
一人〈乃未也〉慶〈之岐〉貴〈岐〉御命受賜〈牟〉。卿等庶〈母〉共喜
〈牟止〉為〈弖奈母〉、一二治賜〈倍岐〉家家門門人等〈爾〉、冠位上
賜〈比〉治賜〈久止〉宣天皇御命、衆聞食宣。又御命坐〈世〉、宣
〈久〉。大保〈乎波〉多他〈仁〉卿〈止能味波〉不念。朕父〈止〉、復
藤原伊良豆売〈乎波〉婆々〈止奈母〉念。是以、治賜〈武等〉勅〈倍
止〉、遍重〈天〉辞〈備〉申〈爾〉依〈天〉默在〈牟止〉為〈礼止毛〉、
止事不得。然此家〈乃〉子〈止毛波〉朕波良何良〈仁〉在物〈乎夜〉親
王〈多知〉治賜〈夫〉日〈仁〉治不賜在〈牟止〉為〈弖奈母〉、汝
〈仁〉冠位上賜治賜〈夫〉。又此家自〈久母〉藤原〈乃〉卿等〈乎波〉、
掛畏聖天皇御世重〈弖〉於母自〈岐〉人〈乃〉自門〈波〉慈賜〈比〉上
賜来〈流〉家〈奈利〉。今又無過仕奉人〈乎波〉慈賜〈比〉治賜〈比〉
不忘賜〈之止〉宣天皇御命、衆聞食宣。」従三位船王。池田王並授三品。
正四位上諱従三位。従五位下御方王。御使王。無位林王。笠王。宗形王
並従四位下。従五位下河内王従五位上。正四位下紀朝臣飯麻呂。藤原朝
臣真楯並正四位上。従四位上藤原朝臣巨勢麻呂正四位下。従四位下藤原
朝臣御楯従四位上。正五位下阿倍朝臣嶋麻呂。大伴宿禰犬養。石川朝臣
名人。正六位上岡真人和気。従五位下仲真人石伴。従五位上藤原恵美朝

119

臣真光。従五位下藤原恵美朝臣久須麻呂並従四位下。正五位下中臣朝臣
清麻呂。従五位上藤原朝臣魚名並正五位上。従五位下藤原恵美朝臣朝狩
正五位下。従五位下都努朝臣道守。阿倍朝臣毛人。大伴宿禰御依。豊野
真人出雲並従五位上。正六位上三嶋真人廬原。阿倍朝臣許智。藤原朝臣
雄田麻呂。藤原恵美朝臣小弓麻呂。藤原恵美朝臣薩雄。橘宿禰綿裳並従
五位下。従四位下室女王。飛鳥田女王並四品。従五位下弓削女王。無位
川辺女王。加豆良女王。従五位下藤原恵美朝臣児従並従四位下。」以従
四位上藤原朝臣御楯任参議。

Tenpyō Hōji 3.6.16 庚戌 *kanoe-inu*

[July 14, 759]

The Emperor Junnin went to the Private Palace[277], summoned the officials from the Clerks on up, and gave an edict [*Senmyō 25*]:

"Let all – imperial princes, princes, ministers, the hundred officials, and all nobles in the realm – give heed to the words spoken as an edict by the Emperor, Beloved Child of Yamato, who rules the land of the Great Eight Islands as a manifest god. Recently the Empress Dowager Kōmyō spoke to Us the following words:

'When at the beginning of your reign affairs were still unsettled, We named you, Our child,[278] as Crown Prince, and then to the rank of Emperor, and the peoples' fears were calmed. Until then We forebore speaking on another matter. But now the days and months of your governing as Emperor have

---

[277] Here *Naianden* 内安殿. SNIII, p 314, n 5 – location uncertain, but likely a building within the the imperial living quarters.

[278] Junnin was of course not her actual child, and the *Shoku Nihongi* record does not give Kōmyō credit for naming him Crown Prince.

mounted up. Now your deceased father should be named Emperor[279], and your mother named Great Imperial Consort.[280] Your elder and younger brothers and sisters should be named imperial princes.'

"Upon receiving these august words, We trembled with joy, and went to the saintly Retired Empress Kōken, Our Sovereign whose name is invoked with fear, and reported this matter, informing her that these were the words of the Dowager Empress Kōmyō, and saying:

'We Ourselves have received the blessing of being appointed to the imperial rank, but it is a problematic matter whether this award should end with my own reign. The issue of whether We should bestow it on my descendants in order that they should receive it in perpetuity is one with which We struggle day and night. Moreover, whether the imperial appellation should be bestowed upon Our parents is a matter which is extremely grave, and on which I cannot make a decision.' -- thus I reported to Retired Empress Kōken.

"We have also reflected on the fact that when Shōmu *Tennō* designated a Crown Prince, and at the time when We ascended to the High Throne of Heavenly Sun Succession, We wondered fearfully whether Our parents and siblings should be designated. This was indeed a fearful thing. We did not know what to do, and declined to speak.

---

[279] Imperial Prince Toneri 舍人親王 (676 – 735). A son of Emperor Tenmu 天武天皇. Zachert comments that it had been customary in China since Emperor Wu of the Zhou dynasty to posthumously designate a dynastic founder's ancestors as emperors themselves. Zachert, 105.
[280] *Ohomiyoya* (*Daibunin* 大夫人).

"However, the Dowager Empress has advised that if We say nothing, then others will also say nothing. Moreover, that one's child escapes misfortune and receives good fortune is due to the parents. Since We have been blessed with the rank of Emperor, We should also confer distinction on the Imperial Prince.[281] This is what has been advised."

We thus proclaim:

"Henceforth Our father Imperial Prince Toneri will be designated an Emperor, and will be called "Sovereign of the Lofty Way who is to be Endlessly Revered."[282] Our mother Imperial Consort Tagima[283] will be called Great Imperial Consort. Our elder and younger brothers and sisters will all be designated imperial princes and princesses. Let all hearken to these words of the Emperor."

On another matter, We pronounce the following:

"Shall We alone rejoice in the words of the Empress Dowager? We believe that the aristocracy should also rejoice, and thus promotions in cap and rank shall be given to members of several noble families. Let all hearken to the words of the Emperor."

Further, We proclaim:

---

[281] Toneri, his father.
[282] *Sudō Jinkyō Ōtai (Kōtei)* 崇道尽敬皇帝.
[283] 当麻夫人

"The Grand Guardian[284] is no ordinary subject. We think of him as Our father[285], and of Fujiwara no Iratsume[286], his consort, as our mother. Thus while we are speaking of bestowing rewards, although we have hesitated thus far to speak of it, since Oshikatsu and Iratsume are like my parents, their children are my sisters and brothers. Along with naming Imperial Prince Toneri's children[287] as imperial princes, shall we not also award cap and rank to Oshikatsu's children? Moreover, the Fujiwara house have as a noble family down through the reigns of the saintly emperors, whose names are invoked with awe and fear, produced weighty retainers, and its members have been blessed with the bestoyal of court rank. These members of Oshikatsu's family who serve without fault should also not be forgotten at this time –let all hearken to the words of the Emperor."

Jr 3 Prince Fune and Prince Ikeda both awarded Third Cap Rank.[288]

Sr 4 Upper Prince Shirakabe[289] awarded Jr 3 Rank.

Jr 5 Lower Prince Mikata, Prince Mitsukai, and no-rank Prince Hayashi, Prince Kasa and Prince Munakata[290] all awarded Jr 4 Lower Rank.

Jr 5 Lower Prince Kawachi awarded Jr 5 Upper Rank.

---

[284] 大保 -- Fujiwara no Nakamaro. On TPHJ 2.8.25 the Emperor Junnin bestowed the rank of 紫微大保 on Nakamaro and gave him the honorary name Emi no Ason Oshikatsu 恵美朝臣押勝. *Daihō* was the equivalent of Great Minister of the Right.

[285] Nakamaro was actually Junnin's father-in-law, having married the widow (Muroawata Morohime 室粟田諸姉) of Nakamaro's son Mayori 真従. Junnin was living in Nakamaro's Tamura mansion previous to being named Crown Prince.

[286] 藤原伊良豆売

[287] Junnin's actual brothers (sons of Toneri).

[288] 三品. Both were sons of Imperial Prince Toneri.

[289] Imina 諱 - later Kōnin *Tennō*.

[290] Grandchildren of Imperial Prince Toneri.

Sr 4 Lower Ki no Asomi Iimaro and Fujiwara no Asomi Matate both awarded Sr 4 Upper Rank.

Jr 4 Upper Fujiwara no Asomi Kosemaro to Sr 4 Lower Rank.

Jr 4 Lower Fujiwara no Asomi Mitate to Jr 4 Upper Rank.

Sr 5 Lower Abe no Asomi Shimamaro, Ōtomo no Sukune Inukai, Ishikawa no Asomi Nahito, Sr 6 Upper Oka no Mahito Wake, Jr 5 Lower Naka no Mahito Iwatomo, Jr 5 Upper Fujiwara Emi no Asomi Masaki, and Jr 5 Lower Fujiwara Emi no Asomi Kusumaro all awarded Jr 4 Lower Rank.

Sr 5 Lower Nakatomi no Asomi Kiyomaro and Jr 5 Upper Fujiwara no Asomi Uona both awarded Sr 5 Upper Rank.

Jr 5 Lower Fujiwara Emi no Asomi Asakari awarded Sr 5 Lower Rank.

Jr 5 Lower Tsuno no Asomi Michimori, Abe no Asomi Emishi, Ōtomo no Sukune Miyori, and Toyo no Mahito Izumo all awarded Jr 5 Upper Rank.

Sr 6 Upper Mishima no Mahito Iohara, Abe no Asomi Kochi, Fujiwara no Asomi Odamaro, Fujiwara Emi no Asomi Koyumimaro, Fujiwara Emi no Asomi Satsuo, and Tachibana no Sukune Watamo all awarded Jr 5 Lower Rank.

Jr 4 Lower Princess Muro and Princess Asukata both awarded Fourth Cap Rank.

Jr 5 Lower Princess Yuge, no-rank Princess Kawabe, Princess Kazura, and Jr 5 Lower Fujiwara Emi Asomi Koyori all awarded Jr 4 Lower Rank.

Jr 4 Upper Fujiwara no Asomi Mitate appointed Imperial Advisor.

天平宝字三年（七五九）六月壬子【十八】○壬子。令大宰府造行軍式。以将伐新羅也。

Tenpyō Hōji 3.6.18 壬子 *mizunoe-ne*

[July 16, 759]

The Kyushu Government Headquarters was ordered to compile the Regulations for Military Affairs.[291] This was for the purpose of preparing for the attack on Silla.

天平宝字三年（七五九）六月丙辰【廿二】○丙辰。勅。如聞。治国之要。
不如簡人。簡人任能。民安国富。窃見内外官人景迹。曾無廉恥。志在貪
盗。是宰相訓導之怠。非為人皆稟愚性。宜加誘誨、各立令名。其維城典
訓者。叙為政之規模。著修身之検括。律令格式者。録当今之要務。具庶
官之紀綱。並是窮安上治民之道。尽済世弼化之宜。其濫不殺生。能矜貧
苦、為仁。断諸邪悪、修諸善行、為義。事上尽忠、撫下有慈、為礼。遍
知庶事、断決是非、為智。与物不妄、触事皆正、為信。非分希福、不義
欲物、為貪。心無弁了、強逼悩人、為嗔。事不合理、好是自愚、為痴。
不愛己妻、喜犯他女、為婬。人所不与、公取窃取、為盗。父兄不誠。斯
何以導子弟。官吏不行。此何以教士民。若有修習仁義礼智信之善。戒慎
貪嗔痴淫盗之悪。兼読前二色書者。挙而察之。随品昇進。自今以後。除
此色外。不得任用。史生已上。庶令懲悪勧善、重名軽物。普告天下。知
朕意焉。是日。百官及師位僧等。奉去五月九日勅。各上封事。以陳得失。
正三位中納言兼文部卿神祇伯勲十二等石川朝臣年足奏曰。臣聞、治官之
本。要拠律令。為政之宗。則須格式。方今、科条之禁。雖著篇簡。別式
之文。未有制作。伏乞作別式。与律令並行。」参議従三位出雲守文室真
人智努及少僧都慈訓奏。伏見。天下諸寺。毎年正月悔過。稍乖聖願。終
非功徳。何者。修行護国、僧尼之道。而今或曾不入寺。計官供於七日。
或貪規兼得。着空名於両処。由斯。讒及三宝。無益施主。伏願。自今以
後。停官布施。令彼貪僧無所希望。」参議従三位氷上真人塩焼奏。臣伏
見、三世王已下給春秋禄者。是矜王親。而今計上日。不異臣姓。伏乞。
依令優給、勿求上日。」播磨大掾正六位上山田連古麻呂奏。臣窃見。正
丁百姓或生五男已上。其年並登廿已上。乃輸庸調、父子倶従課役。臣謂。
合有優矜。伏乞。庶民生丁男五口已上者。免其課役。」並付所司施行。
其緇侶意見。略拠漢風。施於我俗。事多不穏。雖下官符。不行於世。故
不具載。

Tenpyō Hōji 3.6.22 丙辰 *hinoe-tatsu*

[July 20, 759]

The Emperor gave an edict:

---

[291] *Kōgunshiki* 行軍式

"We have heard that 'Choosing men of ability is the cornerstone of governing the country. If men of ability are selected, the people will be pacified and the country will prosper.' As We examine intently the conduct of the inner and outer officials, it seems that they have known no shame and have done nothing but stolen wantonly. The great ministers[292] have taught and led the functionaries in this negligence. It is not that the people's nature is inherently foolish. The officials should each be properly evaluated and instructed according to their titles in the codes. The *Yicheng Dianxun*[293] set a standard for conducting government, and made clear the standards for assessing oneself. Furthermore the Penal Code, Civil Code, Ordinances and Regulations[294] record important matters for the present and detail the duties and laws of the ordinary official. Together these should regulate the government and provide the proper way for governing the people. They are fundamental for promoting the national welfare and for edification.

"Thus refraining from the reckless killing of living beings, and having compassion for the peoples' poverty and suffering – this is benevolence. Preventing evil and practicing good works – this is righteousness. Serving one's superiors with complete loyalty, and nurturing inferiors with compassion – this is propriety. Having a wide knowledge of affairs and deciding and judging the

---

[292] 宰相. Here presumably not Oshikatsu. SNIII p 321 n 16 -- it may refer to the Great Council of State.
[293] 維城典訓 – SNIII p 321 n 18 -- a document Wu Zetian had had written for admonition of the crown prince and various princes.
[294] *Ritsu, Ryō, Kyaku* and *Shiki* 律令格式

good and evil – this is wisdom. Bestowing favor appropriately, and rectifying offenses – this is trustworthiness.

"By contrast, striving after good fortune and craving immoral things – this is covetousness. Insatiably and forcefully oppressing others – this is anger. Acting without propriety and according to one's own foolish wants – this is stupidity. Not cherishing one's own wife, and taking illicit pleasure with other women – this is lewdness. Brazenly taking what should be given to others, and stealing secretly – this is theft. If one does not act with sincerity towards fathers and elder brothers, how will he be able to lead the children and younger brothers? If the officials do not act with rectitude, how will they be able to instruct the people?

"If there are those who cultivate and practice the virtues of benevolence, righteousness, propriety, wisdom, and fidelity, and attentively guard against the evils of covetousness, anger, stupidity, lewdness and theft, and in addition study the aforementioned texts, they should be proposed for office and nominated for advancement. From now on those who do otherwise should not be employed as teachers, students or officials. What We wish is that evil be discouraged and good commended, so that good behavior is valued. Let this be widely propagated thoughout the empire as Our desire."

On this day the Hundred Officials and the high level Buddhist priests in response to the edict of the previous month (5.9), submitted a memorial stating their opinions about the strong and weak points of government.

The Sr 3 Middle Counsellor, Head of the Ministry of Civil Affairs and Head of the Department of Deity Affairs, 12th Rank Order of Merit Ishikawa no Asomi Toshitari memorialized:

"Your subject has heard 'The cornerstone of the practice of government is the *Ritsuryō*, and the particular rules lie in the ordinances and regulations.' At present the basic prohibitions have been compiled, but the special regulation documents[295] have not yet been drawn up. What I respectfully request is that these special regulations be written and used along with the *Ritsuryō*."

The Imperial Advisor Jr 3 Izumo Governor Fumuya no Mahito Chino and the Junior Assistant High Priest Jikin memorialized:

"What we have respectfully observed is that every New Year's Day the Repentance Ritual[296] is performed at the various temples of the empire. However, gradually it has not been carried out according to the Emperor's original wishes and it has finally lost its meritorious effect. This is because the Buddhist practice of protecting the country is the business of the monks and nuns. But now there are those who without officially entering a temple obtain

---

[295] *betsushiki* 別式之文
[296] *keka* 悔過

government support for the seven-day period, or merely desire alms, and thus sully the reputation of the Buddhist order. Because of this the Three Treasures are demeaned, and no benefit will be produced by the alms given by the Emperor. What we respectfully beg is that government alms for these persons be stopped, and that the evil desires of greedy priests be thwarted."

Imperial Advisor Jr 3 Hikami no Mahito Shioyaki memorialized:

"Your servant has reverently observed that the three generations of imperial princes are paid a sparing stipend in spring and autumn. However at present this stipend does not differ from the rate of an ordinary subject for the number of days of attendance at work. I respectfully ask that this stipend be liberalized."

The Harima Senior Secretary Sr 6 Upper Yamada no Muraji Komaro memorialized:

"Your servant has observed that in the case of adults[297] with five children where the age of the children is twenty or over, father and children are subject to both tax in kind and commuted tax. Your servant reverently asks that in those cases there should be special consideration and that adults with five children be exempted from corvee."

These petitions were all referred to the appropriate office. However, the opinions of the Buddhist priests conformed to the customs of China, and in

---

[297] *shōtei* 正丁 – ages 20-60

many cases are difficult to apply to our country's society. Although government pronouncements[298] be handed down, it may not be possible to put them into actual practice in detail.

天平宝字三年（七五九）七月丁卯【乙丑朔三】o秋七月丁卯。勅。准令。弾正尹者従四位上官。官位已軽。人豈能畏。自今以後。改為従三位官。」以従四位下阿倍朝臣嶋麻呂為左大弁。従四位下大伴宿禰犬養為右大弁。従五位上石川朝臣豊成為左中弁。従四位下佐味朝臣虫麻呂為中宮大夫。備前守如故。従五位下佐佐貴山君親人為亮。従五位下橘宿禰綿裳為左大舎人助。従四位下岡真人和気為内匠頭。従四位下御方王為木工頭。三品池田親王為糺政尹。外従五位下食朝臣三田次為西市正。従五位下阿倍朝臣許智為山背介。外従五位下陽侯史玲珎為伊賀守。鎮国衛次将従五位下田中朝臣多太麻呂為兼上総員外介。従五位下三嶋真人廬原為武蔵介。従三位百済王敬福為伊予守。

Tenpyō Hōji 3.7.3 丁卯 Autumn *hinoto-u*

[July 31, 759]

The Emperor gave an edict:

"According to the civil code[299] the official rank of the Head of the Board of Censors corresponds to Jr 4 Upper. But this rank is too low, and the people do not fear him. Therefore from now on it should be changed to Jr 3 Rank."

Jr 4 Lower Abe no Asomi Shimamaro appointed Major Controller of the Left.

Jr 4 Lower Ōtomo no Sukune Inukai appointed Major Controller of the Right.

Jr 5 Upper Ishikawa no Asomi Toyonari appointed Middle Controller of the Left.

---

[298] *kanfu* 官符
[299] SNIII p 325 n 21 -*Kan'iryō* 官位 令 9.

Jr 4 Lower Sami no Asomi Mushimaro appointed Master of the Middle Palace, while remaining Hizen Governor.

Jr 5 Lower Sasakiyama no Kimi Oyabito appointed Assistant Head of the Middle Palace.

Jr 5 Lower Tachibana no Sukune Watamo appointed Assistant Head of the Left Imperial Attendants.

Jr 4 Lower Oka no Mahito Wake appointed Head of Craft Industries.

Jr 4 Lower Prince Mikata appointed Head of Carpentry.

Third Cap Rank Imperial Prince Ikeda appointed Head of the Board of Censors.

Outer Jr 5 Lower Hami no Asomi Mitasuki appointed Head of the Western Market.

Jr 5 Lower Abe no Asomi Kochi appointed Yamashiro Assistant Governor.

Outer Jr 5 Lower Yako no Fuhito Ryōchin appointed Iga Governor.

Irregular Minor Captain of the Imperial Middle Guard Jr 5 Lower Tanaka no Asomi Tadamaro appointed concurrently Kazusa Irregular Assistant Governor.

Jr 5 Lower Mishima no Mahito Iohara appointed Musashi Assistant Governor.

Jr 3 Kudara no Konikishi Kyōfuku appointed Iyo Governor.

天平宝字三年（七五九）七月己巳【五】○己巳。夫人正二位広岡朝臣古那可智薨。正四位上橘宿禰佐為之女也。天平勝宝九歳閏八月十八日。有勅賜姓広岡朝臣。

Tenpyō Hōji 3.7.5 己巳 *tsuchinoto-mi*

[August 2, 759]

The late Emperor Shōmu's concubine Sr 2 Hirooka no Asomi Konakachi died. She was the daughter of Sr 4 Upper Tachibana no Sukune Sai. In an edict of TPSH 9 8.18 she was granted the *kabane* Hirooka.

天平宝字三年（七五九）七月丁丑【十三】○丁丑。内薬佐従七位下粟田臣道麻呂賜姓朝臣。

Tenpyō Hōji 3.7.13 丁丑 *hinoto-ushi*

[August 10, 759]

The Assistant Head of the Palace Medical Office Jr 7 Lower Awata no Omi Michimaro was granted the *kabane* of Asomi.

天平宝字三年（七五九）七月庚辰【十六】○庚辰。左京人中臣朝臣楫取詐造勅書。＝［言＋圭］誤民庶。配出羽国柵戸。」授従七位上川上忌寸宮主外従五位下。

Tenpyō Hōji 3.7.16 庚辰 *kanoe-tatsu*

[August 13, 759]

A person of the Left Capital, Nakatomi no Asomi Kajitori, forged an edict to deceive and confuse the common people. He was exiled to a fortress in Dewa.

Jr 7 Upper Kawakami no Imiki Miyatate awarded Outer Jr 5 Lower Rank.

天平宝字三年（七五九）八月己亥【甲午朔六】○八月己亥。遣大宰帥三品船親王於香椎廟。奏応伐新羅之状。

Tenpyō Hōji 3.8.6 己亥 *tsuchinoto-i*

[September 1, 759]

The Governor-General of the Kyushu Headquarters Third Cap Rank Imperial Prince Fune was dispatched to the *Kashiibyō*[300] to announce the matter of the forthcoming attack on Silla.

天平宝字三年（七五九）九月丁卯【甲子朔四】○九月丁卯。勅大宰府。頃年、新羅帰化、舳艫不絶。規避賦役之苦。遠棄墳墓之郷。言念其意。豈無顧変。宜再三引問。情願還者。給糧放却。

Tenpyō Hōji 3.9.4 丁卯 *hinoto-u*

[September 29, 759]

The Emperor sent the following edict to the Kyushu Government Headquarters:

"In recent years, immigrants from Silla have not had sufficient ships. To avoid the misery of forced labor they abandoned the tombs of their ancestors. In speculating about their sympathies, can it not be that they think of returning to their homeland? They should be repeatedly questioned, and if there are those who wish to return home, they should be given food and freely allowed to return.

天平宝字三年（七五九）九月丙子【十三】○丙子。大宰府言。去八月廿九日南風大吹。壊官舎及百姓廬舎。

Tenpyō Hōji 3.9.13 丙子 *hinoe-ne*

[October 8, 759]

The Kyushu Headquarters reported:

---

[300] 香椎廟 the Kashii Shrine 香椎宮 where Emperor Chūai and Empress Jingū were enshrined.

"On the 29th day of the past eighth month the southern wind blew strongly and destroyed some government buildings and peoples' homes."

天平宝字三年（七五九）九月戊寅【十五】○戊寅。乾政官奏。百姓輸調。其価不同。理須折中以均賦役。又停廃品部。混入公戸。其世業相伝者。不在此限。伏聴天裁。奏可。事在別式。

Tenpyō Hōji **3.9.15** 戊寅 *tsuchinoe-tora*

[October 10, 759]

The Heavenly Council of State memorialized:

"When the people's tax grain is gathered, its value differs. The price difference should be reasonably stabilized, and the burden equalized. We think that the occupational group of tax grain transporters[301] should be eliminated, and that this work be included among public duties. An exception should be made only for those who have traditionally done this as the work of their ancestors. We respectfully beg this of the Emperor's officials."

This petition was granted. It was entered as a special regulation.

天平宝字三年（七五九）九月壬午【十九】○壬午。造船五百艘。北陸道諸国八十九艘。山陰道諸国一百＝五艘。山陽道諸国一百六十一艘。南海道諸国一百五艘。並逐閑月営造。三年之内成功。為征新羅也。

Tenpyō Hōji **3.9.19** 壬午 *mizunoe-uma*

[October 14, 759]

---

[301] *shinabe* 品部

Five hundred ships were constructed: eighty-nine from the provinces of *Hokurikudō*; one hundred forty-five from the provinces of *San'indō*; one hundred sixty-one from the provinces of *San'yōdō*; one hundred five from the provinces of *Nankaidō*. All were constructed in the period after the close of the harvest, and they were completed within three years. They were for the purpose of attacking Silla.

天平宝字三年（七五九）九月己丑【廿六】○己丑。勅。造陸奥国桃生城。出羽国雄勝城。所役郡司。軍毅。鎮兵。馬子。合八千一百八十人。従去春月至于秋季。既離郷土。不顧産業。朕毎念茲。情深矜憫。宜免今年所負人身挙税。始置出羽国雄勝。平鹿二郡。及玉野。避翼。平戈。横河。雄勝。助河。并陸奥国嶺基等駅家。

Tenpyō Hōji 3.9.26 己丑 *tsuchinoto-ushi*

[October 21, 759]

The Emperor gave an edict:

"Momunofu Fortress in Michinooku and Okachi Fortress in Dewa were constructed. Eight thousand one hundred eighty laborers were employed for the work, including district officials, militia, soldiers of the Office for Pacifying *Emishi*, and packhorse drivers, who from spring to autumn of this year were away from home to complete the work. When We consider this Our sympathy is indeed deep. They should be exempted from the tax burden this year."

For the first time, horse station posts were established in the two districts of Okachi and Hiraka in Dewa Province: Tamano, Saruhane, Hirahoko, Yokawa, Okachi and Sukekawa; and Minemoto in Michinooku Province.

135

天平宝字三年（七五九）九月庚寅【廿七】○庚寅。遷坂東八国。并越前。越中。能登。越後等四国浮浪人二千人。以為雄勝柵戸。及割留相摸。上総。下総。常陸。上野。武蔵。下野等七国所送軍士器仗。以貯雄勝・桃生二城。

Tenpyō Hōji 3.9.27 庚寅 *kanoe-tora*

[October 22, 759]

Two thousand unsettled people of the eight provinces of *Kantō* plus the four provinces of Echizen, Etchū, Noto, and Echigo were registered as households of Okachi Fortress. Portions of the military equipment sent from the seven provinces of Sagami, Kazusa, Shimōsa, Hitachi, Kōzuke, Musashi and Shimotsuke were stored at the two fortresses of Okachi and Momunofu.

天平宝字三年（七五九）十月辛丑【甲午朔八】○冬十月辛丑。天下諸姓著君字者。換以公字。伊美吉以忌寸。

Tenpyō Hōji 3.10.8 辛丑 Winter *kanoto-ushi*

[November 2, 759]

In the *kabane* of the realm the character 公 was to replace the character 君 (*kimi*).

Also 忌寸 was to replace 伊美吉 (*imiki*).

天平宝字三年（七五九）十月壬寅【九】○壬寅。以従五位下丈部大麻呂為斎宮頭。

Tenpyō Hōji 3.10.9 壬寅 *mizunoe-tora*

[November 3, 759]

Jr 5 Lower Hasetsukaibe no Ōmaro was appointed Head of the Office of Ise Princess.

天平宝字三年（七五九）十月戊申【十五】○戊申。去天平勝宝五年。遣
左大弁従四位上紀朝臣飯麻呂。限伊勢大神宮之界。樹標已畢。而伊勢・
志摩両国相争。於是。遷尾垂刹於葦淵。遣武部卿従三位巨勢朝臣関麻呂。
神祇大副従五位下中臣朝臣毛人。少副従五位下忌部宿禰告麻呂等。奉幣
帛於神宮。

Tenpyō Hōji 3.10.15 戊申 *tsuchinoe-saru*

[November 9, 759]

Last *Tenpyō Shōhō* 5 the Major Controller of the Left Jr 4 Upper Ki no Asomi

Ihimaro was dispatched to settle the boundaries of Ise *Daijingū* and to set up

boundary landmarks. However the two provinces of Ise and Shima thereafter

contested the boundaries. Thus the boundary of Otari was restored to Ashifuchi.

The Head of the Ministry of Military Affairs Jr 3 Kose no Asomi Sekimaro, the

Senior Assistant, Department of Deity Affairs Jr 5 Lower Nakatomi no Asomi

Emishi and the Junior Assistant Jr 5 Lower Imbe no Sukune Azamaro were sent

to present *mitegura* to the shrine.

天平宝字三年（七五九）十月辛亥【十八】○辛亥。迎藤原河清使判官内
蔵忌寸全成。自渤海却廻。海中遭風。漂着対馬。渤海使輔国大将軍兼将
軍玄菟州刺史兼押衙官開国公高南申相随来朝。其中台牒曰。迎藤原河清
使惣九十九人。大唐禄山先為逆命。思明後作乱常。内外騒荒。未有平殄。
即欲放還。恐被害残。又欲勒還。慮違隣意。仍放頭首高元度等十一人。
往大唐迎河清。即差此使。同為発遣。其判官全成等並放帰卿。亦差此使
随徃。通報委曲。

Tenpyō Hōji 3.10.18 辛亥 *kanoto-i*

[November 12, 759]

The envoy sent to seek Fujiwara no Kiyokawa in Tang, the Secretary Kura no

Imiki Matanari, upon returning from Parhae encountered a great storm and finally landed on Tsushima. He returned to Japan with the Parhae envoy Gao Nanshen – the Bulwark Minister and Generalissimo, Commander of Xuantu Province and Dynasty-Founding Duke.[302] His official dispatch from the Parhae Department of State Affairs read as follows:

"The mission to seek Fujiwara Kiyokawa[303] comprised ninety-nine people. An Lushan of Great Tang rebelled against the command of the Son of Heaven, and Shi Shiming later also launched a revolt. There were disturbances both domestic and international, and peace has not yet been restored. Although the mission was sent to seek Kiyokawa, we feared that he may have been killed and that this would displease our neighbor Japan. Then we sent the Parhae official Gao Yuanduo and eleven others to Tang to search for Kiyokawa, and at the same time we have dispatched this envoy to Japan. We have returned the Secretary Matanari with him. This embassy shall report on the matter in detail."

天平宝字三年（七五九）十月壬子【十九】○壬子。中宮大夫従四位下佐味朝臣虫麻呂卒。

Tenpyō Hōji 3.10.19 壬子 *mizunoe-ne*

[November 13, 759]

The Master of the Middle Palace Jr 4 Lower Sami no Asomi Mushimaro died.

天平宝字三年（七五九）十月丙辰【廿三】○丙辰。徴高麗使於大宰。

---

[302] See TPHJ 2.9.18 for a previous Parhae envoy with similar titles.
[303] SN gives the reading Fujiwara Kasei. He was sent to Tang with the embassy of 750 and was received by the emperor, but when attempting to return to Japan was driven back by storms. He settled in Tang, received an official appointment and died there at the age of 73.

Tenpyō Hōji **3.10.23** 丙辰 *hinoe-tatsu*

[November 17, 759]

The Parhae ambassador was interviewed at the Kyushu Government Headquarters.

天平宝字三年（七五九）十一月甲子【癸亥朔二】○十一月甲子。詔曰。如聞。去十月中大風。百姓盧舎並被破壊。是以。為修其舎。免今年田租。

Tenpyō Hōji **3.11.2** 甲子 *kinoe-ne*

[November 25, 759]

The Emperor gave an edict:

"We have heard that in the tenth month a great wind blew and demolished the peoples' homes. Therefore, that the houses may be repaired, they are exempt from the rice field tax for this year."

天平宝字三年（七五九）十一月丙寅【四】○丙寅。賜大保已下至于百官官人。＝［糸＋施の旁］・綿各有差。以被風害屋舎毀壊也。

Tenpyō Hōji **3.11.4** 丙寅 *hinoe-tora*

[November 27, 759]

The Emperor gave an edict that from the Grand Guardian Nakamaro on down to the Hundred Officials, gifts of plain weave silk and silk floss should be bestowed according to status. This was in order to help repair the damage caused by the wind.

天平宝字三年（七五九）十一月丁卯【五】○丁卯。以従五位上藤原朝臣宿奈麻呂為右中弁。従五位下菅生王為大監物。従五位下文室真人波多麻

呂為右大舍人助。従五位下藤原朝臣楓麻呂為文部少輔。従三位氷上真人
塩焼為礼部卿。従五位上阿倍朝臣毛人為仁部大輔。従三位藤原朝臣乙麻
呂為武部卿。従五位上阿倍朝臣子嶋為大輔。正四位上紀朝臣飯麻呂為義
部卿。河内守如故。正四位下文室真人大市為節部卿。従四位下御使王為
大膳大夫。従五位下和王為正親正。従五位下高橋朝臣子老為内膳奉膳。
外従五位下小田臣枚床為采女正。従四位下佐伯宿禰今毛人為摂津大夫。
従五位上大伴宿禰御依為遠江守。正五位上藤原朝臣魚名為上総守。従五
位下池田朝臣足継為下総介。従五位下藤原恵美朝臣薩雄為越前守。従五
位下藤原朝臣武良自為丹後守。右勇士督従四位下上道朝臣正道為兼備前
守。従五位下藤原朝臣縄麻呂為備中守。正五位下久勢王為備後守。従五
位下田口朝臣水直為土左守。

***Tenpyō Hōji* 3.11.5** 丁卯 *hinoto-u*

[November 28, 759]

Jr 5 Upper Fujiwara no Asomi Sukunamaro appointed Middle Controller of the Right.

Jr 5 Lower Prince Sugafu was appointed Senior Inspector.

Jr 5 Lower Fumuya no Mahito Hatamaro appointed Assistant Head, Right Imperial Attendants.

Jr 5 Lower Fujiwara no Asomi Kaerutemaro appointed Junior Assistant, Ministry of Civil Affairs.

Jr 3 Hikami no Mahito Shioyaki appointed Head, Ministry of Rites.

Jr 5 Upper Abe no Asomi Emishi appointed Senior Assistant, Ministry of Benevolence.

Jr 3 Fujiwara no Asomi Otomaro appointed Head, Ministry of Military Affairs.

Jr 5 Upper Abe no Asomi Kojima appointed Senior Assistant, Ministry of Military Affairs.

Jr 4 Upper Ki Asomi no Ihimaro appointed Head, Ministry of Righteousness, remaining Kawachi Governor as before.

Sr 4 Lower Fumuya no Mahito Ōchi appointed Head, Ministry of Moderation.

Jr 4 Lower Prince Mitsukai appointed Master, Office of the Imperial Table.

Jr 5 Lower Prince Yamato appointed Head, Imperial Family Office.

Jr 5 Lower Takahashi no Asomi Kooyu appointed Chief, Office of the Imperial Table.

Outer Jr 5 Lower Oda no Kimi Hiratoko appointed Head, Office of Palace Women.

Jr 4 Lower Saeki no Sukune Imaemishi appointed Settsu Commissioner.

Jr 5 Lower Ōtomo no Sukune Miyori appointed Tōtōmi Governor.

Sr 5 Upper Fujiwara no Asomi Uona appointed Kazusa Governor.

Jr 5 Lower Ikeda no Asomi Taritsugu appointed Shimōsa Suke.

Jr 5 Lower Fujiwara Emi no Asomi Satsuo appointed Echizen Governor.

Jr 5 Lower Fujiwara no Asomi Muraji appointed Tango Governor.

Head of the Left and Right Brave Soldiers   Jr 4 Lower Kamitsumichi no Asomi Masamichi concurrently appointed Bizen Governor.

Jr 5 Lower Fujiwara no Asomi Nawamaro appointed Bitchū Governor.

Sr 5 Lower Prince Kuse appointed Bingo Governor.

Jr 5 Lower Taguchi no Asomi Minao appointed Tosa Governor.

天平宝字三年（七五九）十一月辛未【九】○辛未。勅坂東八国。陸奥国若有急速、索援軍者。国別差発二千已下兵。択国司精幹者一人。押領速相救援。」頒下国分二寺図於天下諸国。

Tenpyō Hōji 3.11.9 辛未 kanoto-hitsuji
[December 2, 759]

An edict was sent to the eight provinces of Kantō:

"If there should be a crisis in Michinooku Province and reinforcements are needed, each province should send up to two thousand people. Each provincial governor should select one strong man to lead them and hastily send reinforcements."

Maps of the Official Provincial Monasteries and Nunneries[304] were distributed to all the provinces of the empire.

天平宝字三年（七五九）十一月癸酉【十一】○癸酉。四品室内親王薨。一品舎人親王之女也。

---

[304] *Kokubunniji* 国分二寺

Tenpyō Hōji **3.11.11** 癸酉 *mizunoto-tori*

[December 4, 759]

Fourth Cap Rank Imperial Princess Muro Naishinnō died. She was the daughter of First Cap Rank Imperial Prince Toneri.

天平宝字三年（七五九）十一月乙亥【十三】○乙亥。造東大寺判官外従五位下河内画師祖足等十七人賜姓御杖連。

Tenpyō Hōji **3.11.13** 乙亥 *kinoto-i*

[December 6, 759]

Seventeen people including the Secretary for Tōdaiji Construction Outer Jr 5 Lower Kawachi no Eshi Oyatari granted the *kabane* of Mitsue no Muraji.

天平宝字三年（七五九）十一月戊寅【十六】○戊寅。遣造宮輔従五位下中臣丸連張弓。越前員外介従五位下長野連君足。造保良宮。六位已下官五人。

Tenpyō Hōji **3.11.16** 戊寅 *tsuchinoe-tora*

[December 9, 759]

The Assistant Head of Palace Construction Jr 5 Lower Nakatomi Wani no Muraji Yumihari and the Echizen Irregular Assistant Governor Jr 5 Lower Nagano no Muraji Kimitari were dispatched and ordered to build the Hora Palace. In addition five officials of sixth rank and lower were sent.

天平宝字三年（七五九）十一月庚辰【十八】○庚辰。授外従五位下津連秋主従五位下。

Tenpyō Hōji **3.11.18** 庚辰 *kanoe-tatsu*

[December 11, 759]

Outer Jr 5 Lower Tsu no Muraji Akinushi awarded Jr 5 Lower Rank.

天平宝字三年（七五九）十一月壬辰【三十】〇壬辰。勅益大保従二位藤原恵美朝臣押勝帯刀資人廿人。通前＝人。

Tenpyō Hōji **3.11.30** 壬辰 *mizunoe-tatsu*

[December 23, 759]

The Emperor gave an edict:

"An additional twenty sword-bearing retainers are allotted to the Grand Guardian Jr 2 Fujiwara Emi no Asomi Oshikatsu. This brings the total to forty.

天平宝字三年（七五九）十二月甲午【癸巳朔二】〇十二月甲午。置授刀衛。其官員。督一人従四位上官。佐一人正五位上官。大尉一人従六位上官。少尉一人正七位上官。大志二人従七位下官。少志二人正八位下官。

Tenpyō Hōji **3.12.2** 甲午 *kinoe-uma*

[December 25, 759]

The Imperial Guard was established. The officials were one Head, of Jr 4 Upper Rank; one Assistant Head, Sr 5 Upper Rank; one Greater Defender, Jr 6 Upper Rank; one Lesser Defender, Sr 7 Upper Rank; two Greater Recorders, Jr 7 Lower Rank; two Lesser Recorders, Sr 8 Lower Rank.

天平宝字三年（七五九）十二月丙申【四】〇丙申。武蔵国隠没田九百町。備中国二百町。便仰本道巡察使勘検。自余諸道巡察使検田者、亦由此也。其使未至国界。而予自首者免罪。

Tenpyō Hōji **3.12.4** 丙申 *hinoe-saru*

[December 27, 759]

There was developed land not entered on the registers – nine hundred hectares in Musashi; two Hundred hectares in Bitchū. Therefore the Regional Inspectors of those circuits were ordered to investigate. In addition the Regional Inspectors of other circuits were ordered to investigate such land. Those who declared such land before the Inspectors arrived in their provinces were pardoned.

天平宝字三年（七五九）十二月己亥【七】○己亥。散位従四位下大伴宿禰麻呂卒。

Tenpyō Hōji 3.12.7 己亥 *tsuchinoto-i*

[December 30, 759]

Scattered Rank Jr 4 Lower Ōtomo no Sukune Maro died.

天平宝字三年（七五九）十二月壬寅【十】○壬寅。外従五位下山田史白金。外従五位下忌部首黒麻呂等七十四人賜姓連。山田史広名。忌部首虫麻呂。壱岐史山守等四百三人賜姓造。

Tenpyō Hōji 3.12.10 壬寅 *mizunoe-tora*

[January 2, 760]

Seventy-four people including Outer Jr 5 Lower Yamada no Fuhito Shirogane, and Outer Jr 5 Lower Imbe no Obito Kuramaro were granted the *kabane* of Muraji. Four hundred and three people including Yamada no Fuhito Hirona, Imbe no Obito Mushimaro, and Iki no Fuhito Yamamori were granted the *kabane* of Miyatsuko.

天平宝字三年（七五九）十二月辛亥【十九】○辛亥。高麗使高南申。我判官内蔵忌寸全成等、到着難波江口。

Tenpyō Hōji 3.12.19 辛亥 *kanoto-i*

[January 11, 760]

The Parhae envoy Gao Nanshen and our envoy the Secretary Kura no Matanari arrived at Naniwa Harbor.

天平宝字三年（七五九）十二月丙辰【廿四】○丙辰。高南申入京。

Tenpyō Hōji 3.12.24 丙辰 *hinoe-tatsu*

[January 16, 760]

Gao Nanshen entered the capital.

Tenpyō Hōji 4

天平宝字四年（七六〇）正月癸亥朔四年春正月癸亥朔。御大極殿受朝。文武百官及渤海蕃客。各依儀拝賀。是日。宴五位已上於内裏。賜禄有差。

Tenpyō Hōji 4.1.1 癸亥 Spring *mizunoto-i*

[January 23, 760]

The Emperor went to the Imperial Council Hall and received felicitatons. The Hundred Officials of the civil and military and also the Parhae envoy all offered ceremonial felicitations. On this day the officials of fifth rank and up were banqueted in the Inner Palace and received stipends according to status.

天平宝字四年（七六〇）正月甲子【二】○甲子。幸大保第。以節部省＝［糸＋施の旁］・綿。賜五位已上及従官主典已上各有差。

Tenpyō Hōji 4.1.2 甲子 *kinoe-ne*

[January 24, 760]

The Emperor went to the mansion of the Grand Guardian and presented plain weave silk and silk floss to the officials of fifth rank and up, and to their Clerks on up from the Ministry of Moderation.

天平宝字四年（七六〇）正月癸未【廿一】○癸未。以文部少輔従五位下藤原朝臣楓麻呂為東海道巡察使。仁部少輔従五位下石川朝臣公成為東山道使。河内少掾従六位上石上朝臣奥継為北陸道使。尾張介正六位上淡海真人三船為山陰道使。右少弁従五位下布勢朝臣人主為山陽道使。典薬頭外従五位下馬史夷麻呂為南海道使。武部少輔従五位下紀朝臣牛養為西海道使。毎道録事一人。観察民俗。便即校田。」散位従三位多治比真人広足薨。父志麻。藤原朝正二位左大臣。広足、平城朝歴任内外。至中納言。勝宝九歳、坐子姪党逆。而免職帰第。以散位終焉。

Tenpyō Hōji 4.1.21 癸未 *mizunoto-hitsuji*

[February 12, 760]

The Junior Assistant, Ministry of Civil Affairs Jr 5 Lower Fujiwara no Asomi Kaeretemaro appointed *Tōkaidō* Regional Inspector.

The Junior Assistant, Ministry of Benevolence Jr 5 Lower Ishikawa no Asomi Kiminari appointed *Tōsandō* Regional Inspector.

The Kawachi Junior Secretary Jr 6 Upper Isonokami no Asomi Okutsugi appointed *Hokurikudō* Regional Inspector.

Owari Assistant Governor Sr 6 Upper Ōmi no Mahito Mifune appointed *San'indō* Regional Inspector.

Minor Controller of the Right Jr 5 Lower Fuse no Asomi Hitonushi appointed *San'yōdō* Regional Inspector.

Head of the Bureau of Medicine Outer Jr 5 Lower Uma no Fuhito Hinamaro appointed *Nankaidō* Regional Inspector.

Junior Assistan, Ministry of Military Affairs Jr 5 Lower Ki no Asomi Ushikai appointed *Saikaidō* Regional Inspector.

Each Regional Inspector was assigned a stipend. They were to observe the condition of the people and also to investigate the fields.

Scattered Rank Jr 3 Tajihi no Mahito Hirotari died. His father Shima was Sr 1[305] Great Minister of the Left in the Fujiwara court of Monmu *Tennō*. Hirotari served in various posts at the center and elsewhere during the Heijō court of Shōmu and Kōken *Tennō* and reached the rank of Middle Counsellor. In TPSH 9 his son and nephew plotted treachery with the Naramaro conspirators. He was relieved of rank and confined to his mansion. He ended as Scattered Rank.

天平宝字四年（七六〇）正月丙寅【四】o丙寅。高野天皇及帝御内安殿。
授大保従二位藤原恵美朝臣押勝従一位。正四位上藤原朝臣真楯。正四位
下藤原朝臣巨勢麻呂並従三位。従五位上下毛野朝臣稲麻呂正五位上。従
五位上日下部宿禰古麻呂。石川朝臣豊成並正五位下。従五位下田中朝臣
多太麻呂。日置造真卯並従五位上。外従五位下食朝臣三田次。正六位上
田口朝臣大戸。正六位下大原真人継麻呂並従五位下。正六位上下道朝臣
黒麻呂外従五位下。従五位上粟田朝臣深見正五位下。女孺正六位上大伴
宿禰真身。雀部朝臣東女。従六位下布勢朝臣小野。正七位上大神朝臣妹。
無位藤原朝臣薬子並従五位下。」事畢。高野天皇口勅曰。【Ｓ２６】乾
政官大臣〈仁方〉敢〈天〉仕奉〈倍伎〉人無時〈波〉空〈久〉置〈弓〉
在官〈爾阿利〉。然今大保〈方〉必可仕奉〈之止〉所念坐〈世〉。多
〈能〉遍重〈天〉勅〈止毛〉、敢〈未之時止〉為〈弓〉辞〈備〉申、
〈豆良久〉可受賜物〈奈利世波〉祖父仕奉〈天麻自〉。然有物〈乎〉、

---

[305] SNIII p 338 n 9 – should be Sr 2.

知所〈毛〉無〈久〉、怯〈久〉劣〈岐〉押勝〈我〉得仕奉〈倍岐〉官〈爾波〉不在、恐〈止〉申。可久申〈須乎〉、皆人〈仁之毛〉辞〈止〉申〈仁〉依〈弖〉此官〈乎婆〉授不給〈止〉令知〈流〉事不得。又祖父大臣〈乃〉明〈久〉明〈久〉浄〈岐〉心以〈弖〉御世累〈弖〉天下申給〈比〉、朝廷助仕奉〈利多夫〉事〈乎〉、宇牟我自〈弥〉辱〈弥〉念行〈弖〉、挂〈久毛〉畏〈岐〉聖天皇朝、太政大臣〈止之弖〉仕奉〈止〉勅〈部礼止〉。数数辞〈備〉申〈多夫仁〉依〈弖〉受賜〈多婆受〉成〈爾志〉事〈毛〉悔〈止〉念〈賀〉故〈仁〉。今此藤原恵美朝臣〈能〉大保〈乎〉大師〈乃〉官〈仁〉上奉〈止〉授賜〈夫〉天皇御命衆聞食宣。即召大師賜随身契。」又以中納言正三位石川朝臣年足為御史大夫。従三位文室真人智努為中納言。三品船親王為信部卿。従三位藤原朝臣真楯為大宰師。」勅曰。尽命事君。忠臣至節。随労酬賞。聖主格言。昔先帝数降明詔。造雄勝城。其事難成。前将既困。然今陸奥国按察使兼鎮守将軍正五位下藤原恵美朝臣朝猟等。教導荒夷。馴従皇化。不労一戦。造成既畢。又於陸奥国牡鹿郡。跨大河凌峻嶺。作桃生柵。奪賊肝胆。眷言惟績。理応褒昇。宜擢朝猟。特授従四位下。陸奥介兼鎮守副将軍従五位上百済朝臣足人。出羽守従五位下小野朝臣竹良。出羽介正六位上百済王三忠。並進一階。鎮守軍監正六位上葛井連立足。出羽掾正六位上玉作金弓並授外従五位下。鎮守軍監従六位上大伴宿禰益立。不辞艱苦。自有再征之労。鎮守軍曹従八位上韓袁哲、弗難殺身。已有先入之勇。並進三階。自余従軍国郡司・軍毅、並進二階。但正六位上別給正税弐仟束。其軍士・蝦夷俘囚有功者。按察使簡定奏聞。

Tenpyō Hōji 4.1.4 丙寅 *hinoe-tora* [days are out of order]

[January 26, 760]

The Takano *Tennō* (Retired Empress Kōken) and the *Mikado* (Emperor Junnin) went to the Private Palace and conferred the Jr First Rank on the Grand Guardian Jr 2 Fujiwara Emi no Asomi Oshikatsu.

Sr 4 Upper Fujiwara no Asomi Matate and Sr 4 Lower Fujiwara no Asomi Kosemaro both awarded Jr 3 Rank.

Jr 5 Lower Shimotsukeno no Asomi Inamaro awarded Sr 5 Upper Rank.

Jr 5 Upper Kusakabe no Sukune Komaro and Ishikawa no Asomi Toyonari both awarded Sr 5 Lower Rank.

Jr 5 Lower Tanaka no Asomi Tadamaro and Heki no Miyatsuko Mau both awarded Jr 5 Upper Rank.

Outer Jr 5 Lower Hami no Asomi Mitasuki and Sr 6 Upper Taguchi no Asomi Ōto, and Sr 6 Lower Ōhara no Mahito Tsigumaro all awarded Jr 5 Lower Rank.

Sr 6 Upper Shimotsumichi no Asomi Kuromaro awarded Outer Jr 5 Lower Rank.

Jr 5 Upper Awata no Asomi Fukami awarded Sr 5 Lower Rank.

The Female Officials of the Rear Palace Sr 6 Upper Ōtomo no Sukune Mami, Sazakibe no Asomi Azumame, Jr 6 Lower Fuse no Asomi Ono, Sr 7 Upper Ōmiwa no Asomi Imo, No-rank Fujiwara no Asomi Kusuko all awarded Jr 5 Lower Rank.

When the awards of rank were finished, the Takano *Tennō* gave the following edict: [*Senmyō* 26]:[306]

"The office of Great Minister of the Heavenly Council of State[307] is one which is left vacant when there is no specially qualified person to fill it.

---

[306] This is an unusual example of a *senmyō* listed as a *choku* rather than *shō*. Also it is the only senmyō listed as "oral" -- 口勅曰. See SNI, p 445, n 15 for another instance of this rare use of 口勅 in TP 6.9.27, in which case it is also in fact a *choku* rather than a *senmyō*.

[307] *Kenjōkan Daijin* 乾政官大臣 (*Daijōdaijin* 太政大臣). The former was the term chosen by Fujiwara no Nakamaro in a major redesignation of government offices on TPHJ 2.8.25. Reischauer 1967, Part B, p. 113 translates this as "Prime Minister."

However, the present Grand Guardian Oshikatsu has repeatedly been commanded to take it up, but has declined, saying:

'If there was anyone capable of taking the office, it was my grandfather Fuhito. However, I Oshikatsu am too weak and inferior to receive this office. I say this with fear and trembling.'

"Since he has said this, We, as is known, have declared to all 'Since Oshikatsu has declined, there is no one else capable of receiving this office.' Now Our grandfather the Great Minister[308] served with bright and pure heart in the reigns of several *Tennō,* offering up advice on matters of state, and his aid to the court was received gratefully. Then in the court of the Sagely Empress Genshō whose name is invoked with awe and fear she ordered him to serve as Great Minister of the Great Council of State[309]. But he declined repeatedly and died without receiving this office, which was greatly regrettable. Now We appoint the Grand Guardian Fujiwara Emi no Asomi to the office of Grand Preceptor[310]. These are the word of the Empress – let all hearken to these pronouncements."

Thereupon Oshikatsu was summoned, and awarded the emblem of office. Also Middle Counsellor Sr 3 Ishikawa no Asomi Toshitari was appointed Master of

---

[308] *Ohomaetsukimi* 大臣 Fuhito, the grandfather of both Kōken *Tennō* and Nakamaro.
[309] *Ohokimatsurigoto no Ohomahetsukimi* (*Daijōdaijin*).
[310] *Daishi* 大師 The equivalent of *Daijōdaijin.* The 太師 was one of the "Three Dukes" in ancient Chou China, and is sometimes translated as "Grand Preceptor."

Imperial Scribes.[311] Jr 3 Fumuya Mahito Chino appointed Middle Counsellor. Third Cap Rank Imperial Prince Fune appointed Head, Ministry of Fidelity. Jr 3 Fujiwara no Asomi Matate appointed Governor-General, Kyushu Headquarters.

The Empress gave an edict:

"Serving one's lord with complete obedience to commands is the most perfect behavior of a loyal subject. Commendations for hard work comprise the wise words of the sage sovereign. In the past the former emperor Shōmu handed down a wise decree ordering the construction of Fort Okachi. However this work was considerably difficult and it was troublesome for the previous general. But now the Michinooku Regional Inspector and concurrently General of the Office for Pacifying *Emishi* Sr 5 Lower Fujiwara Emi no Asomi Asakari and others, leading and teaching the rough *Emishi*, and bringing them into the imperium without any battles, have completed Fort Okachi. Further, in the Oshika District of Michinooku Province, the great river has been bridged and the high peaks crossed, and Fort Momonou has been built. Thus a vital point against the brigands has been established. As We reflect on this achievement, a promotion in rank should be awarded for this meritorious service. We choose Asakari especially to receive Jr 4 Lower Rank. The Michinooku Assistant Governor and Vice-General for Pacifying *Emishi* Jr 5 Upper Kudara Asomi Taruhito; the Dewa Governor Jr 5 Lower Ono no Asomi Tsukara; and the Dewa

---

[311] *Gyoshi Daibu* 御史大夫 – equivalent of *Dainagon* (Major Counsellor).

Assistant Governor Sr 6 Upper Kudara no Konikishi Sanchū all should ascend one step. The Divisional Commander for Pacifying *Emishi* Sr 6 Upper Fujii no Muraji Tachitari, and the Dewa Special Assistant Governor Sr 6 Upper Tamatsukuri no Kanayumi both awarded Outer Jr 5 Lower Rank. The Divisional Commander for Pacifying *Emishi* Jr 6 Upper Ōtomo no Sukune Mashitate with much privation twice led a laborious conquest; the Regimental Commander for Pacifying *Emishi* Jr 8 Upper Kan no Ontetsu, without fear of being killed, forged ahead with bravery – these two are promoted three steps. The provincial governors, district chiefs, and army commanders are all promoted three steps. However those who by law cannot ascend past Sr 6 Upper Rank are granted two thousand sheaves of rice. The Regional Inspector should select meritorious soldiers and submitted *Emishi* to receive special commendation."

天平宝字四年（七六〇）正月丁卯【五】○丁卯。帝臨軒。渤海国使高南申等貢方物。奏曰。国王大欽茂言。為献日本朝遣唐大使特進兼秘書監藤原朝臣河清上表并恒貢物。差輔国大将軍高南申等。充使入朝。詔曰。遣唐大使藤原河清久不来帰。所鬱念也。而高麗王差南申令齎河清表文入朝。王之款誠。実有嘉焉。是日。高野天皇及帝幸太師第。授正六位上巨勢朝臣広足従五位下。従三位藤原朝臣袁比良正三位。従五位上池上女王正五位上。従五位上賀茂朝臣小鮒。飯高公笠目並正五位下。賜陪従五位已上銭。

Tenpyō Hōji **4.1.5** 丁卯 *hinoto-u*

[January 27, 760]

The Emperor Junnin approached.[312] The Parhae envoy Gao Nanshen and others presented tribute of the products of their country. Then they reported:

"The King of our country Da Qinmao[313] respectfully says: 'We have appointed the Bulwark Minister and Generalissimo Gao Nanshen to present the customary tribute to the Japanese court, and also the report from the Japanese envoy to Tang, Lord Specially Advanced [314] and Special Inspector[315] Fujiwara no Asomi Kiyokawa.'"

In response to this the Emperor gave an edict:

"Since the Tang Envoy Fujiwara no Asomi Kiyokawa has not returned to our country for a long time, we have been greatly concerned. However, now the Parhae King has sent Nanshen south to Our court bearing the report from Kiyokawa. We are greatly pleased by the goodwill and fidelity of the King."

On this day the Takano *Tennō* and the *Mikado* went to the mansion of the Grand Preceptor Oshikatsu and awarded Sr 6 Upper Kose no Asomi Hirotari the Jr 5 Lower Rank.

Jr 3 Fujiwara no Asomi Ohira awarded Sr 3 Rank.[316]

---

[312] That is, left his seat on the throne.

[313] In Korean Dae Heummu.

[314] *Tejin* 特進 – Chinese official office awarded to Kiyokawa.

[315] *Mishujian* 秘書監 – Chinese official office awarded to Kiyokawa. SNIII p 343 n 25 says equivalent to Jr 3 Cap Rank.

[316] The following are women.

Jr 5 Lower Princess Ikenoue awarded Sr 5 Upper Rank.

Jr 5 Upper Kamo no Asomi Kofuna and Iitaka no Kimi Kasame both awarded Sr 5 Lower Rank.

The attending officials of fifth rank and up were given gifts of coins.

天平宝字四年（七六〇）正月戊辰【六】〇戊辰。授無位藤原朝臣久米刀自従五位下。

Tenpyō Hōji 4.1.6　戊辰 *tsuchinoto-tatsu*

[January 28, 760]

No-rank Fujiwara no Asomi Kume Toji awarded Jr 5 Lower Rank.

天平宝字四年（七六〇）正月己巳【七】〇己巳。高野天皇及帝御閤門。五位已上及高麗使依儀陳列。詔授高麗国大使高南申正三位。副使高興福正四位下。判官李能本。解臂鷹。安貴宝並従五位下。録事已下各有差。賜国王＝［糸＋施の旁］卅疋。美濃＝［糸＋施の旁］卅疋。糸二百＝［糸＋句］。調綿三百屯。大使已下各有差。賜宴於五位已上及蕃客。賜禄有差。

Tenpyō Hōji 4.1.7　己巳 *tsuchinoto-mi*

[January 29, 760]

The Takano *Tennō* and the *Mikado* went to the Side Gate[317]. Officials of fifth rank and up and the Parhae envoys stood in ceremonial ranks. The Emperor gave an edict awarding the Parhae Ambassador Gao Nanshen the Jr 3 Rank. The Vice-Envoy Gao Xingfu was awarded Sr 4 Lower Rank. The Secretaries Li Naiben, Xie Biying, and An Guibao were all awarded Jr 5 Lower Rank. The

---

[317] *Kōmon* 閤門 - a south gate of the *Daigokuden*.

lower functionaries were awarded rank according to their status. The Parhae King was given gifts – thirty rolls of plain weave silk; thirty rolls of plain weave silk from Mino Province; two hundred skeins of silk thread; three hundred hanks of special tribute silk floss. The members of the embassy from the ambassador on down were given gifts according to their status. The officials of fifth rank and up and the Parhae embassy members were given a banquet and awarded stipends according to their status.

天平宝字四年（七六〇）正月戊寅【十六】〇戊寅。以従五位下大野朝臣広立為少納言。従三位藤原朝臣弟貞為坤宮大弼。但馬守如故。従五位下大原真人継麻呂為少忠。正四位下高麗朝臣福信為信部大輔。従五位下阿陪朝臣許知為少輔。従五位下阿倍朝臣意宇麻呂為内蔵助。従五位下奈癸王為内礼正。従五位下路真人野上為兵馬正。従五位上河内王為義部大輔。従四位下石川朝臣名人為造宮卿。従四位下仲真人石伴為河内守。従五位下紀朝臣小楫為和泉守。外従五位下高元度為能登守。正四位上紀朝臣飯麻呂為美作守。従五位下多治比真人木人為薩摩守。

Tenpyō Hōji 4.1.16 戊寅 *tsuchinoe-tora*
[February 7, 760]

Jr 5 Lower Ōno no Asomi Hirotate appointed Minor Counsellor.

Jr 3 Fujiwara no Asomi Otosada appointed Senior Assistant, Earthly Council, continuing as Tajima Governor.

Jr 5 Lower Ōhara no Mahito Tsugimaro appointed Lesser Devotion, Earthly Council.

Sr 4 Lower Koma no Asomi Fukushin appointed Senior Assistant, Ministry of Fidelity.

Jr 5 Lower Abe no Asomi Kochi appointed Junior Assistant, Ministry of Fidelity.

Jr 5 Lower Abe no Asomi Oumaro appointed Assistant Head, Imperial Storehouse.

Jr 5 Lower Prince Naki appointed Head, Imperial Ceremonies Office.

Jr 5 Lower Michi no Mahito Nokami appointed Head of Cavalry.

Jr 5 Upper Prince Kawachi appointed Senior Assistant, Ministry of Righteousness.

Jr 4 Lower Ishikawa no Asomi Nahito appointed Head of Palace Construction.

Jr 4 Lower Naka no Mahito Iwatomo appointed Kawachi Governor.

Jr 5 Lower Ki no Asomi Okaji appointed Izumi Governor.

Outer Jr 5 Lower Kō no Gendo appointed Noto Governor.

Sr 4 Upper Ki no Asomi Iimaro appointed Mimasaka Governor.

Jr 5 Lower Tajihi no Mahito Kihito appointed Satsuma Governor.

天平宝字四年（七六〇）正月丁丑【十五】○丁丑。授正六位上蜜奚野外従五位下。無位藤原朝臣姉従五位下。

***Tenpyō Hōji* 4.1.15 丁丑 *hinoto-ushi* [days out of order]**
[February 6, 760]

Sr 6 Upper Mitsukeiya awarded Outer Jr 5 Lower Rank. No-rank Fujiwara Asomi Ane awarded Jr 5 Lower Rank.

平宝字四年（七六〇）正月己卯【十七】○己卯。饗文武百官主典已上於朝堂。是日、内射。因召蕃客令観射礼。

Tenpyō Hōji **4.1.17** 己卯 *tsuchinoto-u*

[February 8, 760]

The Clerks on up of the civil and military Hundred Officials were invited to a banquet at the Administrative Palace. On this day there was an archery match. The Parhae envoys were invited to view the archery.[318]

天平宝字四年（七六〇）正月辛卯【廿九】○辛卯。従二位藤原夫人薨。贈正一位太政大臣房前之女也。

Tenpyō Hōji **4.1.29** 辛卯 *kanoto-u*

[February 20, 760]

Jr 2 Rank Concubine Fujiwara died.[319] She was the daughter of Fujiwara no Fusasaki, who was posthumously awarded Sr 1 Rank First Minister, Great Council of State.

天平宝字四年（七六〇）二月壬寅【壬辰朔十一】○二月壬寅。従五位下石川朝臣広成賜姓高円朝臣。

Tenpyō Hōji **4.2.11** 壬寅 *mizunoe-tora*

[March 2, 760]

---

[318] SNIII p 346 notes 13 -15 -- *Uchinoikui* 内射. An archery match held within the *Dairi*. In SN, these were only held when Parhae envoys came to court, and perhaps invited to participate. The *Jarai* 射礼 or 大射 were supposedly regular events on the 17th day of the first month.
[319] She had been a concubine of Emperor Shōmu.

Jr 5 Lower Ishikawa no Asomi Hironari was granted the *kabane* of Takamado no Asomi.

天平宝字四年（七六〇）二月辛亥【二十】〇辛亥。以従四位下笠王。為左大舎人頭。従五位下豊野真人尾張為内蔵頭。在唐大使正四位下藤原朝臣河清為文部卿。従五位下高円朝臣広成為少輔。従五位下石川朝臣人成為仁部少輔。従五位下巨勢朝臣広足為節部少輔。従五位上当麻真人広名為遠江員外介。従五位下藤原朝臣楓麻呂為但馬介。是日。渤海使高南申等帰蕃。

Tenpyō Hōji 4.2.20 辛亥 *kanoto-i*

[March 11, 760]

Jr 4 Lower Prince Kasa appointed Head of the Left Imperial Attendants.

Jr 5 Lower Toyo no Mahito Owari appointed Head of the Imperial Storehouse.

The Tang Ambassador residing in China Sr 4 Lower Fujiwara no Asomi Kiyokawa appointed Head of the Ministry of Civil Affairs.[320]

Jr 5 Lower Takamado noAsomi Hironari appointed Junior Assistant, Ministry of Civil Afairs.

Jr 5 Lower Ishikawa no Asomi Hitonari appointed Junior Assistant, Ministry of Benevolence.

Jr 5 Lower Kose Asomi no Hirotari appointed Junior Assistant, Ministry of Moderation.

Jr 5 Upper Tagima Mahito Hirona appointed Tōtōmi Irregular Assistant Governor.

---

[320] An honorary appointment. Kiyokawa never returned from China.

Jr 5 Lower Fujiwara Asomi Kaerutemaro appointed Tamba Assistant Governor

On this day the Parhae envoy Gao Nanshen and embassy returned to their country.

天平宝字四年（七六〇）二月庚申【廿九】○庚申。設仁王会於宮中及東大寺。

Tenpyō Hōji 4.2.29 庚申 *kanoe-saru*

[March 20, 760]

The ritual for the *Sutra of Humane Kings* was carried out at in the palace and at *Tōdaiji*.

天平宝字四年（七六〇）三月癸亥【壬戌朔二】○三月癸亥。散位従四位下多治比真人家主卒。

Tenpyō Hōji 4.3.2 癸亥 *mizunoto-i*

[March 23, 760]

Scattered-rank Jr 4 Lower Tajihi no Mahito Yakanushi died.

天平宝字四年（七六〇）三月辛未【十】○辛未。没官奴二百卅三人。婢二百七十七人。配雄勝柵。並従良人。

Tenpyō Hōji 4.3.10 辛未 *kanoto-hitsuji*

[March 31, 760]

Two hundred thirty-three male slaves and two hundred seventy-seven female slaves who had lost rank due to crimes were moved to Fort Okachi. They were all released from slavery and made free people.

天平宝字四年（七六〇）三月甲戌【十三】○甲戌。詔曰。比来。皇太后御体不予。宜祭天神地祇。諸祝部等各祷其社。欲令聖体安穏平復。是以。

自太神宮禰宜・内人・　。至諸社祝部。賜爵一級。普告令知之。授外従五位上神主首名外正五位下。外正六位上神主枚人外従五位下。

Tenpyō Hōji 4.3.13 甲戌 *kinoe-inu*

[April 3, 760]

The Emperor gave an edict:

"Recently the Dowager Empress Kōmyō's health has not been good. We desire that the priests[321] and other officials of the various shrines which enshrine the *kami* of heaven and the *kami* of earth offer prayers at the shrines for the recovery of her health. For this purpose the priests of various shrines, beginning with the Ise *Daijingū negi*, *uchihito*, and *monoimi*[322] are awarded one step of promotion in rank. Let this be proclaimed throughout the whole country."

The Outer Jr 5 Upper *Kannushi*[323] Obitona of Ise awarded Outer Sr 5 Lower Rank. Outer Sr 6 Upper *Kannushi* Hirahito to Outer Jr 5 Lower Rank.

天平宝字四年（七六〇）三月丁丑【十六】〇丁丑。勅。銭之為用。行之已久。公私要便、莫甚於斯。頃者。私鋳稍多。偽濫既半。頓将禁断。恐有騒擾。宜造新様与旧並行。庶使無損於民、有益於国。其新銭文曰万年通宝。以一当旧銭之十。銀銭文曰大平元宝。以一当新銭之十。金銭文曰開基勝宝。以一当銀銭之十。

Tenpyō Hōji 4.3.16 丁丑 *hinoto-ushi*

[April 6, 760]

The Emperor gave an edict:

---

[321] *hafuribe* 祝部
[322] *negi* 禰宜 *uchihito* 内人 and *monoimi* 物忌
[323] 神主 – a Shinto priestly rank.

"Coins have been used and in circulation for a long time. Nothing is more fundamental and convenient than their use for public and private purposes. However recently counterfeiting has become rampant, and counterfeit coins already amount to half of the coins in circulation. We fear that if their use is suddenly suppressed there will be disorder, and so We wish to manufacture new coins and use them together with the old. We desire not to harm the people and to benefit the country. The new coins will be inscribed 'Bannen Tsūhō'.[324] One new coin will be worth ten of the old.[325] The silver coins inscribed 'Taihei Genhō'[326] will be worth ten of the new coins. The gold coins inscribed 'Kaiki Shōhō'[327] will be worth ten of the silver coins."

天平宝字四年（七六〇）三月庚辰【十九】〇庚辰。以外従五位下漆部直伊波為佐渡守。

Tenpyō Hōji 4.3.19 庚辰 *kanoe-tatsu*

[April 8, 760]

Outer Jr 5 Lower Nuribe no Atai Iwa appointed Sado Governor.

天平宝字四年（七六〇）三月丁亥【廿六】〇丁亥。上野国飢。賑給之。伊勢。近江。美濃。若狭。伯耆。石見。播磨。備中。備後。安芸。周防。紀伊。淡路。讃岐。伊予等一十五国疫。賑給之。

Tenpyō Hōji 4.3.26 丁亥 *hinoto-i*

[April 16, 760]

---

[324] 万年通宝 'Bannen' meaning 'ten thousand years,' an auspicious phrase. Note the reference to *nengō* (*Wadō*, *Shōhō*) and 'Great Peace' 大平 and 'Treasure' 宝 in the names of the coins.
[325] *Wadō Kaichin* 和同開珎
[326] 大平元宝
[327] 開基勝宝

Famine in Kōzuke Province. Relief supplies granted. Epidemic in fifteen provinces – Ise, Ōmi, Mino, Wakasa, Hōki, Iwami, Harima, Bitchū, Bingo, Aki, Suhō, Kii, Awaji, Sanuki, Iyo. Relief supplies granted.

天平宝字四年（七六〇）四月丁巳【辛卯朔廿七】o夏四月丁巳。志摩国疫。賑給之。

Tenpyō Hōji **4.4.27** 丁巳 **Summer** *hinoto-mi*

[May 16, 760]

Epidemic in Shima Province. Relief supplies granted.

天平宝字四年（七六〇）四月戊午【廿八】o戊午。置帰化新羅一百卅一人於武蔵国。

Tenpyō Hōji **4.4.28** 戊午 *tsuchinoe-uma*

[May 17, 760]

One hundred thirty-one immigrants from Silla were settled in Musashi Province.[328]

天平宝字四年（七六〇）閏四月壬午【庚申朔廿三】o閏四月壬午。転読大般若経於宮中。

Tenpyō Hōji **4.INT4.23** 壬午 *mizunoe-uma*

[June 10, 760]

The *Sutra of Great Wisdom* [329] was chanted in the palace.

---

[328] SNIII p 350 n 2. See repatriation of Silla immigrants in 9th month of previous year. This may reflect a desire to relocate them in light of the planned attack on Silla. Musashi was the site of previous relocations of Silla and Paekche immigrants. In TPHJ 2.8 a district named 新羅 was created.

[329] *Daihannyakyō* 大般若経 – short title for *Skt. Mahāprajñāpāramitā-sūtra* 大般若波羅蜜經

天平宝字四年（七六〇）閏四月丁亥【廿八】○丁亥。仁正皇大后遣使於五大寺。每寺施雑薬二櫃。蜜缶一缶。以皇太后寝膳乖和也。

Tenpyō Hōji 4.INT4.28 丁亥 *hinoto-i*

[June 15, 760]

The Dowager Empress Kōmyō sent messengers to the Five Great Temples[330] donating two containers of various kinds of medicine and one container of honey. These were to be offered at the altar to restore her health.

天平宝字四年（七六〇）五月壬辰【庚寅朔三】○五月壬辰。授従三位河内王正三位。従五位下岡田王従五位上。従五位上気太公十千代正五位上。従五位下石上朝臣国守従五位上。

Tenpyō Hōji 4.5.3 壬辰 *mizunoe-tatsu*

[June 20, 760]

Jr 3 Princess Kawachi awarded Sr 3 Rank.

Jr 5 Lower Princess Okada awarded Jr 5 Upper Rank.

Jr 5 Upper Keda no Kimi Tōchiyo to Sr 5 Upper Rank.

Jr 5 Lower Isonokami no Asomi Kunimori awarded Jr 5 Upper Rank.

天平宝字四年（七六〇）五月丙申【七】○丙申。以従五位下巨勢朝臣広足為安房守。」大膳大夫従四位下御使王。命婦従四位下県犬養宿禰八重並卒。

Tenpyō Hōji 4.5.7 丙申 *hinoe-saru*

[June 24, 760]

---

[330] *Tōdaiji, Daianji, Yakushiji, Gangōji, Kōfukuji*

Jr 5 Lower Kose no Asomi Hirotari appointed Awa Governor.

The Master of the Office of Palace Table Jr 4 Lower Prince Mitsukai and the Noblewoman[331] Jr 4 Lower Agata Inukai no Yae both died.

天平宝字四年（七六〇）五月戊戌【九】○戊戌。右大舎人大允正六位下大伴宿禰上足坐記災事十条伝行人間。左遷多＝嶋掾。告人上足弟矢代任但馬目。

Tenpyō Hōji **4.5.9** 戊戌 *tsuchinoe-inu*

[June 26, 760]

The Assistant, Right Imperial Attendants Sr 6 Lower Ōtomo no Sukune Kamitari wrote ten articles of curses[332] and spread them widely among the people. Therefore he was exiled to be Irregular Assistant Governor of Taneshima. His younger brother Yashiro who had reported this was appointed Tajima Assistant Governor.

天平宝字四年（七六〇）五月丁未【十八】○丁未。於京内六大寺誦経。

Tenpyō Hōji **4.5.18** 丁未 *hinoto-hitsuji*

[July 5, 760]

Sutras were ordered read at the Six Great Temples of the capital.[333]

---

[331] SNIII p 351 n 15. *Myōbu* 命婦 – women of fifth rank and up, or married to a man of that status.
[332] 災事 SNIII p 351 n 18. 妖書 Perhaps these were actually criticisms of the government for its handling of disasters.
[333] The previously noted five plus possibly *Hokkeji*.

天平宝字四年（七六〇）五月戊申【十九】〇戊申。勅。如聞。頃者。疾疫流行。黎元飢苦。宜天下高年。鰥寡孤独。癈疾及臥疫病者。量加賑恤。当道巡察使与国司。視問患苦。賑給。若巡察使已過之処者。国司専当賑給。務従恩旨。

Tenpyō Hōji 4.5.19 戊申 *tsuchinoe-saru*

[July 6, 760]

The Emperor gave an edict:

"We have heard that recently epidemic has been rampant and the common people have been suffering from hunger. Relief aid should be granted to those eighty years of age and older, widows, orphans, the elderly without children, the disabled, and those bedridden from the epidemic, according to their circumstances. The Regional Inspectors of the circuits and the provincial governors should inquire about illness and dispense benefits accordingly. If the Regional Inspector has already passed through, then this is the sole responsibility of the governors. Let it be done in accordance with Our will."

天平宝字四年（七六〇）六月乙丑【己未朔七】〇六月乙丑。天平応真仁正皇太后崩。姓藤原氏。近江朝大織冠内大臣鎌足之孫。平城朝贈正一位太政大臣不比等之女也。母曰贈正一位県犬養橘宿禰三千代。皇太后幼而聡恵。早播声誉。勝宝感神聖武皇帝儲弐之日。納以為妃。時年十六。接引衆御。皆尽其歓。雅閑礼訓。敦崇仏道。神亀元年。聖武皇帝即位。授正一位。為大夫人。生高野天皇及皇太子。其皇太子者。誕而三月立為皇太子。神亀五年天而薨焉。時年二。天平元年。尊大夫人為皇后。湯沐之外、更加別封一千戸。及高野天皇東宮封一千戸。太后仁慈。志在救物。創建東大寺及天下国分寺者。本太后之所勧也。又設悲田・施薬両院。以療養夭下飢病之徒也。勝宝元年、高野天皇受禅。改皇后宮職曰紫微中台。妙選勲賢、並列台司。宝字二年。上尊号曰天平応真仁正皇太后。改中台曰坤宮官。崩時春秋六十。以三品船親王。従三位藤原朝臣永手。藤原朝臣弟貞。従四位上藤原朝臣御楯。従四位下安倍朝臣嶋麻呂。藤原恵美朝臣久須麻呂等十二人。為裝束司。六位已下官十三人。以三品池田親王。
從三位諱。文室真人智努。氷上真人塩焼。正五位下市原王。正四位上坂
上忌寸犬養。從四位下佐伯宿禰今毛人。岡真人和気等十二人。為山作司。
六位已下官十三人。以從五位下大蔵忌寸麻呂。外從五位下上毛野公真人。
為養民司。六位已下官五人。以從三位氷上真人塩焼。從三位諱。正五位
下石川朝臣豊成。從五位下大原真人継麻呂等。為前後次第司。判官・主
典各二人。天下諸国挙哀三日。服期三日。

Tenpyō Hōji 4.6.7 乙丑 kinoto-ushi

[July 23, 760]

The *Tenpyō Ōshin Ninshō* Dowager Empress Kōmyō[334] passed away. Her *kabane* was Fujiwara. She was the granddaughter of the Greater Woven Cap Great Minister of the Middle Kamatari of the Ōmi Court of Tenji *Tennō*, and the daughter of Fuhito of the Heijō Court of Genshō *Tennō*, who was posthumously appointed Sr 1 Rank, First Minister of the Great Council of State. Her mother was Agata Inukai no Tachibana no Sukune Michiyo, posthumously appointed Sr 1 Rank. From her youth the Dowager Empress was wise and compassionate, and her fame was soon made known. On the day that *Shōhō Kanjin Shōmu Kōtei* Shōmu[335] was made Heir Apparent, she was welcomed into the palace and became his Empress. At the time she was 16 years of age. She served as a guide to the masses and they were joyous and content. She instructed in the correct etiquette and deeply revered the way of the Buddha. In *Jinki* 1, at the time of Shōmu's accession, she was granted the Sr 1 rank and the title of Great Consort. She gave birth to the Takano Empress Kōken and the Crown

---

[334] 天平応真仁正皇太后
[335] 勝宝感神聖武皇帝 – Emperor Shōmu

Prince. He was made Crown Prince three months after his birth but died young in Jinki 5. At the time he was two years old. In *Tenpyō* 1 the Great Consort was honored and named Empress. In addition to two thousand sustenance fiefs due to the office of Empress, she was granted special fiefs of one thousand households. To these were added one thousand households for the Eastern Palace of the Takano Empress. The Dowager Empress was benevolent and compassionate and wished to succor the people. The projects of constructing the *Tōdaiji* and the Official Provincial Temples throughout the realm were fundamentally due to her encouragement. [336] In addition she had medical dispensaries and fields for their support[337] prepared to minister to the people suffering from hunger and sickness. In *TPSH* 1, when the Takano Empress received the abdication of Emperor Shōmu, she had the name of the *Kōgōgūshiki* changed to *Shibi Chūdai*.[338] She appointed wise and meritorious officials to staff it. In TPHJ 2, her honorary name was elevated to *Tenpyō Ōshin Ninshō Kōtaigō*, and the name of the *Shibi Chūdai* was changed to the Earthly Palace Council.[339] When she died she was sixty years of age. To prepare the funeral, twelve men were appointed as officials to prepare funerary clothing, including 3rd Cap Rank Imperial Prince Fune, Jr 3 Fujiwara no Asomi Nagate and Fujiwara no Asomi Otosada, Jr 4 Upper Fujiwara no Asomi Mitate, Jr 4

---

[336] SNIII p 553 n 60. This supplemental note details her efforts and suggests that these projects were due to her work more than/as much as that of Shōmu.

[337] *Hiden* and *Seyaku* 悲田・施薬両院

[338] 皇后宮職 to 紫微中台

[339] *Kongūkan* 坤宮官

Lower Abe no Asomi Shimamaro and Fujiwara Emi no Asomi Kusumaro. Thirteen officials of sixth rank and lower were also appointed. Twelve men including 3rd Cap Rank Imperial Prince Ikeda, Jr 3 Prince Shirakabe, Fumuya no Mahito Chino, and Hikami no Mahito Shioyaki, Sr 5 Lower Prince Ichihara, Sr 4 Upper Sakanoue no Imiki Inukai, Jr 4 Lower Saeki no Sukune Imaemishi and Oka no Mahito Wake were appointed as officials in charge of constructing the tomb. Thirteen officials of sixth rank and lower were also appointed. Jr 5 Lower Ōkura no Imiki Maro, Outer Jr 5 Lower Kamitsukeno no Kimi Mahito, were appointed as officials to prepare food and clothing for the funeral. Five officials of sixth rank and lower were also appointed. Jr 3 Hikami no Mahito Shioyaki, Jr 3 Prince Shirakabe, Sr 5 Lower Ishikawa no Asomi Toyonari, and Jr 5 Lower Ōhara no Mahito Tsugimaro were appointed as officials to arrange the funeral procession. Two men were appointed as Secretary and Clerk. In all the provinces of the realm, three days of mourning was commanded in which people were to wear mourning clothes.

天平宝字四年（七六〇）六月癸卯（この月なし。）○癸卯。葬仁正皇太后於大和国添上郡佐保山。武部卿従三位藤原朝臣弟麻呂薨。平城朝贈正一位太政大臣武智麻呂之第四子也。

Tenpyō Hōji **4.6.28** 癸卯 *mizunoto-u* [day not found in sixth month]
[August 13, 760]

The Dowager Empress was buried in the Sahoyama tomb in the Sōnokami district of Yamato Province.

The Head of the Ministry of Military Affairs Jr 3 Fujiwara no Asomi Otomaro died. He was the fourth son of Muchimaro, who served in the Nara court and was posthumously awarded Sr 1 Rank, First Minister of the Great Council of State.

《巻尾続日本紀　巻第廿二

[End of *Shoku Nihongi Maki* 22]

《巻首続日本紀巻第廿三〈起天平宝字四年七月、尽五年十二月。〉
　　右大臣従二位兼行皇太子傅中衛大将臣藤原朝臣継縄等奉勅撰」

　廃帝 **Haitei (Deposed Emperor Junnin)**

Shoku Nihongi Maki 23 (*Tenpyō Hōji* 4.7 –5.12)

Selected and presented by the Great Minister of the Right and concurrently Crown Prince Tutor and General of the Middle Imperial Guards Jr 2 Fujiwara Asomi Tsugutada et. al.

天空宝字四年（七六〇）七月戊子朔秋七月戊子朔。日有蝕之。

Tenpyō Hōji 4.7.1 Autumn 戊子 *tsuchinoe-ne*

[August 15, 760]

Solar eclipse.

天平宝字四年（七六〇）七月庚戌【廿三】○庚戌。大僧都良弁。少僧都慈訓。律師法進等奏曰。良弁等聞。法界混一。凡聖之差未著。断証以降。行住之科始異。三賢十地。所以開化衆生。前仏後仏。由之勧勉三乗。良知。非酬勲庸。無用証真之識。不差行住。＝［言＋巨］勧流浪之徒。今者。像教将季。緇侶稍怠。若無褒貶。何顕善悪。望請。制四位十三階。以抜三学六宗。就其十三階中。三色師位并大法師位。准勅授位記式。自外之階。准奏授位記式。然則、戒定恵行、非独昔時。経・論・律旨、方

盛当今。庶亦永息濫位之譏。以興敦善之隆。良弁等。学非渉猟。業惟浅
近。輒以管見。略事採択。叙位節目。具列別紙。」勅報曰。省来表知具
示。勧誡緇徒。実応利益。分置四級。恐致労煩。故其修行位。誦持位。
唯用一色。不為数名。若有誦経忘却。戒行過失者。待衆人知。然後改正。
但師位等級。宜如奏状。」又勅曰。東大寺封五千戸者。平城宮御宇後太
上天皇・皇帝・皇太后。以去天平勝宝二年二月廿三日。専自参向於東大
寺。永用件封入寺家訖。而造寺了後。種種用事、未宣分明。因茲。今追
議定営造修理塔寺精舎分一千戸。供養三宝并常住僧分二千戸。官家修行
諸仏事分二千戸。

Tenpyō Hōji 4.7.23 庚戌 kanoe-inu

[September 6, 760]

The Senior Assistant Abbot Rōben, the Junior Assistant Abbot Jikin, and the
Master of Buddhist Precepts Hōshin memorialized:

"Rōben and others have heard 'In an age when the Buddhist law has become
confused, the difference between sages and ordinary men is no longer evident.
Since the Buddha's attainment of enlightenment, the stages of the Bodhisattva
practice have been distinguished. Thus the stages of the three wisdoms and the
ten grounds have been opened to the masses, and the former Buddhas and the
latter Buddhas have been exhorted to undertake the three vehicles for the
purpose of enlightenment of sentient beings'.

"In ignorance, not being recompensed for merit and effort, and unable to realize
the truth, the priests cannot discern the path and wander aimlessly; now in the
last stages of this period of the Semblance Dharma[340] the priests have become

---

[340] SNIII p 367 n 17 像教--像法

lazy. They do not know how to assess praise and blame; how shall they clarify what is good and what is evil?

"What we ask is that the priesthood be established as four ranks with thirteen steps. Together with priestly ranks for the three disciplines[341], the rank of Great Law Master[342] should be prescribed by imperial edict, and the lower ranks also be prescribed. Thus the three disciplines of precepts, meditation and wisdom[343] will no longer be a thing of the past, but the purport of the sutras, commentaries and discipline will flourish in the present. What we wish is that there will no longer be difficulty in establishing the rank of priests, and good works will flourish again. Our learning is not sufficiently deep, and our practice is also weak. Humbly we suggest this plan. The details of the awarding of ranks are in the attached document."

The Emperor gave the following edict in response:

"We have viewed your memorial and understand its details. To have priests strive for the good is indeed beneficial. However, to divide the priestly categories into four parts is overly complex. Thus the rank of practicing monks and chanting monks[344] should be one category, and there should not be numerous ranks. If there are those who forget the sutras to be memorized, or those who break the discipline, this will be noticed by the people and shall be

---

[341] SNIII p 357 n 22 伝灯法師位, 修行法師位, 誦持法師位
[342] *Daihōshii* 大法師
[343] SNIII p 347 n 25 *kai* 戒 *jō* 定 *e* 慧
[344] 修行位 and 誦持位

172

corrected. However, the rest of the priestly levels shall be as you memorialized."

In addition the Emperor gave the following edict:

"As for the five thousand sustenance households of *Tōdaiji*, the Retired Emperor Shōmu who ruled in the Nara palace, the Retired Empress Kōken, and the Dowager Empress on TPSH 2.2.23 went in person to the *Tōdaiji* and donated these fiefs in perpetuity. However since the completion of the temple the division of income from these fiefs has been uncertain. Therefore henceforth the income from one thousand households should be dedicated to the construction and repair of pagodas, temples and monks' lodgings. Income from two thousand should be dedicated for the sustenance of the monks who live perpetually at the temple and to the Buddha image. Income from two thousand should be dedicated to ceremonies performed on behalf of the government."

天平宝字四年（七六〇）七月癸丑【廿六】o癸丑。設皇太后七七斎於東大寺并京師諸小寺。其天下諸国。毎国奉造阿弥陀浄土画像。仍計国内見僧尼。写称讃浄土経。各於国分金光明寺礼拝供養。

Tenpyō Hōji 4.7.26 癸丑 *mizunoto-ushi*
[September 9, 760]

The abstinence rite for the forty-ninth day of the Late Dowager Empress was celebrated at *Tōdaiji* and the smaller temples in the capital. In each province of the realm paintings of Amida's Pure Land were to be completed. The numbers of monks and nuns in each province should be calculated, and they should be made to copy the Blessed Pure Land Sutra[345] and services of veneration held in each Official Provincial Temple of the Golden Light.

天平宝字四年（七六〇）八月甲子【戊午朔七】〇八月甲子。勅曰。子以祖為尊。祖以子亦貴。此則不易之彝式。聖主之善行也。其先朝太政大臣藤原朝臣者。非唯功高於天下。是復皇家之外戚。是以。先朝贈正一位太政大臣。斯実雖依我令。已極官位。而准周礼。猶有不足。窃思、勲績蓋於宇宙。朝賞未允人望。宜依斉太公故事。追以近江国十二郡。封為淡海公。余官如故。継室従一位県狗養橘宿禰贈正一位。以為大夫人。又得大師奏状称。故臣父及叔者。並為聖代之棟梁。共作明時之羽翼。位已窮高。官尚未足。伏願。廻臣所給太師之任。欲譲南北両左大臣者。宜依所請。南卿贈太政大臣。北卿転贈太政大臣。庶使酬庸之典垂跡於将来。事君之臣尽忠於後葉。普告遐邇。知朕意焉。」又勅。大隅。薩摩。壱岐。対馬。多＝等司。身居辺要。稍苦飢寒。挙乏官稲。曾不得利。欲運私物。路険難通。於理商量。良須矜愍。宜割大宰所管諸国地子各給。守一万束。掾七千五百束。目五千束。史生二千五百束。以資遠戌。稍慰覊情。」以従四位下阿倍朝臣嶋麻呂為参議。

Tenpyō Hōji **4.8.7** 甲子 *kinoe-ne*

[September 20, 760]

The Emperor gave an edict:

"Descendants honor ancestors and ancestors esteem their descendants. This is an unchanging principle and constitutes the virtuous action of a sage ruler. The First Minister of the Great Council of State Fujiwara no Asomi Fuhito of a previous court not only was of high merit but was also a maternal relative of the imperial household. Thus in Empress Genshō's court he was posthumously awarded Sr 1 and appointed First Minister of the Great Council of State. Although this is indeed the highest official rank in the codes of our nation, it is not the highest according to the *Zhou Li*. We consider that although Fuhito's

---

[345] *Shōsan Jōdōkyō* 称讃浄土経

merits were so lofty as to uphold the universe, he has not received the highest reward one could wish for. In antiquity Duke Tai of Qi was granted land for merit. Hence twelve districts in Ōmi province are reserved as special fiefs in Fuhito's name.[346] Other offices will remain as they are. Fuhito's widow Jr 2 Agata Inukai no Tachibana no Sukune Michiyo is to be posthumously awarded Sr 1 Rank and named Great Consort.[347]

"Also the Grand Preceptor[348] Oshikatsu has petitioned:

'My deceased father Muchimaro and uncle Fusasaki both served as chief supports in the reigns of sage emperors and assisted the sagely rule. Although their rank is extremely high, their office is not sufficiently high. Thus I humbly beg that the same rank bestowed upon me, Grand Preceptor also be bestowed upon the north and south Great Ministers of the Left.'[349]

"It shall be as he wishes. The rank of First Minister, Great Council of State, is bestowed posthumously on both the Southern Great Minister of the Left and the Northern Great Minister of the Left. What We desire for the future is to establish the means by which We reward merit. We desired that subjects serve their lords with eternal loyalty. Let this be announced far and near and let it be known that it is Our will."

---

[346] *Tankaikō* 淡海公

[347] *Daibunin* 大夫人 SNIII p 361 n 14 Kōmyō had also held this title before becoming Empress.

[348] *Daishi* 大師 = *Daijōdaijin* (First Minister, Great Council of State).

[349] Southern Fujiwara house (Muchimaro) and northern Fujiwara house (Fusasaki).SNIII p 361 n 17 regarding the four Fujiwara houses.

The Emperor also gave an edict:

"The governors of Ōsumi, Satsumi, Iki, Tsushima, Tane and others, who perform vital service at our borders, are suffering from hunger and cold. The official rice is scarce, and they are not able to benefit from it. Even if private stuffs are transported, the roads are narrow and the passage difficult. This is not right and We commiserate with them. Thus the Kyushu Headquarters is to allot income from fields in the provinces it governs in order to support them. To each Governor ten thousand sheaves; to each Assistant Governor seven thousand five hundred sheaves; to each Clerk five thousand sheaves; to the Lesser Clerks two thousand five hundred sheaves. Thus the burden of guarding our distant borders will be alleviated, and they will be to some extent encouraged."

Jr 4 Lower Abe no Asomi Shimamaro appointed Imperial Advisor.

天平宝字四年（七六〇）八月辛未【十四】○辛未。転播麻国糒一千斛。備前国五百斛。備中国五百斛。讃岐国一千斛。以貯小治田宮。

Tenpyō Hōji* 4.8.14 辛未 *kanoto-hitsuji

[September 27, 760]

One thousand bushels of dried boiled rice from Harima, five hundred bushels from Bizen, five hundred bushels from Bitchū, and one thousand bushels from Sanuki are to be laid in stock at Oharida Palace.

天平宝字四年（七六〇）八月乙亥【十八】○乙亥。幸小治田宮。天下諸国当年調庸。便即収納。

Tenpyō Hōji* 4.8.18 乙亥 *kinoto-i

[October 1, 760]

The Emperor went to Oharida Palace. This year's taxes in kind and commuted tax from all provinces in the realm were to be collected and sent to that Palace.

天平宝字四年（七六〇）八月己卯【廿二】o己卯。賜新京諸大小寺。及僧綱・大尼。諸神主。百官主典已上新銭。各有差。

Tenpyō Hōji **4.8.22** 己卯 *tsuchinoto-u*

[October 5, 760]

New coins were awarded to the temples great and small of the new capital[350] and to the Buddhist priests, upper level nuns, the Shinto priests[351], and to the hundred officials of the rank of Clerk and up. They were to be distributed according to status.

天平宝字四年（七六〇）八月癸未【廿六】o癸未。施新京高年僧尼曜蔵。延秀等卅四人＝［糸＋施の旁］・綿。

Tenpyō Hōji **4.8.26** 癸未 *mizunoto-hitsuji*

[October 9, 760]

Plain weave silk and silk floss were donated to thirty-four people in the new capital – the elderly monks and nuns of two categories.[352]

天平宝字四年（七六〇）九月癸卯【戊子朔十六】o九月癸卯。新羅国遣級＝［彳＋食］金貞巻朝貢。使陸奥按察使従四位下藤原恵美朝臣朝猟等問其来朝之由。貞巻言曰。不脩職貢。久積年月。是以。本国王令齎御調貢進。又無知聖朝風俗言語者。仍進学語二人。問曰。凡是執玉帛行朝聘。

---

[350] SNIII p 363 n 9 – It is not clear whether this refers to the new capital at Hora, or the palace at Oharida.

[351] *kannushi* 神主

[352] 曜蔵 and 延秀 SNIII p 363 notes 12 and 13. The first is otherwise not mentioned in SN; the second is mentioned in *Hōki* 3.

本以副忠信通礼義也。新羅既無言信。又闕礼義。棄本行末。我国所賤。又王子泰廉入朝之日。申云。毎事遵古迹。将供奉。其後遣小野田守時。彼国闕礼。故田守不行使事而還帰。王子尚猶無信。況復軽使。豈足為拠。貞巻曰。田守来日。貞巻出為外官。亦復賤人不知細旨。於是。告貞巻曰。使人軽微不足賓待。宜従此却迴。報汝本国。以専対之人。忠信之礼。仍旧之調。明驗之言。四者備具。乃宜来朝。

Tenpyō Hōji 4.9.16 癸卯 *mizunoto-u*

[October 19, 760]

Silla dispatched Kim Jeonggwon, a high-ranking official,[353] to present tribute. The Michinooku Regional Inspector Jr 4 Lower Fujiwara Emi no Asomi Asakari and others were sent to question him about the reason for coming to Japan. Jeonggwon responded as follows:

"Many long years have passed without our sending tribute. Hence the king of our country is now sending tribute. Also, since there is nobody who understands the language and customs of your sagely court, we are sending two men to study them."

In response Asakari asked:

"Bringing jewels and cloth to present as tribute and seeking an audience with the emperor, these are in accordance with correct protocol and show the heart of a loyal subject. However, until now Silla has not used words to inspire confidence and has lacked correct etiquette. Neglecting the fundamentals and carrying out only minor things is to disrespect our country. Also when the Prince T'aeryŏm

---

[353] SNIII p 363 n 14. Ninth rank in Silla's seventeen rank system.

formerly came to our country[354], he said "Continuing the ancient ways, I mean to serve." However, later, when Ono no Tamori was dispatched to Silla,[355] your country was lacking in etiquette. Therefore Tamori was unable to achieve his duties and returned home. How can we have confidence even if the messenger is Prince T'aeryŏm?

Jeonggwon responded:

"When Tamori came I was serving away from the capital. Also I was of lowly rank and not privy to the details of these affairs."

Then Jeonggwon was informed:

"Since you are of such low rank we cannot accept you as a guest. You should return home and inform your government of the situation. When there is a sufficiently high-ranking person, with the proper protocol, with tribute as of old, with clearly articulated words – when these four conditions are met, then he may proceed to our court."

天平宝字四年（七六〇）十月癸酉【丁巳朔十七】○冬十月癸酉。陸奧柵戸百姓等言。遠離郷関。傍無親情。吉凶不相問。緩急不相救。伏乞。本居父母・兄弟・妻子。同貫柵戸。庶蒙安堵。許之。

Tenpyō Hōji 4.10.17 癸酉 **Winter** *mizunoto-tori*

[November 28, 760]

The people of a fortress in Michinooku petitioned:

---

[354] SNIII p 364 n 1 TPSH 4 Int 3 – landed at Dazaifu, entered the capital in the 6th month
[355] SNIII p 364 n 2 TPSH 5 2

"We are far from our homelands and do not have close family with us. We have no way of knowing of the weal and woe of family nor of aiding them in crises. What we humbly beg is that our parents, elder and younger brothers, wives and children be moved from their original dwelling place to be with us in this fortress, and that we receive this relief."

This was granted.

天平宝字四年（七六〇）十一月壬辰【丁亥朔六】○十一月壬辰。勅。先歳逆徒。家挂羅網。今年巡察。人畏憲章。古人有言。盗窺財主有自来焉。撫躬自訟。責帰元首。静言興念。憂心如灼。書不云乎。德惟善政。政在養民。今陽気初萌。日南既至。地惟育物。天道更生。思承地施仁。順天降恵。俾茲＝庶与時競新。其自天平宝字四年十一月六日昧爽已前天下罪無軽重。已発覚。未発覚。繋囚・見徒。并逋租調官物未納已言上者、悉赦除之。但犯八虐。故殺人。私鋳銭。叛徒隠不首者。不在免限。前年已赦。今歳亦除。窃恐。人習寛容。終無懲改。冀令悉停前悪。皆従後善。其七道巡察使所勘出田者。宜仰所司随地多少。量加全輸。正丁若有不足国者。以為乗田。遂使貧家継業。憂人息肩。普告遐邇。知朕意焉。

Tenpyō Hōji 4.11.6 壬辰 *mizunoe-tatsu*
[December 17, 760]

The Emperor gave an edict:

"In recent years, various households were ensnared by the law due to the rebellion by the evil bandits Naramaro and company. Thus this year when We dispatched Regional Inspectors, people were afraid of the law. The ancients said, "If property is not properly secured, it is as if the owner were inviting thieves."[356] It is the ruler's responsibility not to cause the people to complain about their lot. Contemplating these words quietly causes Us to burn with anxiety. Do not the old writings say "Virtue improves government, and government consists in nurturing the people." Now the *yang* energy of spring has begun, and the sun comes from the furthest south. On the great earth crops spring up, and the heavenly principle is born. We consider that following earth We should dispense benevolence. Following heaven We should hand down compassion. We should behave toward the people in emulation of the new times. Thus We pardon crimes for which people are held in jail and undetected crimes committed before today's dawn, and We remit taxes evaded and not yet collected. However, crimes of the eight abominations, premeditated murder, counterfeiting, and harboring treasonous rebels are not included. Although we fear that due to previous years' amnesties and this one that perhaps people have become used to forbearance and not corrected their ways, We desire that from now on they will reform their previous evil ways and from now on practice the good. As for those hidden fields which the Regional Inspectors of the seven circuits have discovered, the government officials who have them in their jurisdiction should measure their size and collect the appropriate taxes. If there are provinces where there are not enough adults, the poor farmers should be made to cultivate them and the burden on those suffering be lightened. This should be announced far and wide, and Our will be made known.

---

[356] SNIII p 365 n 16 – from the *Yijing*.

天平宝字四年（七六〇）十一月丙申【十】〇丙申。遣授刀舎人春日部三関。中衛舎人土師宿禰関成等六人於大宰府。就大弐吉備朝臣真備。令習諸葛亮八陳。孫子九地及結営向背。

Tenpyō Hōji **4.11.10** 丙申 *hinoe-saru*

[December 20, 760]

The Sword-Bearing Retainer Kasukabe no Miseki and the Middle Imperial Palace Retainer Haji no Sukune Sekinari and others, six in all, were sent to the Kyushu Headquarters to study with the Senior Assistant Governor-General Kibi no Asomi Makibi. They were to study the eight military formations of Ge Liang[357], and the Nine Earths tactics of Sunzi,[358] and also the methods of fortification for warfare.

天平宝字四年（七六〇）十一月丁酉【十一】〇丁酉。送高南申使外従五位下陽侯史玲＝至自渤海。授従五位下。余各有差。

Tenpyō Hōji **4.11.10** 丁酉 *hinoto-tori*

[December 21, 760]

Outer Jr 5 Lower Yako no Fuhito Ryōgu and others sent to accompany Gao Nanshen, returned from Parhae. For meritorious service he was awarded Jr 5 Lower Rank. The other members of the embassy were given promotions according to status.

天平宝字四年（七六〇）十一月丙午【二十】〇丙午。大臣已下参議已上。夏冬衣服。節級作差。

Tenpyō Hōji **4.11.20** 丙午 *hinoe-uma*

[December 31, 760]

---

[357] Ge Liang is noted in the *Hou Han Shu*.
[358] Often translated as the "Nine Variables."

The summer and winter clothing for the Imperial Advisors on up to Great Ministers was prepared to reflect difference in status.

天平宝字四年（七六〇）十二月戊辰【丁巳朔十二】〇十二月戊辰。勅。准令、給封戸事。女悉減半者。今尚侍・尚蔵。職掌既重。宜異諸人。量須全給。其位田、資人。並亦如此。又勅。太皇太后宮。皇太后御墓者。自今以後。並称山陵。其忌日者亦入国忌例。設斎如式。

Tenpyō Hōji 4.12.12 戊辰 *tsuchinoe-tatsu*

[January 22, 761]

The Emperor gave an edict:

"According to the codes, in the management of enfoeffed households, women should have only half. However, the officials of the rear palace[359] find this onerous. Thus it shall be different for them than ordinary people. Their rank land and people shall be the same as others of the same rank."[360]

The Emperor gave a further edict:

"The tombs of the late Dowager Empresses Miyako and Kōmyō from now on shall be designated imperial tombs. Their death anniversaries shall be made national observances and abstinence rites shall be prepared according to protocol."

天平宝字四年（七六〇）十二月戊寅【廿二】〇戊寅。薬師寺僧華達。俗名山村臣伎婆都。与同寺僧範曜。博戯争道。遂殺範曜。還俗配陸奥国桃生柵戸。

---

[359] *Shōji* 尚侍 and *Shōzō* 尚蔵
[360] SNIII pp 368 -369 notes 2-7 for a detailed explanation.

Tenpyō Hōji 4.12.22 戊寅 *tsuchinoe-tora*

[February 1, 761]

The Buddhist priest Ketatchi of *Yakushiji* was secularized and given the name Yamamura no Ōmi Kihatsu. He was involved in a gambling dispute with the *Yakushiji* priest Bon'yō and killed him. Therefore Ketachi was deprived of his priestly status and exiled to work at Fort Momonou in Michinooku.

Tenpyō Hōji 5

天平宝字五年（七六一）正月丁亥朔五年春正月丁亥朔。廃朝。以新宮未就也。

Tenpyō Hōji 5.1.1 丁亥 Spring *hinoto-i*

[February 10, 761]

The New Year's day audience was cancelled. This was because the new palace was not completed.[361]

天平宝字五年（七六一）正月戊子【二】○戊子。帝臨軒。文武百官主典巳上、依儀陪位。」授従三位文室真人浄三正三位。従五位下林王従五位上。無位高嶋王。布勢王。忍坂王並従五位下。従四位下阿倍朝臣嶋麻呂従四位上。正五位上藤原朝臣魚名従四位下。従五位下粟田朝臣人成。藤原朝臣縄麻呂並従五位上。正六位上藤原恵美朝臣辛加知。安曇宿禰石成。粟田朝臣足人。石川朝臣弟人。佐味朝臣伊与麻呂。阿倍朝臣広人。当麻真人高庭。淡海真人御船。藤原朝臣田麻呂。藤原朝臣黒麻呂。石川朝臣名足並従五位下。正六位上坂上忌寸老人。村国連虫麻呂。山田連古麻呂並外従五位下。」正四位下小長谷女王正四位上。正五位上池上女王。無位置始女王。小葛女王並従四位下。無位川上女王従五位下。従五位上阿倍朝臣石井正五位下。無位藤原恵美朝臣東子従五位上。無位藤原恵美朝

---

[361] SNIII p 370 n 20 - The Oharida palace mentioned in the 8th month of the previous year.

臣額。橘宿禰真都我並従五位下。正六位上御間名人黒女。正七位下壬生
直小家主女。従七位上稲蜂間連仲村女並外従五位下。

Tenpyō Hōji 5.1.2 戊子 *tsuchinoe-ne*
[February 11, 761]

The Emperor approached. The Hundred Officials, civil and military, from Clerk
on up, attended in order of precedence prescribed by law.

Jr 3 Fumuya no Mahito Jōsamu awarded Sr 3 Rank.

Jr 5 Lower Prince Hayashi awarded Jr 5 Upper Rank.

No-rank Prince Takashima, Prince Fuse, and Prince Osaka all awarded Jr 5
Lower Rank.

Jr 4 Lower Abe no Asomi Shimamaro awarded Jr 4 Upper Rank.

Sr 5 Upper Fujiwara no Asomi Uona awarded Jr 4 Lower Rank.

Jr 5 Lower Awata no Asomi Hitonari and Fujiwara no Asomi Nahamaro both
awarded Jr 5 Upper Rank.

Sr 6 Upper Fujiwara Emi no Asomi Karakachi, Azumi no Sukune Iwanari,
Awata no Asomi Taruhito, Ishikawa no Asomi Otohito, Sami no Asomi
Iyomaro, Abe no Asomi Hirohito, Tagima no Mahito Takaniwa, Ōmi no Mahito
Mifune, Fujiwara no Asomi Tamaro, Fujiwara no Asomi Kuromaro, and
Ishikawa no Asomi Natari all awarded Jr 5 Lower Rank.

Sr 6 Upper Sakanoue no Imiki Okina, Murakuni no Muraji Mushimaro, and Yamada no Muraji Komaro all awarded Outer Jr 5 Lower Rank.

Sr 4 Lower Princess Ohatsuse awarded Sr 4 Upper Rank.

Sr 5 Upper Princess Ikenoue, no-rank Princess Okisome and Princess Ofuji all awarded Jr 4 Lower Rank.

No-rank Princess Kawakami awarded Jr 5 Lower Rank.

Jr 5 Upper Abe no Asomi Iwai awarded Sr 5 Lower Rank.

No-rank Fujiwara Emi no Asomi Azumako awarded Jr 5 Upper Rank.

No-rank Fujiwara Emi no Asomi Hitai, and Tachibana no Sukune Matsuga both awarded Jr 5 Lower Rank.

Sr 6 Upper Mima no Nahito Kurome, Sr 7 Lower Mibu no Atai Oyakanushime, and Jr 7 Upper Inahachima no Muraji Nakamurame all awarded Outer Jr 5 Lower Rank.

天平宝字五年（七六一）正月癸巳【七】○癸巳。詔曰。依有大史局奏事。暫移而御小治田岡本宮。是以。大和国国司史生已上。恪勤供奉者。賜爵一階。郡司者賜物。百姓者免今年之調。授守従四位下藤原恵美朝臣真光従四位上。介外従五位下山辺県主男笠外従五位上。大掾正六位下布勢朝臣清道巳下。史生巳上。爵人一級。賜郡司・軍毅＝［糸＋施の旁］・綿各有差。

Tenpyō Hōji 5.1.7 癸巳 *mizunoto-mi*

[February 16, 761]

The Emperor gave a *shō*:

"Due to a memorial from the Department of the Great Historian[362] We moved to the Oharida no Okamoto Palace for a short while. Thus the provincial officials of Yamato Province, from the lesser clerks on up, had to work extremely hard, and so we award one step of rank. Also we bestow gifts on the district officials, and the peoples' taxes for this year are remitted.

The Yamato Governor Jr 4 Lower Fujiwara Emi no Asomi Masaki awarded Jr 4 Upper Rank.

The Yamato Assistant Governor Outer Jr 5 Lower Yamabe no Agatanushi Okasa awarded Outer Jr 5 Upper Rank.

The Yamato Senior Secretary Sr 6 Lower Fuse no Asomi Kiyomichi on down to the lesser clerks were each awarded one step of rank. The district officials and troops were given gifts of plain weave silk and silk floss according to status.

天平宝字五年（七六一）正月乙未【九】○乙未。令美濃。武蔵二国少年。毎国廿人習新羅語。為征新羅也。

Tenpyō Hōji* 5.1.9　乙未　*kinoto-hitsuji

[February 18, 761]

Twenty youth in the provinces of Mino and Musashi each were made to study the language of Silla. This was to prepare for the attack on Silla.

---

[362] *Daishikyoku* 大史局. SNIII p 371 n 26 The *Onmyōryō* – the name had been changed in *Tenpyō Hōji* 2.8.

天平宝字五年（七六一）正月丁酉【十一】○丁酉。車駕至自小治田宮。
以武部曹司為御在所。

Tenpyō Hōji 5.1.11　丁酉　_hinoto-tori_

[February 20, 761]

The court returned to Nara from Oharida Palace. It lodged in the headquarters of

the head of the Head of Military Affairs.

天平宝字五年（七六一）正月壬寅【十六】○壬寅。以従五位下粟田朝臣
足人為斎宮長官。従五位下藤原朝臣浜足為大判事。外従五位下茨田宿禰
枚野為鋳銭次官。従四位下藤原恵美朝臣久須麻呂為大和守。従五位下淡
海真人御船為参河守。外従五位下御杖連祖足為相模介。従五位上石上朝
臣宅嗣為上総守。外従五位下上毛野公牛養為美濃介。従五位下紀朝臣僧
麻呂為信濃介。従五位上藤原朝臣宿奈麻呂為上野守。従五位下石川朝臣
名足為下野守。従五位下高橋朝臣人足為若狭守。外従五位下高丘連比枝
麻呂為越前介。従五位下阿倍朝臣広人為越中守。外従五位下高松連笠麻
呂為備後介。従五位下大伴宿禰益立為陸奥鎮守副将軍鎮国驍騎将軍。従
四位上藤原恵美朝臣真光為兼美濃。飛騨。信濃按察使。授刀督従四位上
藤原朝臣御楯為兼伊賀。近江。若狭按察使。

Tenpyō Hōji 5.1.16　壬寅　_mizunoe-tora_

[February 25, 761]

Jr 5 Lower Awata no Asomi Taruhito appointed Head of the Office of the Ise

Priestess.

Jr 5 Lower Fujiwara no Asomi Hamatari appointed Major Judge, Ministry of

Justice.

 Outer Jr 5 Lower Mamuta no Sukune Hirano appointed Assistant Director of

the Mint.

Jr 4 Lower Fujiwara Emi no Asomi Kusumaro appointed Yamato Governor.

Jr 5 Lower Ōmi no Mahito Mifune appointed Mikawa Governor.

Outer Jr 5 Lower Mitsue no Muraji Oyatari appointed Sagami Governor.

Jr 5 Upper Isonokami no Asomi Yakatsugu appointed Kazusa Governor.

Outer Jr 5 Lower Kamitsukeno no Kimi Ushikai appointed Mino Assistant Governor.

Jr 5 Lower Ki no Asomi Hōshimaro appointed Shinano Assistant Governor.

Jr 5 Upper Fujiwara no Asomi Sukunamaro appointed Kōzuke Governor.

Jr 5 Lower Ishikawa no Natari appointed Shimotsuke Governor.

Jr 5 Lower Takahashi no Asomi Hitotari appointed Wakasa Governor.

Outer Jr 5 Lower Takaoka no Muraji Hiramaro appointed Echizen Assistant Governor.

Jr 5 Lower Abe no Asomi Hirohito appointed Etchū Governor.

Outer Jr 5 Lower Takamatsu no Muraji Kasamaro appointed Bingo Assistant Governor.

Jr 5 Lower Ōtomo no Sukune Mashitate appointed Michinooku Vice-General for Pacifying *Emishi*.

General of Cavalry for Pacifying *Emishi* Jr 4 Upper Fujiwara Emi no Asomi Masaki concurrently appointed Regional Inspector of Mino, Hida, and Shinano.

Head of the Sword-Bearing Attendants Jr 4 Upper Fujiwara no Asomi Mitate concurrently appointed Regional Inspector of Iga, Ōmi, and Wakasa.

天平宝字五年（七六一）正月癸卯【十七】○癸卯。以従五位下参河王為和泉守。従五位下賀茂朝臣塩管為土左守。

Tenpyō Hōji 5.1.17 癸卯 *mizunoto-u*

[February 26, 761]

Jr 5 Lower Prince Mikawa appointed Izumi Governor.

Jr 5 Lower Kamo no Asomi Shiotsutsu appointed Tosa Governor.

天平宝字五年（七六一）正月丁未【廿一】○丁未。使司門衛督正五位上粟田朝臣奈勢麻呂。礼部少輔従五位下藤原朝臣田麻呂等。六位已下官七人、於保良京。班給諸司史生已上宅地。

Tenpyō Hōji 5.1.21 丁未 *hinoto-hitsuji*

[March 3, 761]

Head of the Outer Palace Guards Sr 5 Upper Awata no Asomi Nasemaro, Senior Assistant of Ministry of Rites Jr 5 Lower Fujiwara no Asomi Tamaro, plus seven officials of sixth rank and lower were dispatched to the Hora Capital to manage the distribution of housing for officials of lesser clerk rank and up.

天平宝字五年（七六一）二月丙辰朔○二月丙辰朔。勅。朕以余閑歴覧前史。皆降親王之礼。並在三公之下。是以、別預議政者。月料・馬料。春秋季禄。夏冬衣服等。其一品・二品准御史大夫。三品・四品准中納言給之。」又勅。中納言。准格正四位上。此則職掌既重。季禄尚少。自今以後。宜改為従三位官。其管左右京。並任一人。長官者。名以為尹。官位准正四位下官。

Tenpyō Hōji 5.2.1 丙辰 *hinoe-tatsu*

[March 11, 761]

The Emperor gave an edict:

"As We review historical documents of previous ages concerning the administration of government, we see that in regard to the protocol of Imperial Princes, they were placed lower than the three Great Ministers.[363] Therefore a special arrangement is made for Imperial Princes of First and Second Cap Ranks – their monthly stipends, horse stipends, spring and autumn stipends, and their summer and winter clothes should be like those of the Master of Imperial Scribes.[364] Those of the Imperial Princes of Third and Fourth Cap Ranks should be like those of Middle Counsellor."

The emperor gave a further edict:

"The rank of Middle Counsellor, according to the ordinance, should be Sr 4 Upper Rank. Although their duties are onerous, their seasonal stipends are small. From now on they should be changed to equal those of Jr 3 Rank.

An official should be appointed to administer the Left and Right Capital, and the position should be called 'In'[365]. The rank should be Sr 4 Lower."

天平宝字五年（七六一）二月戊午【三】〇戊午。越前国加賀郡少領道公勝石。出挙私稲六万束。以其違勅。没利稲三万束。

---

[363] *Daijōdaijin, Sadaijin, Udaijin*
[364] *Gyoshi Daibu* 御史大夫 – equivalent of *Dainagon* (Major Counsellor).
[365] 尹

Tenpyō Hōji 5.2.3 戊午 *tsuchinoe-uma*

[March 13, 761]

An assistant district magistrate of Kaga district in Echizen Province named Michi no Kimi Katsuiwa lent sixty thousand sheaves of private rice as seed-rice loans. This contravenes the edict on seed-rice loans – they should be limited to thirty thousand sheaves.

天平宝字五年（七六一）三月丙戌朔〇三月丙戌朔。乾政官奏曰。外六位已下。不在蔭親之限。由此。諸国郡司承家者。已無官路。潜抱憂嗟。朝議平章。別許少領已上嫡子出身。遂使堂構無墜。永世継宗。但貢兵衛者、更不得重。奏可。

Tenpyō Hōji 5.3.1 丙戌 *hinoe-inu*

[April 4, 761]

The Heavenly Council of State petitioned:

"Those of Outer 6th Rank and lower do not fall within the appropriate scope of shadow rank. For this reason the descendants of households of district officials do not have a path to serve as officials, and they secretly harbor feelings of resentment. The result of deliberation at court is that legitimate heirs of assistant district magistrates and up should have a special provision to be permitted to serve as officials. They should not lose the status of their fathers and should be allowed to inherit in the main line in perpetuity. However, in cases where sons and younger brothers are already serving in the Military Guards, they should not be able to serve concurrently.

The petition was granted.

天平宝字五年（七六一）三月乙未【十】○乙未。参議正四位下安倍朝臣嶋麻呂卒。藤原朝右大臣従二位御主人之孫。奈良朝中納言従三位広庭之子也。

Tenpyō Hōji 5.3.10 乙未 *kinoto-hitsuji*

[April 19, 761]

The Imperial Advisor Sr 4 Lower Abe no Asomi Shimamaro died. He was the grandson of the Great Minister of the Right Miushi of Jr 2nd Rank who served in the court of Monmu at Fujiwara. He was the son of the Middle Counsellor Jr 3rd Rank Hironiwa who served in the court of Shōmu at Nara.

天平宝字五年（七六一）三月庚子【十五】○庚子。百済人余民善女等四人賜姓百済公。韓遠智等四人中山連。王国嶋等五人楊津連。廿良東人等三人清篠連。刀利甲斐麻呂等七人丘上連。戸浄道等四人松井連。憶頼子老等＝一人石野連。竹志麻呂等四人坂原連。生河内等二人清湍連。面得敬等四人春野連。高牛養等八人浄野造。卓杲智等二人御池造。延爾豊成等四人長沼造。伊志麻呂福地造。陽麻呂高代造。烏那竜神水雄造。科野友麻呂等二人清田造。斯＝国足等二人清海造。佐魯牛養等三人小川造。王宝受等四人楊津造。答他伊奈麻呂等五人中野造。調阿気麻呂等廿人豊田造。高麗人達沙仁徳等二人朝日連。上部王虫麻呂豊原連。前部高文信福当連。前部白公等六人御坂連。後部王安成等二人高里連。後部高呉野大井連。上部王弥夜大理等十人豊原造。前部選理等三人柿井造。上部君足等二人雄坂造。前部安人御坂造。新羅人新良木舎姓県麻呂等七人清住造。須布呂比満麻呂等十三人狩高造。漢人伯徳広足等六人雲梯連。伯徳諸足等二人雲梯造。

Tenpyō Hōji 5.3.15 庚子 *kanoe-ne*

[April 24, 761]

Four people from Paekche including Yonomi Yoshime granted the *kabane* of Kudara no Kimi.[366]

Four people including Kan no Ochi granted the *kabane* of Nakayama no Muraji.

Five people including Ō no Kunishima granted the *kabane* of Yanagitsu no Muraji.

Three people including Kara no Azumahito granted the *kabane* Kiyoshi no Muraji.

Seven people including Tori no Kaimaro granted the *kabane* Okanoe no Muraji.

Four people including He no Kiyomichi granted the *kabane* Matsui no Muraji.

Forty-one people including Okurai no Kooyu granted the *kabane* Iwano no Muraji.

Four people including Tsukushi no Maro granted the *kabane* Sakahara no Muraji.

Two people including Shō no Kafuchi granted the *kabane* Kiyose no Muraji.

Four people including Men no Tokukyō granted the *kabane* Haruno no Muraji.

Eight people including Kō no Ushikai granted the *kabane* Kiyono no Miyatsuko.

---

[366] SNIII p 377 n 2 –people of Paekche down to Tsuki no Akimaro. See the edict of TPHJ 1.4.4 naturalizing immigrants from Paekche, Koguryō, and Silla.

Two people including Taku no Kuwachi granted the *kabane* Miike no Miyatsuko.

Four people including Eni no Toyonari granted the *kabane* Naganuma Miyatsuko.

Ishi no Maro granted the *kabane* Fukuchi no Miyatsuko.

Yō no Maro granted the *kabane* Takashiro no Miyatsuko.

Una no Ryūjin granted the *kabane* Minoo no Miyatsuko.

Two people including Shinano no Tomomaro granted the *kabane* Kiyota no Miyatsuko.

Two people including Shirafu no Kunitari granted the *kabane* Kiyomi no Miyatsuko.

Three people including Saro no Ushikai granted the *kabane* Ogawa no Miyatsuko.

Four people including Ō no Hōju granted the *kabane* Yanagitsu no Miyatsuko.

Five people including Tafuta no Inamaro granted the *kabane* Nakano no Miyatsuko.

Twenty people including Tsuki no Akemaro granted the *kabane* Toyota no Miyatsuko.

Two Koma people of Koguryō [367] including Tachisa no Nintoku granted the *kabane* Asahi no Muraji.

Shōhō no Ōmushimaro granted the *kabane* Toyohara no Muraji.

Zenbō no Kōmonshin granted the *kabane* Futagi no Muraji.

Six people including Zenbō no Shirakimi granted the *kabane* Misaka no Muraji.

Two people including Kōhō no Ōansei granted the *kabane* Takasato no Muraji.

Kōhō no Kōkureno granted the *kabane* Ōi no Muraji.

Ten people including Shōhō no Ōmiyatari granted the *kabane* Toyohara no Miyatsuko.

Three people including Zenbō no Senri granted the *kabane* Kakii no Miyatsuko.

Two people including Shōhō no Kimitari granted the *kabane* Osaka no Miyatsuko.

Zenbō no Yasuhito granted the *kabane* Misaka no Miyatsuko.

Seven people of Silla[368] including Shirakinosa no Agatamaro granted the *kabane* Kiyosumi no Miyatsuko.

Thirteen people including Sufurohi no Mamaro granted the *kabane* Karitaka no Miyatsuko.

---

[367] SNIII p 377 n 47 – people of Koguryō origin down to Zenbō no Yashuhito below.
[368] SNIII p 377 n 64 – people of Silla down to Sufurohi no Mamaro.

Six people of China[369] including Hakatoko no Hirotari granted the *kabane* Unade no Muraji.

Two people including Hakatoko no Morotari granted the *kabane* Unade no Miyatsuko.

天平宝字五年（七六一）三月甲辰【十九】○甲辰。京戸百姓、規避課役。浮宕外国。習而為常。其数実繁。各在所占著。給其口田。

Tenpyō Hōji 5.3.19 甲辰 *kinoe-tatsu*

[April 28, 761]

The number of people registered in households in the capital who have skillfully evaded taxes and corvee, fled to provinces outside the Kinai and gotten used to life there, has become extremely high. Their numbers should be ascertained and they should be assigned sustenance rice fields where they now reside.

天平宝字五年（七六一）三月丁未【廿二】○丁未。以外従五位下完人朝臣和麻呂為佐渡守

Tenpyō Hōji 5.3.22 丁未 *hinoto-hitsuji*

[May 1, 761]

Outer Jr 5 Lower Shishihito no Asomi Yamatomaro appointed Sado Governor.

天平宝字五年（七六一）三月戊申【廿三】○戊申。賜従六位下大神東女等十六人播磨国稲人六百束。優高年也。

Tenpyō Hōji 5.3.23 戊申 *tsuchinoe-saru*

[May 2, 761]

---

[369] Aya 漢人 SNIII p 377 n 73 – people of China down to Hakatoko no Morotari.

Sixteen people including Jr 6 Lower Ōmiwa no Azumame were granted six hundred sheaves of rice each in Harima Province. This was because of their care for the elderly.

天平宝字五年（七六一）三月己酉【廿四】○己酉。葦原王坐以刃殺人。賜姓竜田真人。流多＝嶋。男女六人復令相随。葦原王者。三品忍壁親王之孫。従四位下山前王之男。天性凶悪。喜遊酒肆。時与御使連麻呂。博飲忽発怒。刺殺、屠其股完。便置胸上而膾之。及他罪状明白。有司奏請其罪。帝以宗室之故。不忍致法。仍除王名配流。

Tenpyō Hōji 5.3.24 己酉 *tsuchinoto-tori*

[May 3, 761]

Prince Ashihara killed a person with a sword. For this crime he was given the kabane of Tatsuta no Mahito and exiled to Taneshima. His six sons and daughters were exiled with him. He was the grandson of Third Cap Rank Imperial Prince Osakabe and the son of Jr 4 Lower Prince Yamasaki. The Prince's nature was evil and he enjoyed patronizing drinking establishments. One time when he was gambling with Mitsukai no Muraji Maro he was drinking wine and suddenly became angry. He stabbed Maro to death, butchering his groin and making mincemeat of his breast. In addition he was clearly guilty of other crimes. Official functionaries reported his crimes. Because Prince Ashihara belonged to the imperial family, the Emperor could not bear to punish him according to the law. Thus he stripped him of his royal status and exiled him.

天平宝字五年（七六一）四月癸亥【乙卯朔九】○夏四月癸亥。散位従三位巨勢朝臣関麻呂薨。難破長柄豊崎朝大臣大繍徳太古曾孫。従五位上小邑治之子也。其伯父中納言正三位邑治養之為子。遂承其後。頻歴顕職。
遂拝参議。以病帰休。仮満解任。

Tenpyō Hōji 5.4.9 Summer 癸亥 *mizunoto-i*

[May 17, 761]

Scattered Rank Jr 3 Kose no Asomi Sekimaro died. He was the great-grandson
of the Great Minister *Daishu*[370] Tokudaiko of the court of *Naniwa Nagara
Toyosaki* (Kōtoku *Tennō*), and the son of Jr 5 Upper Kohoji. His uncle Oji, the
Middle Counsellor who succeeded to the Sr 3 rank, adopted him as his
legitimate heir and Sekimaro succeeded him. He was appointed to various posts
and eventually became Imperial Advisor. Due to illness he had retired from
office and was then released from his duties.

天平宝字五年（七六一）四月乙亥【廿一】○乙亥。外従五位下稲蜂間連
仲村売。親族稲蜂間首醜麻呂等八人。賜姓稲蜂間連。

Tenpyō Hōji 5.4.21 乙亥 *kinoto-i*

[May 29, 761]

Eight people including Inarihachima no Obito Shikomaro from the family of
Outer Jr 5 Lower Inahachima no Muraji Nakamurame were granted the *kabane*
Inahachima no Muraji.

天平宝字五年（七六一）四月辛巳【廿七】○辛巳。授正五位下石川朝臣
豊成正五位上。

Tenpyō Hōji 5.4.27 辛巳 *kanoto-mi*

[June 4, 761]

---

[370] 3rd rank in the old 19 cap rank system.

Sr 5 Lower Ishikawa no Asomi Toyonari awarded Sr 5 Upper Rank.

天平宝字五年（七六一）五月壬辰【甲申朔九】〇五月壬辰。従五位下高円朝臣広世為摂津亮。従五位下紀朝臣伊保為相摸守。

Tenpyō Hōji* 5.5.9 壬辰 *mizunoe-tatsu

[June 15, 761]

Jr 5 Lower Takamado no Asomi Hiroyo appointed Settsu Assistant Governor.

Jr 5 Lower Ki no Asomi Iho appointed Sagami Governor.

天平宝字五年（七六一）五月丙申【十三】〇丙申。左兵衛河内国志紀郡人正八位上達沙仁徳。散位正六位下達沙牛養二人、賜姓朝日連。後改為嶋野連。

Tenpyō Hōji* 5.5.13 丙申 *hinoe-saru

[June 19, 761]

Two persons of Kawachi Province, Shiki District Left Military Guards Sr 8 Upper Tachisa no Nintoku and Scattered Rank Sr 6 Lower Tachisa no Ushikai had been granted the *kabane* Asahi no Muraji. Later it was changed to Shimano no Muraji.

天平宝字五年（七六一）五月丙午【廿三】〇丙午。使散位外従五位下物部山背。正六位下曰佐若麻呂。行視五畿内陂池・堰堤・溝洫之所宜。

Tenpyō Hōji* 5.5.23 丙午 *hinoe-uma

[June 29, 761]

Scattered rank Outer Jr 5 Lower Mononobe no Yamashiro and Sr 6 Lower Osa no Wakamaro were dispatched to the five Kinai provinces to investigate suitable sites for levees, dikes, and ditches.

天平宝字五年（七六一）六月庚申【甲寅朔七】〇六月庚申。設皇太后周忌斎於阿弥陀浄土院。其院者在法華寺内西南隅。為設忌斎所造也。其天下諸国。各於国分尼寺。奉造阿弥陀丈六像一躯。脇侍菩薩像二躯。

Tenpyō Hōji 5.6.7 庚申 *kanoe-saru*

[July 13, 761]

The death anniversary ceremonies for the late Dowager Empress Kōmyō were prepared at the Amida *Jōdōin*. This hall had been constructed in the southwest corner of the *Hokkeji* for these cereemonies. It was commanded that in the Official Monasteries and Nunneries of all the provinces of the realm, one six-foot statue of Amida Buddha and two flanking *Bodhisattva*[371] statues were to be constructed.

天平宝字五年（七六一）六月辛酉【八】〇辛酉。於山階寺。毎年皇太后忌日。講梵網経。捨京南田＝町以供其用。又捨田十町。於法華寺。毎年始自忌日。一七日間、請僧十人。礼拝阿弥陀仏。

Tenpyō Hōji 5.6.8 辛酉 *kanoto-tori*

[July 14, 761]

The court ordered that the *Brahma's Net Sutra* was to be lectured on annually on the death anniversary of the late Dowager Empress Kōmyō at the *Yamashinadera*.[372] Forty hectares of land in the south of the capital were donated to support this expense. Also ten hectares of land were donated to the

---

[371] SNIII p 380 n 13 – perhaps Kannon?
[372] *Kōfukuji.*

Hokkeji to support a seven-day period of veneration of the Amida Buddha by ten priests upon her annual death anniversary.

天平宝字五年（七六一）六月庚午【十七】〇庚午。以従五位下大野朝臣広立為若狭守。」賜大和国介従五位上日置造真卯没官稲一千束。賞廉勤也。

Tenpyō Hōji 5.6.17 庚午 *kanoe-uma*

[July 23, 761]

Jr 5 Lower Ōno Asomi Hirotate appointed Wakasa Governor.

The Yamato Assistant Governor Jr 5 Upper Heki no Miyatsuko Mau was given one thousand sheaves of rice. This was a reward for serving with honesty and integrity.

天平宝字五年（七六一）六月己卯【廿六】〇己卯。賜正四位下文室真人大市。従五位上国中連公麻呂。従五位下長野連公足爵人一級。従三位粟田女王。正四位上小長谷女王並進一階。従四位下紀女王授従三位。正五位下粟田朝臣深見従四位下。正五位下飯高公笠目。蔵毘登於須美。従五位上熊野直広浜。多気宿禰弟女。多可連浄日並進一階。外従五位上錦部連河内。外従五位下忍海連致。尾張宿禰若刀自並従五位下。従七位上大鹿臣子虫外従五位下。以供奉皇太后周忌御斎也。

Tenpyō Hōji 5.6.26 己卯 *tsuchinoto-u*

[August 1, 761]

Sr 4 Lower Fumuya no Mahito Ōchi, Jr 5 Upper Kuninaka no Muraji Kimimaro, and Jr 5 Lower Nagano no Muraji Kimitari were all awarded one level of promotion in rank.

Jr 3 Princess Awata and Sr 4 Upper Princess Ohatsuse were both awarded one level of promotion in rank.

Jr 4 Lower Princess Ki awarded Jr 3 Rank.

Sr 5 Lower Awata no Asomi Fukami awarded Jr 4 Lower Rank.

Sr 5 Lower Iitaka no Kimi Kasame, Kura no Ohito Osumi, Jr 5 Upper Kumano no Atai Hirohama, Take no Sukune Otome, and Taka no Muraji Kiyohi all awarded one level of promotion in rank.

Outer Jr 5 Upper Nishigori no Muraji Kawachi, Outer Jr 5 Lower Oshinumi no Muraji Itasu, and Owari no Sukune Wakatoji all awarded Jr 5 Lower Rank.

Jr 7 Upper Ōka no Omi Komushi awarded Outer Jr 5 Lower Rank.

This was because they had served in the death anniversary ceremonies for the late Dowager Empress Kōmyō.

天平宝字五年（七六一）六月辛巳【廿八】○辛巳。。供奉御斎雑工将領等。随其労効。賜爵与考各有差。其未出身者。聴預当官得考之例。

Tenpyō Hōji **5.6.28** 辛巳 *kanoto-mi*

[August 3, 761]

The Emperor gave an edict:

"The officials in charge of the construction workers for the death anniversary rites should be given one level of rank according to their service, and given a meritorious evaluation for their service. Also those who have not yet received evaluation as officials should receive a meritorious evaluation for this work."

天平宝字五年（七六一）七月癸未朔○秋七月癸未朔。日有蝕之。

Tenpyō Hōji* 5.7.1 Autumn 癸未 *mizunoto-hitsuji

[August 5, 761]

Solar eclipse.

天平宝字五年（七六一）七月甲申【二】○甲申。西海道巡察使武部少輔
従五位下紀朝臣牛養等言。戎器之設。諸国所同。今西海諸国。不造年料
器仗。既曰辺要。当備不虞。於是。仰筑前。筑後。肥前。肥後。豊前。
豊後。日向等国。造備甲刀弓箭。各有数。毎年送其様於大宰府。

Tenpyō Hōji* 5.7.2 甲申 *kinoe-saru

[August 6, 761]

The *Saikaidō* Regional Inspector and Junior Assistant, Ministry of Military Affairs Jr 5 Lower Ki no Asomi Ushikai and others submitted the following petition:

"The preparation of military equipment should be the same in all provinces. However now in the various provinces of the *Saikaidō* the annual production of military equipment is insufficient. These are important provinces on the frontier, and should prepare for the unexpected."

It is commanded to Chikuzen, Chikugo, Hizen, Higo, Buzen, Bungo and Hyuga that the requisite number of armor, swords, bows and arrows be produced. Evidence should be submitted annually to the Kyushu Government Headquarters."

天平宝字五年（七六一）七月辛丑【十九】○辛丑。遠江国荒玉河堤決三百余丈。役単功卅万三千七百余人。充糧修築。

Tenpyō Hōji **5.7.19** 辛丑 *kanoto-ushi*

[August 23, 761]

The dike along the Aratama River in Tōtōmi Province collapsed along a distance of over three hundred feet. Thus over thirty-three thousand seven hundred workers were sent to repair it and food was provided.

天平宝字五年（七六一）八月癸丑朔○八月癸丑朔。勅曰。頃見七道巡察使奏状。曾無一国守領政合公平。窃思貪濁人多。清白吏少。朕聞。授非賢哲。万事咸邪。任得其材。千務悉理。上如国司。一色親管百姓籍。其奨導風俗字撫黎民。特須精簡。必合称職。其居家無孝。在国無忠。見利行非。臨財忘恥。上交違礼。下接多＝。施政不仁。為民苦酷。差遣辺要。詐称病重。任使勢官。競欲自拝。匪聞教義。靡率典章。措意属心。唯利是視。巧弄憲法。漸汚皇化。如此之流。傷風乱俗。雖有周公之才。朕不足観也。自今已後。更亦莫任。還却田園。令勤耕作。若有悔過自新。必加褒賞。迷塗不返。永須貶黜。普告遐邇教喩衆諸。」美作介従五位下県犬養宿禰沙弥麻呂。不経官長。恣行国政。独自在館。以印公文。兼復不拠時価。抑買民物。為守正四位上紀朝臣飯麻呂所告失官。

Tenpyō Hōji **5.8.1** 癸丑 *mizunoto-ushi*

[September 4, 761]

The Emperor gave an edict:

"Recently, in reviewing the reports of the Regional Inspectors of the Seven Circuits, We see that there is not even one provincial governor who is governing fairly. We think privately that there are many who are deeply greedy and impure, and those officials who are upright are few. We have heard 'If one does not appoint people who are wise and upright there will be wickedness in all things. If one appoints those who are talented all will be rightly governed.' Officials like governors intimately administer the household registers of the people, exhort and lead the people in good customs, and nurture and take care of the masses. In particular they need to carefully select people and must appoint suitable people to office. Those who are not filial at home will not be loyal to the nation. Those concerned with their own benefit will commit evil deeds, and will have no shame with regard to property. Those who lack propriety regarding their superiors will tend to be flattered by their inferiors. In governing they will not have compassion and will make the people suffer. If such people are dispatched to our borders, they will lie and cause trouble. If appointed to positions of power they will compete to advance themselves. They will not heed the righteous teachings and will not follow the laws. Their hearts will be warped by thinking only of their own profit. They will flaunt the laws and disgrace the imperial government. Such people will harm the customs and disorder the conventions. Even if that sort of person had the ability of the Duke of Zhou, we would not be able to judge them clearly. Hereafter such people shall not be appointed. They should be returned to the farms and made to work as agricultural labor. If there are those who repent of their behavior and correct themselves, then they should be rewarded. If those who have lost their way do not reform, they should be demoted permanently and removed from office. This matter should be announced near and far and taught to all the people."

The Mimasaka Assistant Governor Jr 5 Lower Agata Inukai no Sukune Samimaro, without permission from the governor, acted selfishly in the provincial administration. He used the seal in the governor's mansion on official documents, and forced the people to buy at higher than the current prices. The Mimasaka Governor Sr 4 Upper Ki no Asomi Iimaro discovered this and took away his official appointment.

天平宝字五年（七六一）八月甲子【十二】○甲子。高野天皇及帝幸薬師寺礼仏。奏呉楽於庭。施綿一千屯。還幸授刀督従四位上藤原朝臣御楯第。宴飲。授御楯正四位上。其室従四位下。藤原恵美朝臣児従正四位下。

Tenpyō Hōji 5.8.3 甲子　[not 5.8.12] *kinoe-ne*

[September 6, 761]

The Takano Empress and the Emperor went to the *Yakushiji* and venerated the Buddha statues. Music and dance of China[373] were performed in the garden. One thousand hanks of silk floss were donated to the *Yakushiji*. Then they went to the mansion of the Head of Sword-Bearing Attendants Jr 4 Upper Fujiwara no Asomi Mitate and a banquet was presented. Mitate was awarded Sr 4 Upper Rank. His wife, Jr 4 Lower Fujiwara Emi no Asomi Koyori, was awarded Sr 4 Lower Rank.

天平宝字五年（七六一）八月甲子【十二】○甲子。迎藤原河清使高元度等至自唐国。初元度奉使之日。取渤海道。随賀正使揚方慶等。往於唐国。事畢欲帰。兵仗様。甲冑一具。伐刀一口。槍一竿。矢二隻分付元度。又有内使。宣勅曰。特進秘書監藤原河清。今依使奏。欲遣帰朝。唯恐残賊未平。道路多難。元度宜取南路、先帰復命。即令中謁者謝時和押領元度等向蘇州。与刺史李＝［山＋古］平章。造船一隻長八丈。并差押水手官越州浦陽府折衝賞紫金魚袋沈惟岳等九人、水手。越州浦陽府別将賜緑陸張什等卅人、送元度等帰朝。於大宰府安置。

Tenpyō Hōji 5.8.12 甲子　*kinoe-ne*

---

[373] *kuregaku* 呉楽 – *gigaku*.

[September 15, 761]

Ko Gendo and others who had been sent to seek Fujiwara no Kiyokawa returned from Tang. When Gendo was appointed ambassador he had gone via Parhae and had been accompanied to China by the Hezheng envoy Yang Fangqing. When he returned home, Tang presented him with samples of military weapons – one suit of armor, one sword, one spear, two quivers of arrows.

Also the direct emissary from the Chinese emperor gave the following edict:

"The Secretary Inspector Fujiwara no Kiyokawa was requested by the messenger Ko Gendo to return to Japan. However, the rebel army not yet being subdued, the direct route was extremely dangerous. Gendo was commanded to return to Japan by the southern route."

The Chinese Emperor's close aide Xie Shihe commanded Gendo to proceed to Suzhou where the Prefect Lihu was to prepare a ship of eighty feet in length. He was also to send some sailors and some men – sailors and border functionaries of Yue Prefecture – and the Chinese envoy Chen Weiyue [374] – to accompany Gendo home.

The whole party reached Kyushu Government Headquarters safely.

天平宝字五年（七六一）八月己卯【廿七】○己卯。以今良三百六十六人。編附左右京。大和。山背。伊勢。参河。下総等職・国。

[374] 沈惟岳 SNIII p 387 n 25 for detailed description of these personnel.

Tenpyō Hōji 5.8.27 己卯 *tsuchinoto-u*

[September 30, 761]

Three hundred sixty-six freedmen were entered on the house registers of the Right and Left Capital, Yamato, Yamashiro, Ise, Mikawa and Shimōsa Provinces.

天平宝字五年（七六一）八月辛巳【廿九】○辛巳晦。大祓。以斎内親王将向伊勢也。

Tenpyō Hōji 5.8.29 辛巳 *kanoto-mi* 晦 [*misoka* or *tsugumori* – dark of the moon, last day of month]

[October 2, 761]

There was a Great Purification rite.[375] This was because the Imperial Princess, the *Saigū*, was being sent to Ise.

天平宝字五年（七六一）九月乙酉【壬午朔四】○九月乙酉。命婦従三位曾禰連伊賀牟志薨。

Tenpyō Hōji 5.9.4 乙酉 *kinoto-tori*

[October 6, 761]

The Noblewoman Jr 3 Sone no Muraji Ikamushi died.

天平宝字五年（七六一）十月壬子朔○冬十月壬子朔。以従五位下菅生王為少納言。従五位下紀朝臣牛養為信部少輔。従五位下尾張王為大監物。従五位下石川朝臣弟人為玄番頭。従五位上粟田朝臣人成為仁部大輔。従五位下榎井朝臣小祖父為少輔。従五位下柿本朝臣市守為主計頭。明法博士外従五位下山田連銀為兼助。従五位下大伴宿禰東人為武部少輔。従五位下石川朝臣人成為節部大輔。外従五位下陽侯毘登玲珍為漆部正。従五位下県犬養宿禰沙弥麻呂為大膳亮。従五位下忌部宿禰鳥麻呂為木工助。従五位下阿倍朝臣意宇麻呂為大炊頭。従五位下大坂王為正親正。従五位下布施王為内染正。正五位下国中連公麻呂為造東大寺次官。従五位下高

---

[375] *Ōharae* 大祓

円朝臣広世為尾張守。従五位下山口忌寸沙弥麻呂為甲斐守。従五位下高麗朝臣大山為武蔵介。外従五位下上毛野公牛養為能登守。外従五位下蜜奚野為越中員外介。従五位上長野連公足為丹後守。正四位上文室真人大市為出雲守。従五位上甘南備真人伊香為美作介。従五位上豊野真人出雲為安芸守。従五位上県犬養宿禰古麻呂為筑後守。従五位下池田朝臣足継為豊後守。

Tenpyō Hōji 5.10.1 Winter 壬子 *mizunoe-ne*

[November 2, 761]

Jr 5 Lower Prince Sugafu appointed Minor Counsellor.

Jr 5 Lower Ki no Asomi Ushikai appointed Junior Assistant, Ministry of Fidelity.

Jr 5 Lower Prince Owari appointed Senior Inspector.

Jr 5 Lower Ishikawa no Asomi Otohito appointed Head of the Bureau of Buddhism and Aliens.

Jr 5 Upper Awata no Asomi Hitonari appointed Senior Assistant, Ministry of Benevolence.

Jr 5 Lower Enoi no Asomi Koōji appointed Junior Assistant, Ministry of Benevolence.

Jr 5 Lower Kakinomoto no Asomi Ichimori appointed Head of the Bureau of Statistics.

Learned Scholar of the Law Outer Jr 5 Lower Yamada no Muraji Shirogane concurrently appointed Assistant Head, Bureau of Statistics.

Jr 5 Lower Ōtomo no Sukune Azumahito appointed Junior Assistant, Military Affairs.

Jr 5 Lower Ishikawa no Asomi Hitonari appointed Senior Assistant, Ministry of Moderation.

Outer Jr 5 Lower Yako no Ohito Ryōchin appointed Head of the Lacquer Office.

Jr 5 Lower Agata Inukai no Sukune Samimaro appointed Assistant, Office of the Palace Table.

Jr 5 Lower Imbe no Sukune Torimaro appointed Assistant Head, Office of Carpentry.

Jr 5 Lower Abe no Asomi Oumaro appointed Head, Palace Kitchen.

Jr 5 Lower Prince Ōsaka appointed Head, Imperial Family Office.

Jr 5 Lower Prince Fuse appointed Head, Office of Dyeing.

Sr 5 Lower Kuninaka no Muraji Kimimaro appointed Assistant Head, Office for *Tōdaiji* Construction.

Jr 5 Lower Takamado no Asomi Hiroyo appointed Owari Governor.

Jr 5 Lower Yamaguchi no Imiki Samimaro appointed Kai Governor.

Jr 5 Lower Koma no Asomi Ohoyama appointed Musashi Assistant Governor.

Outer Jr 5 Lower Kamitsukeno no Kimi Ushikai appointed Noto Governor.

Outer Jr 5 Mitsu no Keiya appointed Etchū Irregular Assistant Governor.

Jr 5 Upper Naganao no Muraji Kimitari appointed Tango Governor.

Sr 4 Upper Fumuya no Mahito Ōchi appointed Izumo Governor.

Jr 5 Upper Kamunabi no Mahito Ikago appointed Mimasaka Assistant Governor.

Jr 5 Upper Toyono no Mahito Izumo appointed Aki Governor.

Jr 5 Upper Agata Inukai no Sukune Komaro appointed Echigo Governor.

Jr 5 Lower Ikeda no Asomi Taritsugu appointed Bungo Governor.

天平宝字五年（七六一）十月辛酉【十】〇辛酉。遣従五位上上毛野公広浜。外従五位下広田連小床。六位已下官六人。造遣唐使船四隻於安芸国。仰東海。東山。北陸。山陰。山陽。南海等道諸国。貢牛角七千八百隻。初高元度自唐帰日。唐帝語之曰。属禄山乱離。兵器多亡。今欲作弓。交要牛角。聞道。本国多有牛角。卿帰国。為求使次相贈。故有此儲焉。

Tenpyō Hōji 5.10.10 辛酉 kanoto-tori
[November 11, 761]

Jr 5 Upper Kamitsukeno no Kimi Hirohama and Outer Jr 5 Lower Hirota no Muraji Otoko and six officials of sixth rank and lower were sent to Aki Province to construct four ships for the embassy to Tang.

The provinces of *Tōkaidō*, *Tōsandō*, *Hokurikudō*, *San'indō*, *San'yōdō*, and *Nankaidō* were ordered to present seven thousand eight hundred head of cattle as tribute. On the day that Ko Gendo returned from Tang, he brought a message from the Chinese emperor saying "Due to the recent rebellion of An Lushan, our military supplies have been depleted. Now we seek the horns of cattle for making bows. We have heard that in your country horned cattle are plentiful. When the emissary returns home, we ask that for our sake you send cattle horns with your next embassy." This is in preparation for that mission.

天平宝字五年（七六一）十月壬戌【十一】○壬戌。内舎人正八位上御方広名等三人、賜姓御方宿禰。又賜大師稲一百万束。三品船親王。池田親王、各十万束。正三位石川朝臣年足。文室真人浄三、各四万束。二品井上内親王、十万束。四品飛鳥田内親王。正三位県犬養夫人。粟田女王。陽侯女王、各四万束。以遷都保良也。

Tenpyō Hōji 5.10.11 壬戌 *mizunoe-inu*
[November 12, 761]

Three people including the Utoneri Sr 8 Upper Mikata no Hirona were awarded the *kabane* of Mikata no Sukune.

Also the Grand Preceptor Oshikatsu was given one hundred thousand sheaves of rice. Third Cap Rank Imperial Prince Fune and Imperial Prince Ikeda were each given ten thousand sheaves. Sr 3 Ishikawa no Asomi Toshitari and Fumuya no Mahito Kiyomi were each given four thousand sheaves. Second Cap Rank Imperial Princess Inoue was given ten thousand sheaves. Fourth Cap Rank Imperial Princess Asukata and Sr 3rd rank Concubine Agata no Inukai,[376] Princess Awata, and Princess Yako Ōkimi were each given four thousand sheaves. This was because the capital was being moved to Hora.

天平宝字五年（七六一）十月甲子【十三】○甲子。行幸保良宮。

---

[376] Shōmu *Tennō*'s concubine Hirotoji.

Tenpyō Hōji 5.10.13 甲子 *kinoe-ne*

[November 14, 761]

The Emperor went to Hora no Miya.

天平宝字五年（七六一）十月庚午【十九】○庚午。幸近江按察使御楯第。転幸大師第。宴飲。賜従官物有差。極歓而罷。

Tenpyō Hōji 5.10.19 庚午 *kanoe-uma*

[November 20, 761]

The Emperor went to the mansion of Fujiwara no Mitate, the Ōmi Regional Inspector. Following that he went to the mansion of the Grand Preceptor Oshikatsu for a banquet with wine, and awarded gifts to the officials who were in attendance according to level. The banquet ended with great joy.

天平宝字五年（七六一）十月癸酉【廿二】○癸酉。以右虎賁衛督従四位下仲真人石伴為遣唐大使。上総守従五位上石上朝臣宅嗣為副使。以武蔵介従五位下高麗朝臣大山為遣高麗使。又以従四位下藤原恵美朝臣朝猟為仁部卿。陸奥出羽按察使如故。従四位下和気王為節部卿。従五位下藤原恵美朝臣辛加知為左虎賁衛督。従四位下仲真人石伴為播磨守。

Tenpyō Hōji 5.10.22 癸酉 *mizunoto-tori*

[November 23, 761]

The Head of the Right Elite Tigers no Kami Jr 4 Lower Naka no Mahito Iwatomo was appointed Ambassador to Tang.

The Kōzuke Governor Jr 5 Upper Isonokami no Asomi Yakatsugu was appointed Vice-Envoy.

The Musashi Assistant Governor Jr 5 Lower Koma no Asomi Ohoyama was appointed Ambassador to Parhae.

Jr 4 Lower Fujiwara Emi no Asomi Asakari was appointed Head of the Ministry of Benevolence. He remained as Michinooku and Dewa Regional Inspector.

Jr 4 Lower Prince Wake was appointed Head of the Ministry of Moderation.

Jr 5 Lower Fujiwara Emi no Asomi Karakachi was appointed Head of the Left Elite Tigers.

Jr 4 Lower Naka no Mahito Iwatomo was appointed Harima Governor.

天平宝字五年（七六一）十月己卯【廿八】○己卯。詔曰。為改作平城宮。暫移而御近江国保良宮。是以。国司史生已上供事者。并造宮使藤原朝臣田麻呂等。加賜位階。郡司者賜物。免当国百姓。及左右京。大和。和泉。山背等国今年田租。又自天平宝字五年十月六日昧爽已前近江国雑犯死罪已下。咸悉赦除。」授正四位上藤原朝臣御楯従三位。従五位下藤原朝臣田麻呂。巨曾倍朝臣難波麻呂。中臣丸連張弓並従五位上。正六位上椋垣忌寸吉麻呂。葛井連根主並外従五位下。是日。勅曰。朕有所思。議造北京。縁時事由。暫移遊覧、此土。百姓頗労差科。仁恕之襟。何無矜愍。宜割近都両郡。永為畿県。停庸輸調。其数准京。

***Tenpyō Hōji* 5.10.28** 己卯 *tsuchinoto-u*

[November 29, 761]

The Emperor gave an edict:

"Since Heijō Palace is being remodeled, We have moved temporarily to Hora Palace in Ōmi Province. Therefore We award promotions in rank to the staff of the Ōmi Governor from the lesser clerks on up, and to the Head of Palace Construction Fujiwara no Asomi Tamaro. We bestow gifts on the district official. This year's rice field taxes for the people of this province, of the Right and Left Capital, Yamato, Izumi, and Yamashiro are remitted. Also those who have commited crimes in Ōmi from TPHJ 5.10.16 [377] from those under death sentence on down are pardoned."

Sr 4 Upper Fujiwara no Asomi Mitate awarded Jr 3 Rank.

Jr 5 Lower Fujiwara no Asomi Tamaro, Kosobe no Asomi Naniwamaro, and Nakatomi Wani no Muraji Yumihari all awarded Jr 5 Upper Rank.

Sr 6 Upper Kurakaki no Imiki Emaro and Fujii no Muraji Nenushi both awarded Outer Jr 5 Lower Rank.

On this day the Emperor gave an edict:

"We have taken thought and planned to construct a Northern Capital. As we have travelled here We have observed that the people of the area are overburdened with labor due to the move. Our heart is deeply moved by their suffering. Therefore the two districts adjoining the new capital shall be designated Inner Districts [378] in perpetuity. Corvee shall be halted and transmuted into tax on products. The tax shall be equal to that of the Nara capital."

天平宝字五年（七六一）十一月癸未【辛巳朔三】〇十一月癸未。授迎藤原河清使外従五位下高元度従五位上。其録事羽栗翔者、留河清所而不帰。

Tenpyō Hōji **5.11.3** 癸未 *mizunoto-hitsuji*

---

[377] SNIII p 393 n 6 – on the basis of this date, perhaps the date is actually the 16th day -丁卯

[378] *Kiken* 畿県

[December 3, 761]

The envoy sent to seek Fujiwara no Kiyokawa, Outer Jr 5 Lower Ko Gendo, was awarded Jr 5 Upper Rank. The Recording Officer Haguri no Kakeru[379] should remain in Tang with Kiyokawa.

天平宝字五年（七六一）十一月丁酉【十七】〇丁酉。以従四位下藤原恵美朝臣朝狩為東海道節度使。正五位下百済朝臣足人。従五位上田中朝臣多太麻呂為副。判官四人。録事四人。其所管遠江。駿河。伊豆。甲斐。相摸。安房。上総。下総。常陸。上野。武蔵。下野等十二国。検定船一百五十二隻。兵士一万五千七百人。子弟七十八人。水手七千五百廿人。数内二千四百人肥前国。二百人対馬嶋。従三位百済王敬福為南海道使。従五位上藤原朝臣田麻呂。従五位下小野朝臣石根為副。判官四人。録事四人。紀伊。阿波。讃岐。伊予。土左。播磨。美作。備前。備中。備後。安芸。周防等十二国。検定船一百廿一隻。兵士一万二千五百人。子弟六十二人。水手四千九百廿人。正四位下吉備朝臣真備為西海道使。従五位上多治比真人土作。佐伯宿禰美濃麻呂為副。判官四人。録事四人。筑前。筑後。肥前。肥後。豊前。豊後。日向。大隅。薩摩等八国。検定船一百廿一隻。兵士一万二千五百人。子弟六十二人。水手四千九百廿人。皆免三年田租。悉赴弓馬。兼調習五行之陳。其所遺兵士者。便役造兵器。

Tenpyō Hōji 5.11.17 丁酉 *hinoto-tori*

[December 17, 761]

Jr 4 Lower Fujikawa Emi no Asomi Asakari appointed *Tōkaidō* Military Instructor.[380] Sr 5 Lower Kudara no Asomi Taruhito and Jr 5 Upper Tanaka no Asomi Tadamaro appointed Deputies. Four Secretaries and four Recording Officers were also appointed.

Their area of administrative responsibility includes the twelve provinces of Tōtōmi, Suruga, Izu, Kai, Sagami, Awa, Kazusa, Shimofusa, Hitachi, Kōzuke,

---

[379] SNIII p 394 n 1 – Ono no Komaro's son.
[380] *Setsudoshi* 節度使.

Musashi, and Shimotsuke. Their duty is to oversee the requisitioning of one hundred fifty-two ships, fifteen thousand seven hundred soldiers, seventy-eight district youth, and four thousand nine hundred twenty sailors. Of these two thousand four hundred will be stationed in Hizen, and two hundred on Tsushima Island.

Jr 3 Kudara no Konikishi Kyōfuku appointed *Nankaidō* Military Instructor. Jr 5 Upper Fujiwara no Asomi Tamaro and Jr 5 Lower Ono no Asomi Iwane appointed Deputies. Four Secretaries and four Recording Officers also appointed.

Their area of administrative responsibility includes the twelve provinces of Kii, Awa, Sanuki, Iyo, Tosa, Harima, Mimasaka, Bizen, Bitchū, Bingo, Aki, and Suo. Their duty is to oversee the requisitioning of one hundred twenty-one ships, twelve thousand five hundred soldiers, sixty-two district youth, and four thousand nine hundred sailors.

Sr 4 Lower Kibi no Asomi Makibi appointed *Saikaidō* Military Instructor. Jr 5 Upper Tajihi no Mahito Hanitsukuri and Saeki no Sukune Minomaro appointed Deputies. Four Secretaries and four Recording Officers also appointed.

Their area of administrative responsibility includes the eight provinces of Chikuzen, Chikugo, Hizen, Higo, Buzen, Bungo, Hyuga, Ōsumi, and Satsuma. Their duty is to oversee the requisitioning of one hundred twenty-one ships, twelve thousand five hundred soldiers, sixty-two district youth, and four thousand nine hundred twenty sailors.

They shall all have their rice field taxes remitted for three years. They should all prepare horses and bows and learn and practice five-rank formations. The remaining soldiers should make weapons.

天平宝字五年（七六一）十二月戊午【辛亥朔八】〇十二月戊午。授正五位上藤原朝臣家児従四位下。無位大伴宿禰諸刀自従五位下。

Tenpyō Hōji **5.12.8** 戊午 *tsuchinoe-uma*

[January 7, 762]

Sr 5 Upper Fujiwara no Asomi Yakako awarded Jr 4 Lower Rank. No-rank Ōtomo no Sukune Morotoji awarded Jr 5 Lower Rank.

天平宝字五年（七六一）十二月丙寅【十六】〇丙寅。唐人外従五位下李元環賜姓李忌寸。

Tenpyō Hōji **5.12.16** 丙寅 *hinoe-tora*

[January 15, 762]

The Tang person, Outer Jr 5 Lower Ri no Genkan, granted the *kabane* of Ri no Imiki.

《巻尾続日本紀　巻第廿三

[End of *Shoku Nihongi Maki* 23]

Tenpyō Hōji 6

《巻首続日本紀　巻第廿四〈起天平宝字六年正月、尽七年十二月。〉

***Shoku Nihongi Maki* 24 (from *Tenpyō Hōji* 6.1 to 7.12)**

右大臣従二位兼行皇太子傅中衛大将臣藤原朝臣継縄等奉勅撰」

Compiled and presented by imperial order by Great Minister of the Right Jr 2 and concurrently Tutor to the Crown Prince and General of the Middle Guard Fujiwara no Asomi Tsugutada.

廃帝　**Haitei (Deposed Emperor Junnin)**

天平宝字六年（七六二）正月庚辰朔六年春正月庚辰朔。廃朝。以宮室未成也。

Tenpyō Hōji* 6.1.1 庚辰　*kanoe-tatsu

[January 29, 762]

The New Year's Audience ceremony was cancelled. This was because the Hora Palace was not yet completed

天平宝字六年（七六二）正月辛巳【二】○辛巳。日有蝕之。

Tenpyō Hōji* 6.1.2 辛巳 *kanoto-mi

[January 30, 762]

Solar eclipse.

天平宝字六年（七六二）正月癸未【四】○癸未。帝臨軒。授三品船親王二品。正四位上紀朝臣飯麻呂従三位。無位榎本王従四位下。荻田王従五位下。正五位上粟田朝臣奈勢麻呂。中臣朝臣清麻呂。石川朝臣豊成並従四位下。従五位上阿倍朝臣子嶋正五位下。従五位下石川朝臣人成。巨勢朝臣浄成並従五位上。正六位上息長丹生真人国嶋。路真人鷹養。中臣朝臣伊加麻呂。阿倍朝臣小路。阿倍朝臣息道。石上朝臣奥継。大伴宿禰田麻呂並従五位下。正六位上守部垣麻呂。船連小楫並外従五位下。」以中納言正三位文室真人浄三為御史大夫。信部卿従三位氷上真人塩焼。鎮国衛驍騎将軍兼美濃飛騨信濃按察使従四位上藤原恵美朝臣真光並為参議。」授従四位上氷上真人陽侯正四位下。正六位上紀朝臣真艫。従六位上安曇宿禰夷女。従七位下車持朝臣塩清。無位当麻真人多玖比礼並従五位下。

Tenpyō Hōji 6.1.4 癸未 *mizunoto-hitsuji*

[February 1, 762]

The Emperor approached and awarded Second Cap Rank to Third Cap Rank Imperial Prince Fune.

Sr 4 Upper Ki no Asomi Iimaro awarded Jr 3 Rank.

No-rank Prince Enomoto awarded Jr 4 Lower Rank.

Prince Ogita awarded Jr 5 Lower Rank.

Sr 5 Upper Awata no Asomi Nasemaro, Nakatomi no Asomi Kiyomaro, and Ishikawa no Asomi Toyonari all awarded Jr 4 Lower Rank.

Jr 5 Upper Abe no Asomi Koshima awarded Sr 5 Lower Rank.

Jr 5 Lower Ishikawa no Asomi Hitonari and Kose no Asomi Kiyonari both awarded Jr 5 Upper Rank.

Sr 6 Upper Okinaganiu no Mahito Kunishima, Michi no Mahito Takakai, Nakataomi no Asomi Ikamaro, Abe no Asomi Komichi, Abe no Asomi Okimichi, Isonokami no Asomi Okutsugi, and Ōtomo no Sukune Tamaro all awarded Jr 5 Lower Rank.

Sr 6 Upper Moribe no Kakimaro and Fune no Muraji Okaji both awarded Outer Jr 5 Lower Rank.

Middle Counsellor Sr 3 Fumuya no Mahito Jōsamu appointed Master of Imperial Scribes.

Head of Ministry of Fidelity Jr 3 Hikami no Mahito Shioyaki; and General of State Protection Guards and Cavalry[381] and Regional Inspector for Mino, Hida, and Shinano Jr 4 Upper Fujiwara Emi no Asomi Masaki both appointed as Imperial Advisor.

Jr 4 Hikami no Mahito Yako awarded Sr 4 Lower Rank.

Sr 6 Upper Ki no Asomi Matoshi and Jr 6 Upper Azumi no Sukune Ebisume and Jr 7 Lower Kurumamochi no Asomi Shiokiyo and no-rank Tagima no Mahito Takuhire all awarded Jr 5 Lower Rank.

天平宝字六年（七六二）正月乙酉【六】○乙酉。遣参議従四位上藤原恵美朝臣真光。饗唐人沈惟岳等於大宰府。賜大使以下禄有差。

Tenpyō Hōji* 6.1.6 乙酉 *kinoto-tori

[February 3, 762]

---

[381] *Chinkokue Gyōki Shōgun* 鎮国衛驍騎将軍

The Imperial Advisor Jr 4 Upper Fujiwara Emi no Asomi Masaki was dispatched to provide a banquet at Kyushu Headquarters for the Chinese envoy Chen Weiyue and others.[382] The envoy and other members of the embassy were awarded stipends according to their level.

天平宝字六年（七六二）正月戊子【九】o戊子。以信部少輔従五位下紀朝臣牛養為兼少納言。従五位上阿倍朝臣毛人為左中弁。従四位下石川朝臣豊成為右大弁。従五位上大伴宿禰家持為信部大輔。外従五位下忌部連黒麻呂為内史局助。従四位下宗形王為右大舎人頭。従五位下淡海真人三船為文部少輔。従五位下中臣朝臣伊加麻呂為礼部少輔。従四位下林王為木工頭。従五位上上毛野公広浜為左京亮。外従五位下茨田宿禰枚野為東市正。従五位下阿倍朝臣許智為摂津亮。従五位上巨曾倍朝臣難破麻呂為造宮大輔。外従五位下椋垣忌寸吉麻呂為右平準令。従五位下笠朝臣真足為右勇士翼。従五位上高元度為参河守。従五位下阿倍朝臣小路為近江介。従五位下阿倍朝臣息道為若狭守。外従五位下日置造蓑麻呂為丹波介。従五位上河内王為丹後守。従五位上長野連公足為因幡守。従五位下石上朝臣奥継為播磨介。従五位下大野朝臣広立為肥前守。従五位下百済王理伯為肥後守。従五位下田口朝臣大戸為日向守。

Tenpyō Hōji 6.1.9 戊子 *tsuchinoe-ne*

[February 6, 762]

Junior Assistant, Ministry of Fidelity Jr 5 Lower Ki no Asomi Ushikai concurrently appointed Minor Counsellor.

Jr 5 Upper Abe no Asomi Emishi appointed Middle Controller of the Left.

Jr 4 Lower Ishikawa no Asomi Toyonari appointed Major Controller of the Right.

Jr 5 Upper Ōtomo no Sukune Yakamochi appointed Senior Assistant, Ministry of Fidelity.

---

[382] They had arrived on TPHJ 5.8.12.

Outer Jr 5 Lower Imbe no Muraji Kuromaro appointed Assistant Head, Department of Palace Classics.

Jr 4 Lower Prince Munakata appointed Head, Right Imperial Attendants.

Jr 5 Lower Ōmi no Mahito Mifune appointed Junior Assistant, Ministry of Civil Affairs.

Jr 5 Lower Nakatomi no Asomi Ikamaro appointed Junior Assistant, Ministry of Rites.

Jr 4 Lower Prince Hayashi appointed Head of the Carpentry Bureau.

Jr 5 Upper Kamitsukeno no Kimi Hirohama appointed Assistant Commissioner, Left Capital.

Outer Jr 5 Lower Mamuta no Sukune Hirano appointed Head of Eastern Market.

Jr 5 Lower Abe no Asomi Kochi appointed Settsu Assistant Governor.

Jr 5 Upper Kosobe no Asomi Naniwamaro appointed Master, Office of Palace Construction.

Outer Jr 5 Lower Kurakaki no Imiki Emaro appointed Head, Right Ever-Normal Granary.

Jr 5 Lower Kasa no Asomi Matari appointed Commander, Right Brave Warriors.

Jr 5 Upper Kō Gendo appointed Mikawa Governor.

Jr 5 Lower Abe no Asomi Komichi appointed Ōmi Assistant Governor.

Jr 5 Lower Abe no Asomi Okimichi appointed Wakasa Governor.

Outer Jr 5 Lower Heki Miyatsuko Minomaro appointed Tanba Assistant Governor.

Jr 5 Upper Prince Kawachi appointed Tango Governor.

Jr 5 Upper Nagano no Muraji Kimitari appointed Inaba Governor.

Jr 5 Lower Isonokami no Asomi Okutsugi appointed Harima Governor.

Jr 5 Lower Ōno no Asomi Hirotate appointed Hizen Governor.

Jr 5 Lower Kudara no Konikishi Rihaku appointed Higo Governor.

Jr 5 Lower Taguchi no Asomi Ōto appointed Hyuga Governor.

天平宝字六年（七六二）正月丁未【廿八】○丁未。造東海。南海。西海
等道節度使料綿襖冑各二万二百五十具於大宰府。其製一如唐国新様。仍
象五行之色。皆画甲板之形。碧地者以朱。赤地者以黄。黄地者以朱。白
地者以黒。黒地者以白。毎四千五十具成一行之色。

Tenpyō Hōji 6.1.28 丁未 *hinoto-hitsuji*
[February 25, 762]

The Military Instructors of the *Tōkaidō*, *Saikaidō* and *Nankaidō* are to oversee the manufacture of twenty thousand two hundred fifty items each of padded armor and helmets for the Kyushu Headquarters. Their pattern is to be of the newest design of Tang China. The colors of the Five Ranks[383] are to be depicted on the armor. Four thousand fifty items each are to be uniformly constructed with these colors –vermilion on a green field, red on a blue field, blue on a red field, white on a black field, black on a white field, white on a black field.

---

[383] green, red, blue, white, black.

天平宝字六年（七六二）二月辛亥【庚戌朔二】○二月辛亥。授従一位藤
原恵美朝臣押勝正一位。

Tenpyō Hōji 6.2.2 辛亥 *kanoto-i*

[March 1, 762]

Jr 1 Fujiwara Emi Asomi Oshikatsu awarded Sr 1 Rank.

天平宝字六年（七六二）二月乙卯【六】○乙卯。造綿甲冑一千領、以貯
鎮国衛府。

Tenpyō Hōji 6.2.6 乙卯 kinoto-u

[March 5, 762]

One thousand items of padded armor and helmets were made and stored in the

Headquarters of the State Protection Guards.

天平宝字六年（七六二）二月辛酉【十二】○辛酉。簡点伊勢。近江。美
濃。越前等四国郡司子弟及百姓。年＝已下廿已上練習弓馬者。以為健児。
其有死闕及老病者。即以与替。仍准天平六年四月廿一日勅。除其身田租
及雑徭之半。其歴名等第。毎年附朝集使送武部省。

Tenpyō Hōji 6.2.12 辛酉 kanoto-tori

[March 11, 762]

From the staff of the governor's and district officials and the people generally of

the four provinces – Ise, Ōmi, Mino, Echizen – men between the ages of 20 and

40 skilled with horse and bow were selected to form the Stalwart Youth.[384] If

members of these units die, or become old or ill, they are to be immediately

replaced. In conformity with the edict of *Tenpyō* 6.4.21 half of the rice tax and

---

[384] *Kondei* 健児 – "any of several incarnations of units established at various times during the 8th century to augment the imperial court's military and police system in the countryside." Karl Friday, 1992, p 223. In this case Oshikatsu's special militia to guard the three barriers.

miscellaneous corvee is to be exempted. Their names and rank are to be submitted each year to the Official for Annual Provincial Reports[385], and sent in to the Ministry of Military Affairs.

天平宝字六年（七六二）二月甲戌【廿五】○甲戌。賜大師藤原恵美朝臣押勝近江国浅井・高嶋二郡鉄穴各一処。

Tenpyō Hōji 6.2.25 甲戌 *kinoe-inu*

[March 24, 762]

The court granted Grand Preceptor Fujiwara Emi no Asomi Oshikatsu two iron mines in Ōmi Province, one each in Asai and Takashima districts.

天平宝字六年（七六二）三月庚辰朔○三月庚辰朔。遣唐副使従五位上石上朝臣宅嗣罷。以左虎賁衛督従五位上藤原朝臣田麻呂為副使。

Tenpyō Hōji 6.3.1 庚辰 *kanoe-tatsu*

[March 30, 762]

The Vice-Envoy to Tang Jr 5 Upper Ishikawa no Asomi Yakatsugu resigned his position. The Head of the Left Elite Tigers Jr 5 Upper Fujiwara no Asomi Tamaro was appointed Vice-Envoy.

天平宝字六年（七六二）三月壬午【三】○壬午。於宮西南。新造池亭。設曲水之宴。賜五位已上禄有差。

Tenpyō Hōji 6.3.3 壬午 *mizunoe-uma*

[April 1, 762]

---

[385] *Chōshūshi* 朝集使

A new pond and arbor were constructed in the southwest of Hora Palace and a winding water banquet was held. Officials of fifth rank and up were given stipends according to status.

天平宝字六年（七六二）三月甲辰【廿五】○甲辰。保良宮諸殿及屋垣。分配諸国。一時就功。

Tenpyō Hōji 6.3.25 甲辰 *kinoe-tatsu*

[April 23, 762]

The duty of constructing the various buildings and roofed enclosures of Hora Palace were assigned to various provinces. The work was completed quickly.

天平宝字六年（七六二）三月戊申【廿九】○戊申。参河。尾張。遠江。下総。美濃。能登。備中。備後。讃岐等九国旱。

Tenpyō Hōji 6.3.29 戊申 *tsuchinoe-saru*

[April 27, 762]

Drought in nine provinces – Mikawa, Owari, Tōtōmi, Shimofusa, Mino, Noto, Bitchū, Bingo, and Sanuki.

天平宝字六年（七六二）四月庚戌朔○夏四月庚戌朔。以外従五位下山田連古麻呂為主税助。従五位上大伴宿禰御依為義部大輔。外従五位下漆部直伊波為贓贖正。従五位上巨勢朝臣浄成為智部大輔。従五位下紀朝臣広名為少輔。従五位下高橋朝臣子老為大膳亮。従五位下高橋朝臣老麻呂為内膳奉膳。従五位下高円朝臣広世為山背守。外従五位下坂上忌寸老人為介。右大弁従四位下石河朝臣豊成為兼尾張守。従四位下粟田朝臣奈勢麻呂為遠江守。従五位上田中朝臣多太麻呂為陸奥守。鎮守副将軍従五位下大伴宿禰益立為兼介。外従五位下下道朝臣黒麻呂為隠岐守。信部卿従三位氷上真人塩焼為兼美作守。外従五位下中臣酒人宿禰虫麻呂為豊前員外介。

Tenpyō Hōji 6.4.1 庚戌 Summer *kanoe-inu*

228

[April 29, 762]

Outer Jr 5 Lower Yamada no Muraji Komaro appointed Assistant Head, Bureau of Taxation.

Jr 5 Upper Ōtomo no Sukune Miyori appointed Senior Assistant, Ministry of Righteousness.

Outer Jr 5 Lower Nuribe no Atai Iha appointed Head of Reclamation.[386]

Jr 5 Upper Kose no Asomi Kiyonari appointed Senior Assistant, Ministry of Wisdom.

Jr 5 Lower Ki no Asomi Hirona appointed Junior Assistant, Ministry of Wisdom.

Jr 5 Lower Takahashi no Asomi Kooyu appointed Assistant, Office of the Palace Table.

Jr 5 Lower Takahashi no Asomi Oimaro appointed Director, Office of the Imperial Table.

Jr 5 Lower Takamado no Asomi Hiroyo appointed Yamashiro Governor.

Outer Jr 5 Lower Sakanoue no Imiki Okina appointed Yamashiro Assistant Governor.

Major Controller of the Right Jr 4 Lower Ishikawa no Asomi Toyonari concurrently appointed Owari Governor.

---

[386] *Zōshoku Kami* 贓贖正 – Head, office for the reclamation of stolen goods.

Jr 4 Lower Awata no Asomi Nasemaro appointed Tōtōmi Governor.

Jr 5 Upper Tanaka no Asomi Tadamaro appointed Michinooku Governor.

Vice-General, Office for Pacifying *Emishi* Jr 5 Lower Ōtomo no Sukune Mashitate concurrently appointed Michinooku Assistant Governor.

Outer Jr 5 Lower Shimotsumichi no Asomi Kuromaro appointed Oki Governor.

Head of Ministry of Fidelity Jr 3 Eigami no Mahito Shioyaki concurrently appointed Mimasaka Governor.

Outer Jr 5 Lower Nakatomi Sakahito no Sukune Mushimaro appointed Buzen Irregular Assistant Governor.

天平宝字六年（七六二）四月丁巳【八】〇丁巳。河内国狭山池堤決。以単功八万三千人修造。

Tenpyō Hōji **6.4.8 丁巳** *hinoto-mi*

[May 6, 762]

The dikes of Sayama Pond in Kawachi Province collapsed. Eighty-three thousand laborers were mobilized to repair them.

天平宝字六年（七六二）四月戊午【九】〇戊午。遠江国飢。賑給之。

Tenpyō Hōji **6.4.9 戊午** *tsuchinoe-uma*

[May 7, 762]

Famine in Tōtōmi Province. Relief supplies granted.

天平宝字六年（七六二）四月癸亥【十四】〇癸亥。尾張国飢。賑給之。

Tenpyō Hōji 6.4.14 癸亥 *mizunoto-i*

[May 12, 762]

Famine in Owari Province. Relief supplies granted.

天平宝字六年（七六二）四月丙寅【十七】〇丙寅。遣唐使駕船一隻自安
芸国到于難波江口。著灘不浮。其柁亦復不得発出。為浪所揺。船尾破裂。
於是。樽節使人、限以両船。授判官正六位上中臣朝臣鷹主従五位下為使。
賜節刀。正六位上高麗朝臣広山為副。

Tenpyō Hōji 6.4.17 丙寅 *hinoe-tora*

[May 15, 762]

When a ship designed for the China embassy from Aki Province arrived at the
river mouth in Naniwa it ran aground due to the swift current. The rudder could
not function due to the force of the waves and the stern was ripped off. As a
result the number of members of the mission was reduced to the number who
could ride in two ships. The Secretary Sr 6 Upper Nakatomi no Asomi
Takanushi was awarded Jr 5 Lower Rank, appointed Ambassador to Tang and
given the Sword of Command. Sr 6 Upper Koma no Asomi Hiroyama was made
Vice-Envoy.

天平宝字六年（七六二）四月辛未【廿二】〇辛未。始置大宰弩師。

Tenpyō Hōji 6.4.22 辛未 *kanoto-hitsuji*
[May 20, 762]

An official in charge of catapults at Kyushu Headquarters was appointed for the

first time.

天平宝字六年（七六二）四月壬申【廿三】○壬申。越前国江沼郡山背郷戸五十煙施入岡寺。

Tenpyō Hōji 6.4.23 壬申 *mizunoe-saru*

[May 21, 762]

The Emperor gave an edict ordering fifty households in Yamashiro Village,

Enuma District, Echizen Province donated to the *Okadera.*

天平宝字六年（七六二）五月壬午【己卯朔四】○五月壬午。京師及畿内。伊勢。近江。美濃。若狭。越前等国飢。遣使賑給之。

Tenpyō Hōji 6.5.4 壬午 *mizunoe-uma*

[May 31, 762]

Famine in the capital and Kinai, Ise, Ōmi, Mino, Wakasa and Echizen.

Messengers were sent out to give relief supplies.

天平宝字六年（七六二）五月丁亥【九】○丁亥。美濃。飛騨。信濃等国地震。賜被損者穀家二斛。」石見国飢。賑給之。

Tenpyō Hōji 6.5.9 丁亥 *hinoto-i*

[June 5, 762]

Earthquakes in Mino, Hida and Shinano. Two bushels of grain were given to

households that suffered damage.

Famine in Iwami. Relief supplies granted.

天平宝字六年（七六二）五月己丑【十一】○己丑。備前国飢。賑給之。

Tenpyō Hōji 6.5.11 己丑 *tsuchinoto-ushi*

[June 7, 762]

Famine in Bizen. Relief supplies granted.

天平宝字六年（七六二）五月丁酉【十九】〇丁酉。大宰府言。唐客副使
紀喬容已下卅八人状云。大使沈惟岳。贓汚已露。不足率下。副使紀喬容。
司兵晏子欽、堪充押領。伏垂進止。府官商量。所申有實。報曰。大使・
副使並是勅使。謝時和与蘇州刺史。相量所定。不可改張。其還郷之禄亦
依旧給。

Tenpyō Hōji 6.5.19 丁酉 *hinoto-tori*

[June 15, 762]

Kyushu Government Headquarters reported:

"The Vice-Envoy and honored guest from Tang Ji Qiaorong with thirty-eight embassy members submitted the following written communication:

'The Ambassador Chen Weiyue took bribes and is no longer fit to lead the embassy. The Vice-Envoy Ji Qiaorong and the military commander Yan Ziqin are the proper persons to assume the leadership. We beg that you appoint them.'

"Then the functionaries of Kyushu Headquarters consulted and decided this was correct."

The court responded:

"The Envoy or Vice-Envoy are the official envoys from Tang, sent by Xie Shihe, the Prefect of Su Prefecture. This has already been established. There should be no change. When they return home, they should be given the usual stipend.

天平宝字六年（七六二）五月辛丑【廿三】〇辛丑。高野天皇与帝有隙。
於是。車駕還平城宮。帝御于中宮院。高野天皇御于法華寺。

Tenpyō Hōji 6.5.23 辛丑 *kanoto-ushi*

[June 19, 762]

There was a rift in relations between the Takano Empress and the *Mikado*. They returned to the Heijō Palace from Hora Palace. The *Mikado* went to the Middle Palace near the Imperial Council Hall. The Takano Empress entered the *Hokkeji*.

天平宝字六年（七六二）五月丙午【廿八】○丙午。賜大師正一位藤原恵美朝臣押勝帯刀資人六十人。通前一百人。其夏・冬衣服者官給之。

Tenpyō Hōji 6.5.28 丙午 *hinoe-uma*

[June 24, 762]

The Grand Preceptor Sr 1 Fujiwara Emi no Asomi Oshikatsu was granted sixty Sword-Bearing Attendants. This made a total of one hundred including those he had previously been granted. The expense for their summer and winter clothes was paid from the public treasury.

天平宝字六年（七六二）六月庚戌【戌申朔三】○六月庚戌。喚集五位已上於朝堂。詔曰。【Ｓ２７】太上天皇御命以〈弖〉卿等諸語〈部止〉宣〈久〉。朕御祖大皇后〈乃〉御命以〈弖〉朕〈爾〉告〈之久〉、岡宮御宇天皇〈乃〉日継〈波〉、加久〈弖〉絶〈奈牟止〉為。女子〈能〉継〈爾波〉在〈止母〉欲令嗣〈止〉宣〈弖〉、此政行給〈岐〉。加久為〈弖〉今帝〈止〉立〈弖〉須麻〈比〉久〈流〉間〈爾〉、宇夜宇也〈自久〉相従事〈波〉無〈之弖〉、斗卑等〈乃〉仇〈能〉在言〈期等久〉、不言〈岐〉辞〈母〉言〈奴〉。不為〈岐〉行〈母〉為〈奴〉。凡加久伊波〈流倍枳〉朕〈爾波〉不在。別宮〈爾〉御坐坐〈牟〉時、自加得言〈也〉。此〈波〉朕劣〈爾〉依〈弖之〉、加久言〈良之止〉念召〈波〉、愧〈自弥〉伊等保〈自弥奈母〉念〈須〉。又一〈爾波〉朕応発菩提心縁〈爾〉在〈良之止母奈母〉念〈須〉。是以、出家〈弖〉仏弟子〈止〉成〈奴〉。但政事〈波〉、常祀〈利〉小事〈波〉今帝行給〈部〉。国家大事賞罰二柄〈波〉朕行〈牟〉。加久〈能〉状聞食悟〈止〉宣御命、衆聞

234

食宣。」尾張国飢。賑給之。

Tenpyō Hōji 6.6.3 庚戌 kanoe-inu

[June 28, 762]

Officials of fifth rank and up were summoned to the Administrative Palace and the Retired Empress Kōken addressed the nobles with these words [*Senmyō 27*]:

"Let all nobles hearken to the words which are pronounced by the Retired Empress. According to the words of Our revered mother the Dowager Empress Kōmyō, what she announced to Us was that 'The line of imperial descendants of the Emperor who ruled the Realm at *Oka no Miya*[387] should remain unbroken. To avoid breaking this line you, even though a young woman, should succeed to Shōmu *Tennō*.'

"Thus We undertook the government. Then We set up Junnin as the current *Mikado*. However, Junnin has not obeyed Us reverently. He has said things that should not have been said, like those of an outsider, and done things that should not have been done. He has spoken wrongfully in Our name. Perhaps he said these things since We were living in a separate palace. Perhaps it is due to Our foolishness that he has spoken, and We are ashamed and disgraced. Or perhaps it is due to Our karma that moved Our heart to Buddhist enlightenment so that We left the world and became a disciple of the Buddha. Now as for the

---

[387] 岡宮-- the Crown Prince Kusakabe 草壁皇子 died before taking the throne. He was the son of Tenmu and Jitō. The title "Emperor who ruled the Realm at *Oka no Miya*" was an honorary posthumous title. Note that Junnin was NOT a descendant in this line.

government, the *Mikado* will carry out the small duties of the usual ceremonies. We shall carry out the fundamental duties of the great things of state, rewards and punishments. Let all hearken to the words which We speak and understand these things."

Famine in Owari. Relief supplies granted.

天平宝字六年（七六二）六月戊辰【廿一】○戊辰。河内国長瀬堤決。発単功二万二千二百余人修造焉。」散位従四位下榎本王卒。

Tenpyō Hōji 6.6.21 戊辰 *tsuchinoe-tatsu*

[July 16, 762]

The dikes collapsed on the Nagase River (Yamato River) in Kawachi. Over twenty-two thousand two hundred laborers were mobilized to repair them.

Scattered Rank Jr 4 Lower Prince Enomoto died.

天平宝字六年（七六二）六月庚午【廿三】○庚午。尚蔵兼尚侍正三位藤原朝臣宇比良古薨。贈太政大臣房前之女也。賻＝［糸＋施の旁］百疋。布百端。鉄百廷。

Tenpyō Hōji 6.6.23 庚午 *kanoe-uma*

[July 18, 762]

The Head of the Imperial Storehouse and concurrently Head of Palace Women Sr 3 Fujiwara no Asomi Uirako died. [388] She was the daughter of the posthumously appointed First Minister of the Great Council of State Fujiwara no Fusasaki. The court donated one hundred rolls of plain weave silk, one hundred

---

[388] Oshikatsu's wife.

lengths of hemp cloth, and one hundred measures of iron as condolence gifts for the memorial service.

天平宝字六年（七六二）七月丙申【戊寅朔十九】○秋七月丙申。散位従三位紀朝臣飯麻呂薨。淡海朝大納言贈正三位大人之孫。平城朝式部大輔正五位下古麻呂之長子也。仕至正四位下左大弁。拝参議。授従三位。病久不損。上表乞骸骨。詔許之。

天平宝字六年（七六二）七月是月○是月。送唐人使従五位下中臣朝臣鷹主等。風波無便、不得渡海。

Tenpyō Hōji 6.7.19 丙申 Autumn *hinoe-saru*

[August 13, 762]

Scattered Rank Jr 3 Ki no Asomi Ihimaro died. He was the grandson of the Major Counsellor Ki no Ushi, posthumously granted Sr 3 Rank, in the Ōmi court of Tenji. He was the eldest son of Senior Assistant, Ministry of Ceremonial Sr 5 Lower Ki no Komaro of Genmei's court. He served the court and was appointed Major Controller of the Left, reaching Sr 4 Lower Rank. When he was appointed Imperial Advisor he was granted Jr 3 Rank. His illness was long and he did not recover. He wrote a memorial begging to resign. The Emperor gave an edict permitting this.

This month the members of the embassy to Tang, Jr 5 Lower Nakatomi no Asomi Takanushi and all, were unable to cross the sea due to wind and waves.

天平宝字六年（七六二）八月乙卯【丁未朔九】○八月乙卯。勅。唐人沈惟岳等着府。依先例安置供給。其送使者。海陸二路、量便咸令入京。其水手者。自彼放還本郷。

Tenpyō Hōji 6.8.9 乙卯 *kinoto-u*

[September 1, 762]

The Emperor gave an edict:

"The Tang person Chen Weiyue and all landed at the Kyushu Headquarters on TPHJ 5.8.12 according to precedent and stayed. They should be supplied with essentials. The messengers sent to escort them gave up trying to cross the ocean and should return to court by the sea and land routes. The sailors are free to return to their home villages and should do so."[389]

天平宝字六年（七六二）八月丁巳【十一】○丁巳。令左右京尹従四位下藤原恵美朝臣訓儒麻呂。文部大輔従四位下中臣朝臣清麻呂。右勇士率従四位下上道朝臣正道。授刀大尉従五位下佐味朝臣伊与麻呂等。侍于中宮院。宣伝勅旨。

Tenpyō Hōji 6.8.11 丁巳 *hinoto-mi*

[September 3, 762]

The Left and Right Capital Commissioner Jr 4 Lower Fujiwara Emi no Asomi Kusumaro, the Senior Assistant, Ministry of Civil Affairs Jr 4 Lower Nakatomi no Asomi Kiyomaro, Head of Right Brave Warriors Jr 4 Lower Kamitsumichi no Asomi Masamichi, and Head of Sword-Bearing Retainers Jr 5 Lower Sami no Asomi Iyomaro were all ordered to serve at the Middle Palace[390] to report and disseminate the edicts of the *Mikado* Junnin.

天平宝字六年（七六二）八月乙丑【十九】○乙丑。陸奥国疫。賑給之。

---

[389] See TPHJ 6.1.6, 6.5.19, 6.7.19 for references to this Tang embassy. The Japanese escorts and the members of this embassy were unsuccessful in trying to return to Tang. See chart in Tōno 2007, 204.

[390] The new residence of Junnin in the Heijō Palace.

Tenpyō Hōji **6.8.19** 乙丑 *kinoto-ushi*

[September 11, 762]

Epidemic in Michinooku. Relief supplies granted.

天平宝字六年（七六二）八月丙寅【二十】○丙寅。御史大夫文室真人浄三。以年老力衰。優詔特聴宮中持扇策杖。

Tenpyō Hōji **6.8.20** 丙寅 *hinoe-tora*

[September 12, 762]

The Master of Imperial Scribes Fumuya no Mahito Jōsamu was aged and declining in strength. In sympathy the Emperor gave an edict especially permitting him to use a fan and a cane while in the Palace.

天平宝字六年（七六二）九月乙巳【丙子朔三十】○九月乙巳。御史大夫正三位兼文部卿神祇伯勲十二等石川朝臣年足薨。時年七十五。詔、遣摂津大夫従四位下佐伯宿禰今毛人。信部大輔従五位上大伴宿禰家持。弔賻之。年足者。後岡本朝大臣大紫蘇我臣牟羅志曾孫。平城朝左大弁従三位石足之長子也。率性廉勤。習於治体。起家補少判事。頻歴外任。天平七年。授従五位下。任出雲守。視事数年。百姓安之。聖武皇帝善之。賜＝［糸＋施の旁］卅疋。布六十端。当国稲三万束。十九年。至従四位下春宮大夫兼左中弁。拝参議。勝宝五年、授従三位。累遷至中納言兼文部卿神祇伯。公務之閑。唯書是悦。宝字二年、授正三位。転御史大夫。時勅公卿、各言意見。仍上便宜。作別式廿巻。各以其政、繋於本司。雖未施行。頗有拠用焉。

Tenpyō Hōji **6.9.30** 乙巳 *kinoto-mi*

[October 21, 762]

The Master of Imperial Scribes Jr 3 Head of the Ministry of Civil Affairs and concurrently Head of the Department of Deity Affairs and holder of the Twelfth Order of Merit Ishikawa no Asomi Toshitari died. At the time he was 75 years old. The Emperor gave an edict dispatching the Settsu Commissioner Jr 4 Lower Saeki no Sukune Imaemishi, and the Senior Assistant, Ministry of Fidelity Jr 5 Upper Ōtomo no Sukune Yakamochi to present condolence gifts. Toshitari was the grandson of the Great Minister and Great Purple[391] Soga no Omi Muraji who served at the Later Okamoto court of Saimei *Tennō*, and the eldest son of the Major Controller of the Left Jr 3 Iwatari who served at the Heijō Court of Shōmu *Tennō*. From birth he was honest and industrious and he diligently learned the ways of administration. His first appointment was as a Minor Judge, and he frequently served as a provincial official. In *Tenpyō* 7 he was awarded Jr 5 Lower Rank and appointed Izumo Governor. During the years of that appointment the people were at peace. Emperor Shōmu was pleased with this and gave him thirty bolts of plain weave silk, sixty lengths of hemp cloth, and thirty thousand sheaves of rice of that province. In *Tenpyō* 19 he attained the rank of Jr 4 Lower and was appointed Master of the Spring Palace, and concurrently Middle Controller of the Left and Imperial Advisor. In TPSH 5 he was awarded Jr 3 Rank and appointed to additional bureaucratic offices – Middle Counsellor, Head of Ministry of Civil Affairs and Head of Ministry of Deity Affairs. When he had respites from official duties he delighted in reading the classics. In TPHJ 2 he was awarded Sr 3 Rank and appointed Master of the Imperial Scribes. At that time the Emperor gave an edict commanding him to give his opinion on matters of state. He presented many beneficial memorials,

---

[391]*Daishi* 大紫 – pre-Ritsuryō rank.

and he compiled the twenty-volume "Special Regulations"[392] that addressed policies regarding each of the offices of the government. Although they have not yet been publicly promulgated, they are exceedingly useful.

天平宝字六年（七六二）十月丙午朔o冬十月丙午朔。正六位上伊吉連益麻呂等。至自渤海。其国使紫綬大夫行政堂左允開国男王新福已下廿三人、相随来朝。於越前国加賀郡安置供給。我大使従五位下高麗朝臣大山。去日船上臥病。到佐利翼津卒。

Tenpyō Hōji 6.10.1 丙午 Winter *hinoe-uma*

[October 22, 762]

Sr 6 Upper Iki no Muraji Masumaro and others returned from Parhae. That country's ambassador Grand Master and Left Official of Hall of Administration and Dynasty Founding Baron Wang Xinfu[393] and twenty-three lower officials accompanied him to Japan. They landed at Kaga District, Echizen Province, and were provided with necessities. Our country's Envoy Jr 5 Lower Koma no Asomi Ōyama had previously taken ill on board ship, and, landing at Sariyoku Harbor in Dewa, had died.

天平宝字六年（七六二）十月甲寅【九】o甲寅。讃岐守従四位下大伴宿禰犬養卒。

Tenpyō Hōji 6.10.9 甲寅 *kinoe-tora*

[October 30, 762]

The Sanuki Governor Jr 4 Lower Ōtomo no Sukune Inukai died.

---

[392] *Besshiki* 別式
[393] Again, Parhae envoys with lengthy and obscure Chinese titles.

天平宝字六年（七六二）十月己未【十四】○己未。夫人正三位県犬養宿禰広刀自薨。賻＝［糸＋施の旁］百疋。糸三百＝［糸＋句］。布三百端。米九十石。夫人者、讃岐守従五位下唐之女也。聖武皇帝儲弐之日。納為夫人。生安積親王。年未弱冠。天平十六年薨。又生井上内親王。不破内親王。

Tenpyō Hōji **6.10.14** 己未 *tsuchinoto-hitsuji*

[November 4, 762]

The former concubine of the late Emperor Shōmu, Jr 3 Agata Inukai no Sukune Hirotoji died. One hundred rolls of plain weave silk, three hundred skeins of silk thread, three hundred lengths of hemp cloth and ninety bushels of rice were bestowed as condolence gifts. She was the daughter of Sanuki Governor Jr 5 Lower Agata Inukai no Morokoshi. She entered service the day Shōmu became Crown Prince, and became chief concubine. She gave birth to Imperial Prince Asaka. The Prince died without having attained maturity in *Tenpyō* 13.[394] She also gave birth to the two imperial princesses Inoue and Fuwa.

天平宝字六年（七六二）十一月乙亥朔○十一月乙亥朔。以正六位上借緋多治比真人小耳。為送高麗人使。

Tenpyō Hōji **6.11.1** 己未 *tsuchinoto-hitsuji*

[November 20, 762]

Sr 6 Upper *Shakuhi* [395] Tajihi no Mahito Omimi was appointed ambassador to Parhae.

---

[394]Imperial Prince Asaka 728-744. SNIII p 414 n 11 – *Tenpyō* 16 in text is a mistake for *Tenpyō* 13.

[395] 借緋 SNIII p 414 n 14 – A sixth rank official allowed to wear the scarlet clothing of the fifth rank.

天平宝字六年（七六二）十一月丁丑【三】○丁丑。遣御史大夫正三位文室真人浄三。左勇士佐従五位下藤原朝臣黒麻呂。神祇大副従五位下中臣朝臣毛人。少副従五位下忌部宿禰告麻呂等四人。奉幣於伊勢太神宮。

Tenpyō Hōji 6.11.3　乙亥　*kinoto-i*

[November 22, 762]

Master of Imperial Scribes Sr 3 Fumuya no Mahito Jōsamu; Assistant Head of Left Brave Warriors Jr 5 Lower Fujiwara no Asomi Kuromaro; Senior Assistant, Department of Deity Affairs Jr 5 Lower Nakatomi no Asomi Emishi; and the Junior Assistant, Department of Deity Affairs Jr 5 Lower Imbe no Sukune Azamaro were sent to present *mitegura* to Ise *Daijingū*.

天平宝字六年（七六二）十一月庚寅【十六】○庚寅。遣参議従三位武部卿藤原朝臣巨勢麻呂。散位外従五位下土師宿禰犬養。奉幣于香椎廟。以為征新羅調習軍旅也。

Tenpyō Hōji 6.11.16　庚寅　*kanoe-tora*

[December 5, 762]

The Imperial Advisor Jr 3 Head of Ministry of Military Affairs Fujiwara no Asomi Kosemaro and Scattered Rank Outer Jr 5 Lower Haji no Sukune Inukai were sent to present *mitegura* to *Kashii Byō* .[396] This was because of military drills in preparation for the attack on Silla.

天平宝字六年（七六二）十一月庚子【廿六】○庚子。奉幣及弓矢於天下神祇。

Tenpyō Hōji 6.11.26　庚子 *kanoe-ne*

[December 15, 762]

Mitegura and bows and arrows were presented to Shinto shrines in all the realm.

---

[396]香椎廟 *Kashii* Shrine near Dazaifu.

天平宝字六年（七六二）十一月壬寅【廿八】○壬寅。遣使奉幣於天下群神。

Tenpyō Hōji 6.11.28　庚子 *kanoe-ne*

[December 17, 762]

The court sent messengers to present *mitegura* to the *kami* in all the realm.

天平宝字六年（七六二）十二月乙巳朔○十二月乙巳朔。授従四位上藤原恵美朝臣真光正四位上。以御史大夫正三位文室真人浄三為兼神祇伯。従三位氷上真人塩焼。従三位諱。従三位藤原朝臣真楯為中納言。真楯為兼信部卿。正四位上藤原恵美朝臣真光為大宰帥。又以従三位藤原朝臣弟貞。従四位下藤原恵美朝臣訓儒麻呂。藤原恵美朝臣朝猟。中臣朝臣清麻呂。石川朝臣豊成為参議。

Tenpyō Hōji 6.12.1　壬寅　*mizunoe-tora*

[December 20, 762]

Jr 4 Upper Fujiwara Emi no Asomi Masaki awarded Sr 4 Upper Rank.

Master of Imperial Scribes Sr 3 Fumuya no Mahito Jōsamu appointed concurrently as Head of Department of Deity Affairs.

Jr 3 Hikami no Mahito Shioyaki, Jr 3 Prince Shirakabe, and Jr 3 Fujiwara no Asomi Matate all appointed Middle Counsellor. Matate was concurrently appointed Head, Ministry of Fidelity.

Sr 4 Upper Fujiwara Emi no Asomi Masaki appointed Governor-General, Kyushu Headquarters.

Also Jr 3 Fujiwara no Asomi Otosada, Jr 4 Lower Fujiwara Emi no Asomi Kusumaro, Fujiwara Emi no Asomi Asakari, Nakatomi no Asomi Kiyomaro, and Ishikawa no Asomi Toyonari all appointed Imperial Advisor.

天平宝字六年（七六二）十二月乙卯【十一】○乙卯。遣高麗大使従五位下高麗朝臣大山贈正五位下。授副使正六位上伊吉連益麻呂外従五位下。判官已下水手已上、各有差。

Tenpyō Hōji 6.12.11 乙卯 *kinoto-u*

[December 30, 762]

The ambassador to Parhae Jr 5 Lower Koma no Asomi Ōyama who died on the return from Parhae was posthumously awarded Sr 5 Lower Rank. The Vice-Envoy Sr 6 Upper Iki no Muraji Masumaro was awarded Outer Jr 5 Lower Rank. All in the embassy from Secretary to sailors were given promotions in rank according to their status.

天平宝字六年（七六二）閏十二月丙子【乙亥朔二】○閏十二月丙子。以中納言従三位氷上真人塩焼。復為兼美作守。

Tenpyō Hōji 6.INT12.2 丙子 *hinoe-ne*

[January 20, 762]

The Middle Counsellor Jr 3 Hikami no Mahito Shioyaki was again concurrently appointed Governor of Mimasaka.

天平宝字六年（七六二）閏十二月丁亥【十三】○丁亥。配乞索児一百人於陸奥国。便即占着。

Tenpyō Hōji 6.INT12.13 丁亥 *hinoto-i*

[January 31, 762]

One hundred beggars were sent to Michinooku, settled and immediately given land.

天平宝字六年（七六二）閏十二月癸巳【十九】○癸巳。高麗使王新福等入京。

Tenpyō Hōji 6.INT12.19 癸巳 *mizunoto-mi*

[February 6, 762]

The Parhae envoy Wang Xinfu and embassy entered Nara.

天平宝字六年（七六二）閏十二月己亥【廿五】○己亥。以従五位上田中朝臣多太麻呂。為陸奥守兼鎮守副将軍。

Tenpyō Hōji 6.INT12.25 己亥 *tsuchinoto-i*

[February 12, 763]

Jr 5 Upper Tanaka no Asomi Tadamaro concurrently appointed as Michinooku Governor and Vice-General for Pacifying *Emishi*.

Tenpyō Hōji 7

天平宝字七年（七六三）正月甲辰朔七年春正月甲辰朔。御大極殿受朝。文武百寮。及高麗蕃客。各依儀拝賀。事畢。授命婦正四位下氷上真人陽侯正四位上。

Tenpyō Hōji 7.1.1 甲辰 Spring *kinoe-tatsu*

[February 17, 763]

The Emperor[397] went to the Imperial Council Hall and held an audience. The hundred civil and military officials and the Parhae guests[398] offered ceremonial

---

[397] Presumably Junnin, who was resident in the *Chūgūin* of the Nara Palace.
[398] 高麗蕃客 literally "barbarian visitors from Koma (Parhae)."

felicitations. This being concluded, the Noblewoman Sr 4 Lower Hikami no Mahito Yako was awarded Sr 4 Upper Rank.

天平宝字七年（七六三）正月丙午【三】〇丙午。高麗使王新福、貢方物。

Tenpyō Hōji 7.1.3 丙午 *hinoe-uma*

[February 19. 763]

The Parhae Ambassador Wang Xinfu presented tribute of products of his land.

天平宝字七年（七六三）正月庚戌【七】〇庚戌。帝御閣門。授高麗大使王新福正三位。副使李能本正四位上。判官楊懐珍正五位上。品官着緋達能信従五位下。余各有差。賜国王及使＝人已上禄亦有差。宴五位已上及蕃客。奏唐楽於庭。賜客主五位已上禄各有差。

Tenpyō Hōji 7.1.7 庚戌 *kanoe-inu*

[February 23, 763]

The *Mikado* Junnin went to the Side Gate and awarded the Parhae Ambassador Wang Xinfu Sr 3 Rank. The Vice-Envoy Li Naiben was awarded Sr 4 Upper Rank. The Secretary Yang Huaijen awarded Sr 5 Upper Rank. The Fifth Rank[399] Da Naishen awarded Jr 5 Lower. Other members of the embassy were awarded rank according to their status. Wang and the subordinates of the embassy were given stipends according to their status. Officials of the fifth rank and up and the Parhae guests were feted at a banquet, and in the garden music of Tang was presented. The members of the embassy of fifth rank and up were given stipends according to status.

---

[399] 品官着緋 SNIII p 417 n 27. Presumably a Parhae rank. Not seen elsewhere in *Shoku Nihongi*. In Japan it denoted the 4ᵗʰ or 5ᵗʰ Rank.

天平宝字七年（七六三）正月壬子【九】○壬子。授従五位下道守王従五位上。無位桑原王。田上王並従五位下。正五位上大和宿禰長岡従四位下。正五位下日下部宿禰子麻呂正五位上。従五位上阿倍朝臣毛人。多治比真人土作並正五位下。従五位下阿倍朝臣御県。布勢朝臣人主並従五位上。従六位上波多朝臣男足。正六位上当麻真人吉嶋。従六位上中臣朝臣宅守。正六位上大伴宿禰小薩。笠朝臣不破麻呂。藤原朝臣継縄。紀朝臣広純。藤原朝臣蔵下麻呂。藤原恵美朝臣執棹並従五位下。正六位上坂合部宿禰斐太麻呂。大友村主広公。村国連子老。浄岡連広嶋。贄土師連沙弥麻呂並外従五位下。無品不破内親王四品。従四位上円方女王正四位上。従四位下秦女王従四位上。無位掃部女王従四位下。無位広河女王。石上朝臣糸手。藤原朝臣乙刀自。藤原朝臣今児。藤原朝臣人数。従六位下大野朝臣中千。県犬養宿禰姉女。外従五位下稲蜂間連仲村女並従五位下。」以従五位下大伴宿禰東人。藤原朝臣蔵下麻呂。並為少納言。外従五位下伊吉連益麻呂為大外記。従四位下中臣朝臣清麻呂為左大弁。従五位上小野朝臣都久良為左中弁。従五位下大原真人今城為左少弁。従五位上粟田朝臣人成為右中弁。従五位下紀朝臣牛養為右少弁。従五位下忌部宿禰鳥麻呂為信部少輔。従五位下県犬養宿禰沙弥麻呂為大監物。従四位下上道朝臣正道為中宮大夫。播磨守如故。従五位下小野朝臣小贄為内蔵助。従五位下伊刀王為縫殿頭。従五位下陽胡毘登玲＝為内匠助。従五位下文室真人高嶋為内礼正。従五位上石上朝臣宅嗣為文部大輔。侍従如故。従五位上藤原朝臣綱麻呂為礼部大輔。侍従如故。従五位下大蔵忌寸麻呂為玄蕃頭。従五位下豊国真人秋篠為雅楽頭。従五位上巨曾倍朝臣難破麻呂為仁部大輔。従五位下阿倍朝臣継人為主税頭。従三位藤原朝臣永手為武部卿。従五位下大伴宿禰小薩為少輔。従五位下田口朝臣大万戸為兵馬正。外従五位下村国連子老為主船正。従五位下藤原朝臣楓麻呂為大判事。外従五位下李忌寸元環為織部正。出雲介如故。外従五位下広田連小床為木工助。従五位下奈紀王為大炊頭。従五位下荻田王為正親正。従五位下当麻真人吉嶋為主油正。従五位下豊野真人尾張為糺政弼。従五位上布勢朝臣人主為右京亮。正五位下市原王為摂津大夫。従四位下佐伯宿禰今毛人為造東大寺長官。従五位上藤原朝臣宿奈麻呂為造宮大輔。上野守如故。従五位下石川朝臣豊人為少輔。従五位下石川朝臣豊麻呂為鋳銭長官。正四位上坂上忌寸犬養為大和守。従五位下阿倍朝臣息道為介。正五位下阿倍朝臣毛人為河内守。従五位下石川朝臣名足為伊勢守。従五位下佐味朝臣宮守為安房守。在唐大使仁部卿正四位下藤原朝臣清河為兼常陸守。従五位上佐伯宿禰美乃麻呂為介。従五位上藤原朝臣田麻呂Ｐ為美濃守。正五位上日下部宿禰子麻呂為上野守。従五位下百済王三忠為出羽守。従五位下高橋朝臣子老為若狭守。従五位下石川朝臣弟人為越後守。正四位下高麗朝臣福信為但馬守。従五位下巨勢朝臣広足為介。従五位下大原真人継麻呂為伯耆守。従五位下阿倍朝臣意宇麻呂為出雲介。外従五位下上毛野公真

248

人為美作介。従五位上甘南備真人伊香為備前守。従五位上道守王為備中守。従五位下小野朝臣石根為長門守。従三位百済王敬福為讃岐守。外従五位下池原公禾守為介。従四位下和気王為伊与守。従五位上中臣丸連張弓為介。従五位下紀朝臣広純為大宰員外少弐。従五位下中臣朝臣鷹主為肥前守。従五位下笠朝臣不破麻呂為日向守。

Tenpyō Hōji 7.1.9 壬子 *mizunoe-ne*

[February 25, 763]

Jr 5 Lower Prince Chimori awarded Jr 5 Upper Rank.

No-rank Prince Kuwahara and Prince Takami awarded Jr 5 Lower Rank.

Sr 5 Upper Yamato no Sukune Nagaoka awarded Jr 4 Lower Rank.

Sr 5 Lower Kusakabe no Sukune Komaro awarded Sr 5 Upper Rank.

Jr 5 Upper Abe no Asomi Emishi and Tajihi no Mahito Hanitsukuri both awarded Sr 5 Lower Rank.

Jr 5 Lower Abe no Asomi Miagata and Fuse no Asomi Hitonushi both awarded Jr 5 Upper Rank.

Jr 6 Upper Hata no Asomi Otari, Sr 6 Upper Tagima no Mahito Yoshishima, Jr 6 Upper Nakatomi no Asomi Yakamori, Sr 6 Upper Ōtomo no Sukune Kosachi, Kasa no Asomi Fuwamaro, Fujiwara no Asomi Tsugutada, Ki no Asomi Hirosumi, Fujiwara no Asomi Kurajimaro, and Fujiwara Emi no Asomi Saotori all awarded Jr 5 Lower Rank.

Sr 6 Upper Sakaibe no Sukune Hidamaro, Ōtomo no Suguri Hirokimi, Muraoka no Muraji Kooyu, Kiyooka no Muraji Hiroshima, and Nienohaji no Muraji Samimaro all awarded Outer Jr 5 Lower Rank.

No-rank Imperial Princess Fuwa awarded 4th Cap Rank.

Jr 4 Upper Princess Matokata awarded Sr 4 Upper Rank.

Jr 4 Lower Princess Hada awarded Jr 4 Upper Rank.

No-rank Princess Kanimori awarded Jr 4 Lower Rank.

No-rank Princess Hirokawa, Isonokami no Asomi Itode, Fujiwara no Asomi Ototoji, Fujiwara no Asomi Imako, Fujiwara no Asomi Hitokazu, Jr 6 Lower Ōno no Asomi Nakachi, Agata Inukai no Sukune Aneme, and Outer Jr 5 Lower Inahachima no Nakamurame all awarded Jr 5 Lower Rank.

Jr 5 Lower Ōtomo no Sukune Azumahito and Fujiwara no Asomi Kurajimaro appointed Minor Counsellor.

Outer Jr 5 Lower Iki no Muraji Masumaro appointed Senior Secretary.

Jr 4 Lower Nakatomi no Asomi Kiyomaro appointed Major Controller of the Left.

Jr 5 Upper Ono no Asomi Tsukura appointed Middle Controller of the Left.

Jr 5 Lower Ōhara no Mahito Imaki appointed Minor Controller of the Left.

Jr 5 Upper Awata no Asomi Hitonari appointed Middle Controller of the Right.

Jr 5 Lower Ki no Asomi Ushikai appointed Minor Controller of the Right.

Jr 5 Lower Imbe no Sukune Torimaro appointed Senior Assistant, Ministry of Fidelity.

Jr 5 Lower Agata Inukai no Sukune Samimaro appointed Senior Inspector.

Jr 4 Lower Kamitsumichi no Asomi Masamichi appointed Master of the Middle Palace, remaining Governor of Harima.

Jr 5 Lower Ono no Asomi Onie appointed Assistant Head, Imperial Storehouse.

Jr 5 Lower Prince Ito appointed Head, Wardrobe Office.

Jr 5 Lower Yako no Hito Ryōgu appointed Assistant Head, Craft Industries.

Jr 5 Lower Fumuya no Mahito Takashima appointed Head, Palace Ceremonies Office.

Jr 5 Upper Isonokami no Asomi Yakatasugu appointed Senior Assistant, Ministry of Civil Affairs, remaining Chamberlain.

Jr 5 Upper Fujiwara no Asomi Nawamaro appointed Senior Assistant, Ministry of Rites, remaining Chamberlain.

Jr 5 Lower Ōkura no Imiki Maro appointed Head, Bureau of Buddhism and Aliens.

Jr 5 Lower Toyokuni no Mahito Akishino appointed Head, Bureau of Music.

Jr 5 Upper Kosobe no Asomi Naniwamaro appointed Senior Assistant, Ministry of Benevolence.

Jr 5 Lower Abe no Asomi Tsugihito appointed Head, Bureau of Taxation.

Jr 3 Fujiwara no Asomi Nagate appointed Head, Ministry of Military Affairs.

Jr 5 Lower Ōtomo no Sukune Kosachi appointed Junior Assistant, Ministry of Military Affairs.

Jr 5 Lower Taguchi no Asomi Ōmato appointed Head of Cavalry.

Outer Jr 5 Lower Murakuni no Muraji Kooyu appointed Head of Shipping.

Jr 5 Lower Fujiwara no Asomi Kaerutemaro appointed Major Judge.

Jr 5 Lower Ri no Imiki Genkai appointed Head, Office of Weaving, remaining Izumo Assistant Governor.

Outer Jr 5 Lower Hirota no Muraji Otoko appointed Assistant Head, Bureau of Carpentry.

Jr 5 Lower Prince Naki appointed Head, Bureau of Palace Kitchen.

Jr 5 Lower Prince Ogita appointed Head, Imperial Family Office.

Jr 5 Lower Tagima no Mahito Yoshishima appointed Head, Oil Office.

Jr 5 Lower Toyono no Mahito Owari appointed Assistant Head, Board of Investigation.

Jr 5 Upper Fuse no Asomi Hitonushi appointed Assistant Commissioner, Right Capital.

Sr 5 Lower Prince Ichihara appointed Settsu Commissioner.

Jr 4 Lower Saeki no Sukune Imaemishi appointed Head, Office of *Tōdaiji* Construction.

Jr 5 Upper Fujiwara no Asomi Sukunamaro appointed Senior Assistant, Office of Palace Construction, remaining Kōzuke Governor.

Jr 5 Lower Ishikawa no Asomi Toyohito appointed Junior Assistant, Office of Palace Construction.

Jr 5 Lower Ishikawa no Asomi Toyomaro appointed Director of the Mint.

Sr 4 Upper Sakanoue no Imiki Inukai appointed Yamato Governor.

Jr 5 Lower Abe no Asomi Okimichi appointed Yamato Assistant Governor.

Sr 5 Lower Abe no Asomi Emishi appointed Kawachi Governor.

Jr 5 Lower Ishikawa no Asomi Natari appointed Ise Governor.

Jr 5 Lower Sami no Asomi Miyamori appointed Awa Governor.

The Ambassador to Tang and Head, Ministry of Benevolence Sr 4 Lower Fujiwara no Asomi Kiyokawa, resident in Tang, appointed concurrently Hitachi Governor.

Jr 5 Upper Saeki no Sukune Minomaro appointed Hitachi Assistant Governor.

Jr 5 Upper Fujiwara no Asomi Tamaro appointed Mino Governor.

Sr 5 Lower Kusakabe no Sukune Komaro appointed Shimotsuke Governor.

Jr 5 Lower Kudara no Konikishi Sanchū appointed Dewa Governor.

Jr 5 Lower Takahashi no Asomi Kooyu appointed Wakasa Governor.

Jr 5 Lower Ishikawa no Asomi Otohito appointed Echigo Governor.

Sr 4 Lower Koma no Asomi Fukushin appointed Tajima Governor.

Jr 5 Lower Kose no Asomi Hirotari appointed Tajima Assistant Governor.

Jr 5 Lower Ōhara no Mahito Tsugimaro appointed Hōki Governor.

Jr 5 Lower Abe no Asomi Oumaro appointed Izumo Assistant Governor.

Outer Jr 5 Lower Kamitsukeno no Kimi Mahito appointed Mimasaka Assistant Governor.

Jr 5 Upper Kannabi no Mahito Ikago appointed Bizen Governor.

Jr 5 Upper Prince Chimori appointed Bitchū Governor.

Jr 5 Lower Ono no Asomi Iwane appointed Nagato Governor.

Jr 3 Kudara no Konikishi Kyōfuku appointed Sanuki Governor.

Outer Jr 5 Lower Ikehara no Kimi Awamori appointed Sanuki Assistant Governor.

Jr 4 Lower Prince Wake appointed Iyo Governor.

Jr 5 Upper Nakatomi Wani no Muraji Yumihari appointed Iyo Assistant Governor.

Jr 5 Lower Ki no Asomi Hirozumi appointed Junior Assistant Governor-General, Kyushu Headquarters.

Jr 5 Lower Nakatomi no Asomi Takanushi appointed Hizen Governor.

Jr 5 Lower Kasa no Asomi Fuwamaro appointed Hyūga Governor.

天平宝字七年（七六三）正月戊午【十五】○戊午。詔曰。如聞。去天平宝字五年。五穀不登。飢斃者衆。宜其五年以前公私債負。貧窮不堪備償公物者。咸従原免。私物者除利収本。又役使造宮。左右京。五畿内及近江国兵士等。宝字六年田租並免之。

Tenpyō Hōji **7.1.15** 戊午 *tsuchinoe-uma*

[March 3, 763]

The Emperor gave an edict:

"We have heard that in TPHJ 5 the five grains did not flourish and many people died of starvation. Thus as for public and private debt incurred from up to five years ago, the public debt which poor people have been unable to pay is completely forgiven. The interest on private debt is forgiven and only the principal shall be collected. Further, the workers and soldiers employed on construction projects in the Left and Right Capital, the *Kinai*, and in Ōmi province[400], are exempted rice tax for TPHJ 6."

天平宝字七年（七六三）正月庚申【十七】○庚申。帝御閣門。饗五位已上及蕃客。文武百官主典已上於朝堂。作唐・吐羅。林邑。東国。隼人等楽。奏内教坊踏歌。客主主典已上次之。賜供奉踏歌百官人及高麗蕃客綿有差。」高麗大使王新福言。李家太上皇・少帝、並崩。広平王摂政。年穀不登。人民相食。史家朝議。称聖武皇帝。性有仁恕。人物多附。兵鋒甚強。無敢当者。＝州・襄陽已属史家。李家独有蘇州。朝聘之路。固未易通。於是。勅大宰府曰。唐国荒乱。両家争雄。平殄未期。使命難通。其沈惟岳等。宜往往安置優厚供給。其時服者、並以府庫物給。如懐土情深。猶願帰郷者。宜給駕船、水手。量事発遣。

Tenpyō Hōji 7.1.17 庚申 *kanoe-saru*

[March 5, 763]

The *Mikado* Junnin went to the Side Gate and gave a banquet for officials of fifth rank and up, the Parhae guests, and the hundred civil and military officials from Clerk and up in the Administrative Palace. Music of Tang, Tora[401], Rinyū,[402] the Eastern provinces, and the Hayato was played. Music and stomping dance by the Palace Music School were performed. The guests and the major officials from Clerk on up also danced. The Emperor awarded floss

---

[400] Construction work on the Hora Capital in Ōmi Province.
[401] 吐羅 SNIII p 424 n 21 – perhaps Tokara 吐火羅 in Central Asia. See Waterhouse1991, Where did *Toragaku* come from?
[402] 林邑 Vietnam.

silk to the Hundred Officials and the Parhae guests who presented dances according to their status.

The Parhae Ambassador Wang Xinfu reported:

"The Tang Retired Emperor Xuanzong and the lesser Emperor Suzong both died. Afterwards Guang Ping Wang[403] took power as regent, but the five grains did not flourish and the people were so hungry they preyed upon one another. Chao Yi of the Shi house[404] took power and styled himself the Shengwu Emperor.[405] His nature was benevolent and magnanimous and many people followed him. The military's power was very strong and none dared challenge them. Deng province and Xiangyang[406] have submitted to the Shi house, and only Su province remains under the Li. Thus the roads to the capital are at present difficult to navigate."

After hearing the Parhae envoy's report, the Emperor sent an edict to the Kyushu Headquarters:

"Tang at present is desolate and chaotic. The two houses, Li and Shi are battling with each other, peace is not expected, and it is difficult for our envoys to get to Tang. Therefore the envoy Chen Weiyue and company shall remain at Kyushu Headquarters for the time being and provisions should be granted. Seasonal

---

[403] 広平王 SNIII p 425 n 33 was the 8th Tang emperor (r 762-779) Li Yu (李豫) or Daizong of Tang (唐代宗).
[404] Son of Shi Shiming.
[405] 聖武皇帝
[406] SNIII p 427 notes 2 and 3 for these Chinese place names.

clothing is to be supplied from the Headquarter's stores. If there are those of the Chinese embassy who have a deep longing for their homeland and wish to return, ships and sailors should be supplied and their needs met."

天平宝字七年（七六三）正月甲子【廿一】○甲子。內射。蕃客堪射者亦預於列。

Tenpyō Hōji 7.1.21 甲子 *kinoe-ne*

[March 9, 763]

An archery match was held. Archers from among the Parhae guests also participated.

天平宝字七年卷（七六三）二月丁丑【甲戌朔四】○二月丁丑。太師藤原惠美朝臣押勝、設宴於高麗客。詔遣使賜以雜色袷衣卅櫃。

Tenpyō Hōji 7.2.4 丁丑 *hinoto-ushi*

[March 22, 763]

The Grand Preceptor Fujiwara Emi no Asomi Oshikatsu gave a banquet for the Parhae envoys. The Emperor gave an edict sending a messenger to present thirty chests of colored silk.

天平宝字七年（七六三）二月癸未【十】○癸未。新羅国遣級＝［氵＋食］金体信已下二百十一人朝貢。遣左少弁従五位下大原真人今城。讃岐介外従五位下池原公禾守等。問以約束貞巻之旨。体信言曰。承国王之教。唯調是貢。至于余事、非敢所知。於是。今城告曰。乾政官処分。此行使人者喚入京都。如常可遇。而使等約束貞巻之旨。曾無所申。仍称。但齎常貢入朝。自外非所知者。是乃為使之人非所宜言。自今以後。非王子者。令執政大夫等入朝。宜以此状告汝国王知。

Tenpyō Hōji 7.2.10 癸未 *mizunoto-hitsuji*

[March 28, 763]

Silla sent Ninth Rank Kim Chesin and twenty-one lower officials to present tribute. The court dispatched the Minor Controller of the Left Jr 5 Lower Ōhara no Mahito Imaki and the Sanuki Assistant Governor Outer Jr 5 Lower Ikehara no Kimi Awamori to inquire about the promise made earlier by Kim Jeonggwon.[407] Kim Chesin replied "I have received the King's instructions to bring tribute, and nothing further. Other than that I know nothing."

Therefore Imaki announced:

'The Heavenly Council of State has decided: 'The envoy this time is invited to enter the capital and to conduct himself according to precedent. However, the envoy knows nothing of Kim Jeonggwon's promise. He says that he comes only to present tribute to the court according to precedent, and knows nothing besides. Therefore he may not speak as an envoy. Henceforth only the King or Prince or high officials of Silla may come to court. He is to report this matter to the King of his country.'

天平宝字七年（七六三）二月癸巳【二十】〇癸巳。高麗使王新福等帰蕃。

Tenpyō Hōji 7.2.20 癸巳 *mizunoto-mi*
[April 7, 763]

The Parhae envoy Wang Xinfu returned home.

天平宝字七年（七六三）二月壬寅【廿九】〇壬寅。出羽国飢。賑給之。

---

[407] See TPHJ 4.9.16. Kim Jeonggwon came to present tribute, but was not allowed to enter the capital.

Tenpyō Hōji 7.2.29　壬寅 *mizunoe-tora*

[April 16, 763]

Famine in Dewa Province. Relief supplies granted.

天平宝字七年巻（七六三）三月丁卯【甲辰朔廿四】○三月丁卯。令天下諸国進不動倉鉤匙。以国司交替因茲多煩也。其随事修造。及似欲湿損。臨時請受。

Tenpyō Hōji 7.3.24　丁卯　*hinoto-u*

[May 11, 763]

The various provinces of the empire were commanded to forward to the capital the keys to the ever-normal granaries. This was because of problems with frequent changeover of the provincial governors. Whenever it is necessary to repair damage or if loss is suffered due to moisture, officials may request the keys on a temporary basis.

天平宝字七年巻（七六三）四月甲戌朔○夏四月甲戌朔。信濃国飢。賑給之。」京師米貴。糶左右京穀。以平穀価。

Tenpyō Hōji 7.4.1　甲戌　**Summer** *kinoe-inu*

[May 18,763]

Famine in Shinano Province. Relief supplies granted.

In the capital the price of rice rose. Rice was sold in the Left and Right Capital to stabilize the prices.

天平宝字七年（七六三）四月癸未【十】○癸未。壱岐嶋疫。賑給之。

Tenpyō Hōji 7.4.10　癸未　*mizunoto-hitsuji*

[May 27, 763]

Epidemic in Ikishima. Relief supplies granted.

天平宝字七年（七六三）四月丙戌【十三】○丙戌。陸奥国飢。賑給之。

Tenpyō Hōji 7.4.13 丙戌 *hinoe-inu*

[May 30, 763]

Famine in Michinooku Province. Relief supplies granted.

天平宝字七年（七六三）四月丁亥【十四】○丁亥。以従五位下石上朝臣
奥継為少納言。従五位下池田朝臣足継為左少弁。従五位上石川朝臣人成
為信部大輔。従五位上布勢朝臣人主為文部大輔。従五位下榎井朝臣小祖
父為仁部少輔。従五位上阿倍朝臣御県為武部大輔。従五位下当麻真人高
庭為鼓吹正。従五位下藤原朝臣浜足為節部大輔。従五位下藤原朝臣雄田
麻呂為智部少輔。従五位下豊野真人篠原為大膳亮。左大弁従四位下中臣
朝臣清麻呂為兼摂津大夫。従五位下石川朝臣豊人為造宮大輔。従五位下
小野朝臣小贄為少輔。正五位下市原王為造東大寺長官。外従五位下山田
連銀為河内介。従五位下津連秋主為尾張介。正五位下阿倍朝臣子嶋為上
総守。従五位下大原真人今城為上野守。参議従四位下藤原恵美朝臣久須
麻呂為兼丹波守。左右京尹如故。外従五位下村国連武志麻呂為播磨介。
従五位下当生王為阿波守。従五位下笠朝臣不破麻呂為豊後守。外従五位
下陽胡毘登玲珍為日向守。

Tenpyō Hōji 7.4.14 丁亥 *hinoto-i*

[May 31, 763]

Jr 5 Lower Isonokami no Asomi Okitsugi appointed Minor Counsellor.

Jr 5 Lower Ikeda no Asomi Taritsugu appointed Minor Controller of the Left.

Jr 5 Upper Ishikawa no Asomi Hitonari appointed Senior Assistant, Ministry of Fidelity.

Jr 5 Upper Fuse no Asomi Hitonushi appointed Senior Assistant, Ministry of Civil Affairs.

Jr 5 Lower Enoi no Asomi Kohoji appointed Junior Assistant, Ministry of Benevolence.

Jr 5 Upper Abe no Asomi Miagata appointed Senior Assistant, Ministry of Military Affairs.

Jr 5 Lower Tagima no Mahito Takaniwa appointed Head, Office of Drums and Fifes.

Jr 5 Lower Fujiwara no Asomi Hamatari appointed Senior Assistant, Ministry of Moderation.

Jr 5 Lower Fujiwara no Asomi Odamaro appointed Junior Assistant, Ministry of Wisdom.

Jr 5 Lower Toyono no Mahito Shinohara appointed Assistant Head, Office of the Palace Table.

Sadaiben Jr 4 Lower Nakatomi no Asomi Kiyomaro concurrently appointed Settsu Commissioner.

Jr 5 Lower Ishikawa no Asomi Toyohito appointed Senior Assistant, Office of Palace Construction.

Jr 5 Lower Ono no Asomi Onie appointed Junior Assistant, Office of Palace Construction.

Sr 5 Lower Prince Ichihara appointed Head, Office of *Tōdaiji* Construction.

Outer Jr 5 Lower Yamada no Muraji Shirokane appointed Kawachi Assistant Governor.

Jr 5 Lower Tsu no Muraji Akinushi appointed Owari Assistant Governor.

Sr 5 Lower Abe no Asomi Kojima appointed Kazusa Governor.

Jr 5 Lower Ōhara no Mahito Imaki appointed Kōzuke Governor.

Sangi Jr 4 Lower Fujiwara Emi no Asomi Kusumaro appointed Tanba Governor and remains as Head Commissioner, Left and Right Capital.

Outer Jr 5 Lower Murakuni no Muraji Mushimaro appointed Harima Assistant Governor.

Jr 5 Lower Prince Sugafu appointed Awa Governor.

Jr 5 Lower Kasa no Asomi Fuwamaro appointed Bungo Governor.

Outer Jr 5 Lower Yakonohito no Ryōchin appointed Hyūga Governor.

天平宝字七年巻（七六三）五月戊申【癸卯朔六】〇五月戊申。大和上鑑真物化。和上者楊州竜興寺之大徳也。博渉経論。尤精戒律。江淮之間、独為化主。天宝二載。留学僧栄叡・業行等、白和上曰。仏法東流、至於本国。雖有其教、無人伝授。幸願。和上東遊興化。辞旨懇至。諮請不息。乃於楊州買船入海。而中途風漂。船被打破。和上一心念仏。人皆頼之免死。至於七載、更復渡海。亦遭風浪、漂着日南。時栄叡物故。和上悲泣失明。勝宝四年。本国使適聘于唐。業行乃説以宿心。遂与弟子廿四人。寄乗副使大伴宿禰古麻呂船帰朝。於東大寺安置供養。于時有勅。校正一切経論。往往誤字諸本皆同。莫之能正。和上諳誦、多下雌黄。又以諸薬物令名真偽。和上一一以鼻別之。一無錯失。聖武皇帝師之受戒焉。及皇太后不＝。所進医薬有験。授位大僧正。俄以綱務煩雑。改授大和上之号。

施以備前国水田一百町。又施新田部親王之旧宅、以為戒院。今招提寺是
也。和上預記終日。至期端坐。怡然遷化。時年七十有七。

Tenpyō Hōji 7.5.6 戊申 tsuchinoe-saru

[June 21, 763]

The Great Esteemed Monk[408] Ganjin passed away. He was an eminent monk of Longxingsi in Yang Prefecture in Tang. He read widely in sutras and their commentaries, and was deeply versed in the precepts and *vinaya*. He was known as the sole authority between the Yangzi and Huai Rivers. In *Tianbao* 2 (*Tenpyō* 15), the foreign student priests Yōei and Gyogyō said the following to him. "The Buddhist law has spread to the east and has been transmitted to our country. But although the teaching exists in our land there is no-one who can properly transmit the ordination. We hope and pray that the Esteemed Monk would travel east to our land and prosper the teaching. He warmly received these words of supplication and inquired of us without resting. He bought a ship in Yang Prefecture and took to the sea. However, on the way he was blown off course by the wind, and his ship was broken up by the waves. Ganjin earnestly beseeched the Buddha, as did the people with him, and they were spared death. In *Tianbao* 7 (*Tenpyō* 20) he again tried to cross the sea, but once again was blown off course by wind and waves and landed in Rinan[409]. At this time Yōei died. Ganjin wept and grieved, and lost his sight. In TPSH 4 an envoy from our country happened to visit Tang. He encountered Gyōgyō, who explained matters.

---

[408] 大和上
[409] SNIII p 431 n 26 – Northern Vietnam.

Ganjin with twenty-four disciples took ship with the Vice-Envoy Ōtomo no Sukune Komaro and returned with him to our country. The court settled Ganjin in the *Tōdaiji* to serve there. At this time the Emperor Shōmu gave an edict to have him examine the whole of the *Issaikyō*, sutras and commentaries, and to correct the numerous errors. Ganjin compared many texts and rectified the whole. The Esteemed Monk recited from memory and gave corrections. He also tested different medicines, using his acute sense of smell to distinguish their accuracy. Emperor Shōmu accepted him as master, and received the precepts from him. When the Dowager Empress Kōmyō became ill, Ganjin prepared medicines, testing their efficacy. The Emperor bestowed on him the rank of Great Chief Abbot. Soon, because of the complexity of the work of the Council of Buddhist Priestly Affairs, he was given the title of Great Esteemed Monk. The Emperor donated one hundred hectares of paddy in Bizen for his support. He was given the mansion of the late Imperial Prince Niitabe[410] as the Precepts Hall. This is the current *Shōdaiji*. He foretold in advance the day of his death. In a posture of seated meditation he joyfully passed from this world. At the time he was 77 years old.

天平宝字七年（七六三）五月癸丑【十一】〇癸丑。伊賀国疫。賑給之。

Tenpyō Hōji 7.5.11 癸丑 *mizunoto-ushi*

[June 26, 763]

Epidemic in Iga Province. Relief supplies granted.

---

[410] Tenmu's son; died in *Tenpyō* 7.9.

265

天平宝字七年（七六三）五月戊午【十六】○戊午。河内国飢。賑給之。

Tenpyō Hōji 7.5.16 戊午 *tsuchinoe-uma*

[July 1, 763]

Famine in Kawachi province. Relief supplies granted.

天平宝字七年（七六三）五月己巳【廿七】○己巳。義部卿従四位下安都王卒。

Tenpyō Hōji 7.5.27 己巳 *tsuchinoto-mi*

[July 12, 763]

The Head of the Ministry of Righteousness Jr 4 Lower Prince Ato died.

天平宝字七年（七六三）五月庚午【廿八】○庚午。奉幣帛于四畿内群神。其丹生河上神者加黒毛馬。旱也。

Tenpyō Hōji 7.5.28 庚午 *kanoe-uma*

[July 13, 763]

The court sent *mitegura* to the *kami* of the four provinces of *Kinai*. Among them the *Nifukawakami Kami* in Yoshino was sent black horses in addition to the *mitegura*. This was because of the drought.

天平宝字七年巻（七六三）六月戊寅【壬申朔七】○六月戊寅。尾張国飢。賑給之。

Tenpyō Hōji 7.6.7 戊寅 *tsuchinoe-tora*

[July 21, 763]

Famine in Owari Province. Relief supplies granted.

天平宝字七年（七六三）六月丙戌【十五】○丙戌。越前国飢。賑給之。

Tenpyō Hōji 7.6.15 丙戌 *hinoe-inu*

[July 29, 763]

Famine in Echizen Province. Relief supplies granted.

天平宝字七年（七六三）六月壬辰【廿一】○壬辰。能登国飢。賑給之。

Tenpyō Hōji 7.6.21 壬辰 *mizunoe-tatsu*

[August 4, 763]

Famine in Noto Province. Relief supplies granted.

天平宝字七年（七六三）六月丙申【廿五】○丙申。大和国飢。賑給之。

Tenpyō Hōji 7.6.25 丙申 *hinoe-saru*

[August 8, 763]

Famine in Yamato Province. Relief supplies granted.

天平宝字七年（七六三）六月戊戌【廿七】○戊戌。美濃国飢。摂津。山
背二国疫。並賑給之。

Tenpyō Hōji 7.6.27 戊戌 *tsuchinoe-inu*

[August 10, 763]

Famine in Mino Province. Epidemic in Settsu and Yamashiro Provinces. Relief

supplies granted.

天平宝字七年巻（七六三）七月乙卯【壬寅朔十四】○秋七月乙卯。以従
五位下大伴宿禰田麻呂為参河守。従五位上高元度為左平準令。従五位上
藤原朝臣田麻呂為陸奥出羽按察使。外従五位下高松連笠麻呂為日向守。
従五位下忌部宿禰告麻呂為斎宮頭。

Tenpyō Hōji 7.7.14 乙卯 Autumn *kinoto-u*

[August 27, 763]

Jr 5 Lower Ōtomo no Sukune Tamaro appointed Mikawa Governor.

Jr 5 Upper Kō no Gendo appointed Head of the Left Ever-Normal Granaries.

Jr 5 Upper Fujiwara no Asomi Tamaro appointed Michinooku and Dewa Regional Inspector.

Outer Jr 5 Lower Takamatsu no Muraji Kasamaro appointed Hyuga Governor.

Jr 5 Lower Inbe no Sukune Azamaro appointed Head, Office of Ise Princess.

天平宝字七年（七六三）七月丁卯【廿六】○丁卯。備前。阿波二国飢。並賑給之。

Tenpyō Hōji 7.7.26 丁卯 *hinoto-u*

[September 8, 763]

Famine in Bizen and Awa Provinces. Relief supplies granted.

天平宝字七年巻（七六三）八月辛未朔○八月辛未朔。勅曰。如聞。去歳霖雨。今年亢旱。五穀不熟。米価踊貴。由是、百姓稍苦飢饉。加以、疾疫。死亡数多。朕毎念茲。情深傷惻。宜免左右京。五畿内。七道諸国今年田租。

Tenpyō Hōji 7.8.1 辛未 kanoto-hitsuji

[September 12, 763]

The Emperor gave an edict:

"We have heard that in past years abundant rains fell, but this year the drought continues, the five grains do not ripen, and the price of rice has increased. Thus the people have already suffered from famine. In addition epidemic has spread and many people have died. Whenever we consider this our heart is full of deep grief and sadness. We remit rice filed tax this year for the Left and Right Capital, the *Kinai*, and the provinces of the seven circuits."

天平宝字七年（七六三）八月壬申【二】〇壬申。近江。備中。備後三国飢。並賑給之。

Tenpyō Hōji 7.8.2 壬申 *mizunoe-saru*

[September 13, 763]

Famine in the three provinces of Ōmi, Bitchū, and Bingo. Relief supplies granted.

天平宝字七年（七六三）八月壬午【十二】〇壬午。初遣高麗国船。名曰能登。帰朝之日。風波暴急。漂蕩海中。祈曰。幸頼船霊。平安到国。必請朝庭。酬以錦冠。至是、縁於宿祷。授従五位下。其冠製、錦表＝［糸＋施の旁］裏。以紫組為纓。

Tenpyō Hōji 7.8.12 壬午 *mizunoe-uma*

[September 23, 763]

The first ship that the court dispatched to Parhae was named "Noto". On the day of its return the winds and waves were violent and wild, and the ship was adrift on the sea. Then the people on the ship prayed:

"If due to the lucky numinous spirit of this ship we reach home without incident, we shall certainly beg the court to grant the ship a braided cap as a reward."

Since the ship reached home without incident, on this day, according to the promise of the prayer, the court granted the ship Jr 5 Lower Rank. The cap was brocade on one side and coarse silk on the other, with purple chin strap.

天平宝字七年（七六三）八月甲申【十四】〇甲申。丹波。伊予二国飢。並賑給之。

Tenpyō Hōji 7.8.14 甲申 *kinoe-saru*

[September 25, 763]

Famine in Tanba and Iyo Provinces. Relief supplies granted.

天平宝字七年（七六三）八月戊子【十八】○戊子。山陽。南海等道諸国旱。停両道節度使。」廃儀鳳暦、始用大衍暦。」丹後国飢。賑給之。

Tenpyō Hōji 7.8.18 戊子 *tsuchinoe-ne*

[September 29, 763]

Drought in the provinces of *Sanyōdō* and *Nankaidō*. The office of Military Instructor in those provinces was abolished.

The court discontinued the *Yifeng* calendar. For the first time it adopted the *Dayan* Calendar.[411]

Famine in Tango Province. Relief supplies granted.

天平宝字七年（七六三）八月己丑【十九】○己丑。糺政台尹三品池田親王上表曰。臣男女五人。其母出自凶族。臣悪其逆党、不預王籍。然今日月稍邁。聖沢頻流。当是時也。不為処置。恐聖化之内。有失所之民。伏乞。賜姓御長真人。永為海内一族。詔許之。

Tenpyō Hōji 7.8.19 己丑 *tsuchinoto-ushi*

[September 30, 763]

The Head of the Board of InvestigationThird Cap Imperial Prince Ikeda petitioned:

---

[411]儀鳳暦, 大衍暦SNIII p 436, n 2-3. The *Yifeng* 儀鳳 calendar devised by Li Chungeng 季淳風 was used in Tang from *Linde* 2 (665) until *Kaiyuan* 16 (728). The term 儀鳳 is not found in Chinese records, where it is referred to as the Linde 麟徳 calendar. Apparently transmitted from Tang via Silla in the *Yifeng* era (676-679). The *Dayan* 大衍 calendar was devised by the monk Yizing 一行 and used from *Kaiyuan* 17 (729) to *Guangde* 1 (763). It is thought to have been brought from Tang by Kibi Makibi in *Tenpyō* 7.4. It is mentioned in the curriculum of 757. It is unclear why it was apparently not formally adopted until now.

"The mother of my five male and female children was of the same family as the evil conspirator Tachibana no Naramaro.[412] Your subject despised the fact that he was a treasonous villain and so removed the children from the imperial register. However now months and days have passed and the imperial grace has spread widely. There are those who lost their places at that time due to the terrible imperial punishment and now have no standing in the registers. Now I humbly beg that the five children be granted the *kabane* of Minaga no Mahito and having standing forever as a family within the seas."[413]

The Emperor gave an edict permitting this.

天平宝字七年（七六三）八月癸巳【廿三】○癸巳。遣使覆損於阿波。讃岐両国。便即賑給飢民。

Tenpyō Hōji 7.8.23 癸巳 *mizunoto-mi*

[October 4, 763]

Messengers were dispatched to carefully investigate the damage in Awa and Sanuki Provinces, and to grant relief to the sufferers from famine.

天平宝字七年（七六三）八月甲午【廿四】○甲午。新羅人中衛少初位下新良木舎姓前麻呂等六人、賜姓清住造。漢人伯徳広道姓雲梯連。

Tenpyō Hōji 7.8.24 甲午 *kinoe-uma*

[October 5, 763]

The Silla person Middle Imperial Guard *Shōso* Rank Lower Shiraki no Sasei Maemaro and others, six in all, were granted the *kabane* of Kiyozumi no

---

[412] SNIII p 437 n 6 -- not clear what the woman's relationship to Naramaro was.
[413] 海内- Japan

271

Miyatsuko. The Aya person Hakatoko no Kōdō was granted the *kabane* of Unade no Muraji.

天平宝字七年巻（七六三）九月庚子朔○九月庚子朔。勅曰。疫死多数。水旱不時。神火屢至。徒損官物。此者。国郡司等不恭於国神之咎也。又一旬亢旱。致無水苦。数日霖雨。抱流亡嗟。此者、国郡司等使民失時。不修堤堰之過也。自今以後。若有此色。自目已上宜悉遷替。不須久居労擾百姓。更簡良材速可登用。遂使拙者帰田。賢者在官。各修其職、務無民憂。

Tenpyō Hōji 7.9.1 庚子 *kanoe-ne*

[October 11, 763]

The Emperor gave an edict:

"Recently a large number of people have died from epidemic disease, and floods and droughts have occurred unexpectedly. In addition 'divine fires'[414] have broken out and damaged government property. This is the fault of the provincial and district officials for not reverently serving the *kami* of the provinces. Further, there have been ten-day periods of drought, and the people suffer from a lack of water. Then there are periods of downpours, and some people have now suffered from erosion. This is due to the errors of the provincial and district officials who have not employed the people in a timely fashion, and have not repaired the dikes and embankments. From now on if there are such occurrences, the district officials from Clerk on up shall be recalled and changed. They must not stay overlong in their posts and cause the people to be fatigued and troubled.

---

[414] *ayashikihi* 神火 SNIII p 437 n 18 – this is the first appearance of the term. A lengthy endnote pp 580-582, with chart, says that these become frequent from late Nara into the 10th century.

Talented personnel must be speedily chosen and employed. Stupid people should be returned to labor in the fields. Wise men should be appointed to office who will work hard at their duties and tend to the suffering of the people."

天平宝字七年（七六三）九月癸卯【四】○癸卯。遣使於山階寺。宣詔曰。少僧都慈訓法師。行政乖理。不堪為綱。宜停其任。依衆所議。以道鏡法師為少僧都。

Tenpyō Hōji 7.9.4 癸卯 *mizunoto-u*

[October 14, 763]

The Empress[415] sent messengers to *Yamashinadera*. They pronounced her edict as follows:

"The Junior Assistant Abbot and Priest Jikin has not been properly carrying out his duties in clerical administration. His appointment shall be terminated. According to the deliberation of the monks, the Priest Dōkyō should be appointed as Junior Assistant Abbot."

天平宝字七年（七六三）九月甲寅【十五】○甲寅。以從五位下奈紀王為石見守。從五位下采女朝臣浄庭為豊後守。

Tenpyō Hōji 7.9.15 甲寅 *kinoe-tora*

[October 25, 763]

Jr 5 Lower Prince Naki appointed Iwami Governor. Jr 5 Lower Uneme no Asomi Kiyoniwa appointed Bungo Governor.

---

[415] Retired Empress Kōken is not specified, but this is the first mention of Dōkyō and his first appointment to office.

天平宝字七年（七六三）九月庚申【廿一】〇庚申。尾張。美濃。但馬。伯耆。出雲。石見等六国年穀不稔。並遣使覆損。」河内国丹比郡人尋来津公関麻呂坐殺母。配出羽国小勝柵戸。

Tenpyō Hōji 7.9.21 庚申 *kanoe-saru*

[October 31, 763]

In the six provinces of Owari, Mino, Tajima, Hōki, Izumo and Iwami the crops did not ripen this year. Messengers were sent to investigate the damage.

In Tajihi district of Kawachi, a man named Hiroki no Tsunokimi Sekimaro was charged with the crime of killing his mother. He was exiled to Fort Okachi in Dewa Province.

天平宝字七年（七六三）九月丙寅【廿七】〇丙寅。授従五位上山村王正五位下。従四位下池上女王正四位下。

Tenpyō Hōji 7.9.27 丙寅 *hinoe-tora*

[November 6, 763]

Jr 5 Upper Prince Yamamura awarded Sr 5 Lower Rank.

Jr 4 Lower Princess Ikegami awarded Sr 4 Lower Rank.

天平宝字七年巻（七六三）十月癸酉【庚午朔四】〇冬十月癸酉。幸山背国。授介外従五位下坂上忌寸老人外従五位上。従五位下稲蜂間連仲村女従五位上。

Tenpyō Hōji 7.10.4 癸酉 **Winter** *mizunoto-tori*

[November 13, 763]

The Emperor visited Yamashiro Province.

The Yamashiro Assistant Governor Outer Jr 5 Lower Sakanoue no Imiki Okina awarded Outer Jr 5 Upper Rank.

Jr 5 Lower Inahachima no Muraji Nakamurame awarded Jr 5 Upper Rank.

天平宝字七年（七六三）十月乙亥【六】○乙亥。左兵衛正七位下板振鎌束至自渤海。以擲人於海。勘当下獄。八年之乱。獄囚充満。因其居住移於近江。初王新福之帰本蕃也。駕船爛脆。送使判官平群虫麻呂等慮其不完。申官求留。於是。史生已上皆停其行。以修理船。使鎌束便為船師。送新福等発遣。事畢帰日。我学生高内弓。其妻高氏。及男広成。緑児一人。乳母一人。并入唐学問僧戒融。優婆塞一人。転自渤海相随帰朝。海中遭風、所向迷方。柁師・水手為波所没。于時鎌束議曰。異方婦女今在船上。又此優婆塞異於衆人。一食数粒。経日不飢。風漂之災、未必不由此也。乃使水手撮内弓妻并緑児・乳母・優婆塞四人。挙而擲海。風勢猶猛。漂流十余日。着隠岐国。

Tenpyō Hōji 7.10.6 乙亥 *kinoto-tatsu*

[November 15, 763]

Head of the Left Military Guards Sr 7 Lower Itafuri Kamatsuka, when he was returning from Parhae, threw some people into the ocean. He was arrested and investigated and placed in jail. In the rebellion of the 8th year[416] the jail was full and he was moved to Ōmi to reside.

Earlier when the Parhae envoy Wang Xinfu returned home, the ship in which he was to travel rotted and became fragile. The accompanying envoy, the Secretary Heguri no Mushimaro and others were anxious about the defects and they begged the officials to delay for a while. Then the lower-level clerks on up remained on board while repairs were made. They appointed Kamatsuka captain and departed again with Xinfu. When they had finished their mission and were about to return there was a Japanese overseas student named Kō Naikyū and his wife Kōshi, and their son Hironari with infants and a wet nurse. There was also

---

[416] *Tenpyō Hōji* 8, rebellion of Fujiwara Nakamaro. An unusual case of the chronicle referring to future events.

the Buddhist priest Kaiyū who had studied in China and a lay Buddhist disciple who had come via Parhae and were returning to Japan. On the open sea there were violent winds and they lost their way. The helmsman and some sailors were washed overboard. At this point Kamatsuka argued "There are foreign women riding on the ship. There is also a lay disciple, who does not belong to the company of monks. Even though they eat a meal of only a few grains of rice, as the days go on they do not starve. The cause of this foul weather must be the presence of these people." So he gave orders to the sailors to seize and throw overboard Naikyū's wife, infants, and wet nurse, and the lay disciple. The strong and ferocious winds continued. They drifted for about ten days, then landed on Oki Island.

天平宝字七年（七六三）十月丙戌【十七】○丙戌。参議礼部卿従三位藤原朝臣弟貞薨。弟貞者、平城朝左大臣正二位長屋王子也。天平元年、長屋王有罪自尽。其男従四位下膳夫王。無位桑田王。葛木王。鉤取王、亦皆自経。時安宿王。黄文王。山背王。并女教勝。復合従坐。以藤原太政大臣之女所生。特賜不死。勝宝八歳。安宿。黄文謀反。山背王陰上其変。高野天皇嘉之。賜姓藤原。名曰弟貞。

Tenpyō Hōji 7.10.17 丙戌 *hinoe-inu*

[November 26, 763]

The Imperial Advisor and Head of the Ministry of Rites Jr 3 Fujiwara no Asomi Otosada died. He was the son of Great Minister of the Left Sr 2 Prince Nagaya who served at the court of Emperor Shōmu. In *Tenpyō* 1 Prince Nagaya committed a crime and killed himself. His sons Jr 4 Lower Prince Kashiwade, Unranked Prince Kuwata, Prince Katsuragi, and Prince Kagitori all hanged themselves. At that time Prince Asukabe, Prince Kibumi, Prince Yamashiro and the woman Kyōshō were also implicated in the crime.[417] However, since she was daughter of the the First Minister, Great Council of State Fujiwara Fuhito's daughter, they were spared. In TPSH 8, when Prince Asukabe and Prince Kibumi plotted treason[418] Prince Yamashiro secretly reported the plot. The Takano Empress rewarded him and gave him the surname Fujiwara and the name Otosada.

天平宝字七年（七六三）十月乙未【廿六】○乙未。淡路国飢。賑給之。

Tenpyō Hōji 7.10.26 乙未 *kinoto-hitsuji*

[December 5, 763]

Famine in Awaji Province. Relief supplies granted.

天平宝字七年（七六三）十月丁酉【廿八】○丁酉。前監物主典従七位上高田毘登足人之祖父、嘗任美濃国主稲。属壬申兵乱。以私馬奉皇駕中美濃・尾張国。天武天皇嘉之。賜封廿戸伝于子。至是、坐殺高田寺僧。下獄奪封。

Tenpyō Hōji 7.10.28 丁酉 *hinoto-tori*

[December 7, 763]

The grandfather of the former Inspector and Clerk Jr 7 Upper Takata no Hitotari had been appointed rice official for Mino Province. In the *Jinshin no Ran* he supplied Emperor Tenmu with horses from Owari and Mino provinces. Tenmu rewarded this and gave Tarihito's grandfather twenty fief households which he

---

[417] SNIII p 441 n 20 The crime was high treason. See note 20 for a discussion of how they were implicated, and the difference between the Tang codes and the Japanese *Ritsu*.
[418] the Tachibana Naramaro conspiracy.

passed down to his sons. However Tarihito killed a priest of *Takataji* and being convicted of the crime he was imprisoned and these households forfeited.

天平宝字七年巻（七六三）十二月己丑【己巳朔廿一】○十二月己丑。摂津。播磨。備前三国飢。並賑給之。

Tenpyō Hōji* 7.12.21 己丑 *tsuchinoto-ushi

[January 28, 764]

Famine in Settsu, Harima and Bizen Provinces. Relief supplies granted.

天平宝字七年（七六三）十二月丁酉【廿九】○丁酉。礼部少輔従五位下中臣朝臣伊加麻呂。造東大寺判官正六位上葛井連根道。伊加麻呂男真助三人、坐飲酒言語渉時忌諱。伊加麻呂左遷大隅守。根道流於隠岐。真助於土左。其告人酒波長歳授従八位下。任近江史生。中臣真麻伎従七位下。但馬員外史生。

Tenpyō Hōji* 7.12.29 丁酉 *hinoto-tori

[February 5, 764]

The Junior Assistant of the Ministry of Rites Jr 5 Lower Nakatomi no Asomi Ikamaro, the Secretary for *Tōdaiji* Construction Sr 6 Upper Fujii no Muraji Nemichi, and Nakatomi's son Masuke all drank sake, and while talking committed some impropriety.[419] Ikamaro was sent to be governor of Ōsumi. Nemichi was exiled to Oki and Masuke to Tosa. The secret informant Sakanami no Osatoshi was awarded Sr 8 Lower Rank, and appointed a lesser clerk of Ōmi. Nakatomi no Mamaki was awarded Jr 7 Lower rank and appointed a lesser clerk of the Tajima Irregular Assistant Governor.

---

[419] SNIII p 443 n 10 – perhaps having to do with Kōken and Dōkyō.

《巻尾続日本紀　巻第廿四

End of *Shoku Nihongi Maki* 24

APPENDIX: Kanji Reference List and Glossary

Abe no Naishinnō 阿倍内親王

Agata Inukai no Tachibana no Michiyo 縣犬養橘 三千世

akitsumikami 現神

amatsuhitsugi 天日嗣

An Rokushan 安禄山 — An Lushan

Anden 安殿 — Hall of Peace in the Middle Palace

Ansatsushi 按察使 — Imperial Investigator

ashiginu 絁 — plain weave silk

Asomi 朝臣

awaseginu 袷衣 — colored silk

Bandō 坂東 — Eastern Provinces (Kantō)

banjō 番上 — officials of the various guards units

Besshiki 別式 — special regulations

Bokkai 渤海 — Parhae

Bonmōkyō 梵網経 — *Brahma's Net Sutra*

bun 分 — extremely small unit of weight for gold or silver

Chibushō 智部省 — Ministry of Wisdom (*Kunaishō*)

Chinju Fukushōgun 鎮守副将軍 — Vice-General, Office for Pacifying *Emishi*

Chinju Gungen 鎮守軍監 — Divisional Commander, Office for Pacifying *Emishi*

Chinju Gunsō 鎮守軍曹 — Regimental Commander, Office for Pacifying *Emishi*

Chinju no Hangan 鎮守判官 — Secretary, Office for Pacifying *Emishi*

Chinju Shōgun 鎮守将軍 — General, Office for Pacifying *Emishi*

Chinkoku Gyōki Shōgun 鎮国驍騎将軍 — General of Cavalry for Pacifying *Emishi*

Chinkokue Gyoki Shōgun 鎮国衛驍騎将軍 — General of Cavalry HQ for Pacifying Emishi

Chinkokue 鎮国衛 — HQ of State Protection Guards (*Chuefu*)

chishiki 知識

Chishikiji 智識寺

chō 町 — hectare

chō 調 — tax in kind

Chōdō 朝堂 — Administrative Palace

Chōkan 長官 — head official

choku 勅 — imperial edict in classical Chinese

Chōyō 重陽 — festival, ninth day of ninth month

Chue Ingai Shōshō 中衛員外少将 — Irregular Minor Captain, Middle Imperial Guards

Chūe Shōshō 中衛少将 — Minor Captain, Middle Imperial Guards

Chue Taishō 中衛大将 — Major Captain, Middle Imperial Guard

Chūefu 中衛府 — Headquarters, Middle Imperial Guards

Chūgū 中宮	Middle Palace in the Heijō Palace
Chūnagon 中納言	Middle Counsellor
Chūzanji 中山寺	
Daianden 大安殿	Hall of Great Peace
Daianji 大安寺	
Daienreki 大衍暦	Dayan Calendar
Daigakuryō 大学寮	Bureau of Education
Daigeki 大外記	Senior Secretary of *Daijōkan*
Daigokuden 大極殿	Imperial Council Hall
Daihanji 大判事	Major Judge
Daiho 大保	Grand Guardian -- Fujiwara no Nakamaro
Daii 大尉	Greater Defender
Daijin/ Ōomi 大臣	Great Minister
Daijō Tennō 太上天皇	Retired Sovereign
Daijo 大掾	Senior Secretary
Daijōdaijin 太政大臣	First Minister of the Great Council of State
Daijōkan 太政官	Great Council of State
Daijōtennō Shami Shōman 太上天皇沙弥勝滿	Buddhist name of Retired Emperor Shōmu
Daikenmotsu 大監物	Senior Inspector
Daikinge 大錦下	Smaller Brocade Lower -- pre-*Ritsuryō* rank
Daikōtaigō 大皇大后	Senior Dowager Empress
Dainagon 大納言	Major Counsellor
Dairi 内裏	Inner Palace
Dairyō 大領	Chief District Magistrate
Daishi 大師	Grand Preceptor – Fujiwara no Nakamaro
Daishi 大志	Greater Recorder
Daishi 大紫	Great Purple - pre-*Ritsuryō* rank.
Daishiguo 大食国	Tang name for Persia/Abbasid Caliphate
Daishikyoku 大史局	Department of the Great Historian (*Onmyōryō*)
Daisho 大初	rank from a pre-*Ritsuryō* system
Daishoku 大織	Greater Woven Cap -- pre-*Ritsuryō* rank
Daisōjō 大僧正	Great Chief Abbott
Daisōzu 大僧都	Senior Assistant Abbott
Daiun 大雲	Great Cloud - pre-*Ritsuryō* rank
Daizen Daibu 大膳大夫	Master, Office of the Palace Table
Daizen Suke 大膳亮	Assistant, Office of the Palace Table
Daizoku 大属	pre-Ritsuryō rank
Danjō Hitsu 弾正弼	Assistant, Board of Censors

Danjō In 弾正尹	Head of Board of Censors
Danjōdai 弾正台	Board of Censors
Dazai Daini 大宰大弐	Senior Assistant Governor-General, Kyushu Headquarters
Dazai Ingaisotsu 大宰員外帥	Irregular Governor-General of Kyushu Headquarters
Dazai Shōni 大宰少弐	Junior Assistant Governor-General, Kyushu Headquarters
Dazai Sotsu 大宰帥	Governor-General, Kyushu Government Headquarters
Dazaifu 大宰府	Kyushu Government Headquarters
denso 田租	rice field tax
dōjō 道場	Buddhist practice halls
Dōkyō 道鏡	
Emi no Oshikatsu 恵美押勝	Fujiwara no Nakamaro
Emon Ingaisuke 衛門員外佐	Irregular Assistant Official, HQ of Outer Palace Guards
Emonfu 衛門府	Headquarters, Outer Palace Guards
enmi 厭魅	one of the Eight Abominations-- sorcery
Etakumi Kami 画工正	Head of Office of Pictorials
fu 符	pronouncement of the *Daijōkan*
fugeki 巫覡	male and female spirit mediums
Fujiwara no Fuhito 藤原不比等	
Fujiwara no Miyako 藤原宮子	
Fujiwara no Nakamaro 藤原仲麻呂	
Fukushi 副使	Vice-Envoy
Gagaku Kami 雅楽頭	Head of the Bureau of Music
Gagakuryō 雅楽寮	Bureau of Music
Gangōji 元興寺	
Ganjin 鑑真	
Genba Kami 玄蕃頭	Head of Bureau of Buddhism and Aliens
Genjōkan 乾政官	Heavenly Council of State - Daijōkan
Genmei *Tennō* 元明天皇	
Genshō *Tennō* 元正天皇	
Gibushō 義部省	Ministry of Righteousness – (Gyōbushō)
Gihōreki 儀鳳暦	Yifeng Calendar
Gosechi Tamae 五節田舞	Five Festivals rice field dance
Gufukuji 弘福寺	
Gunki 軍毅	army commanders
Gyōbushō 刑部省	Ministry of Justice
gyōdō 行道	circumambulation of Buddhist temples or statues
Gyōki 行基	
Gyōki Bodhisattva 行基菩薩	

Gyōki Shōgun 驍騎将軍	General of Cavalry
Gyōshi Daibu 御史大夫	Master of Imperial Scribes (*Dainagon*)
Gyōshin 行信	
Hachigyaku 八虐	Eight Abominations
hafuribe 祝部	Shinto shrine official
Haiga 拝賀	felicitations received by Emperor at New Year
Haitei 廃帝	Deposed Emperor Junnin
Hakase 博士	Learned Scholar
Hakuwata 白綿	white floss silk
Hangan 判官	Secretary
Hayato 隼人	
heihaku 幣帛	Offerings of cloth, bark or paper made only to Shinto shrines
Hidari Ōtoneri Kyō 左大舎人頭	Head of the Left Imperial Attendants
Hidenin 悲田院	Clinic for Compassionate Treatment
hiki 疋	rolls of fabric
Himegami 比売神/比咩神	female consort deity of Usa Hachiman
Hōki 宝亀	770-781
Hokkeji 法花寺	
Hōkō 袍袴	coat and hakama dance
Hokurikudō 北陸道	
Hora no Kyō 保良京	
Hōryūji 法隆寺	
Hōshin 法進	
Hyōbu no Daifu 兵部大輔	Senior Assistant, Ministry of War
Hyōbushō 兵部省	Ministry of War
Hyōbushōfu 兵部少輔	Junior Assistant Ministry of war
Hyōjunshō 平準署	Office of Ever-normal Granaries
Imiki 忌寸	
Imperial Prince Niitabe 新田部親王	a son of Emperor Tenmu
Imperial Prince Toneri 舎人親王	a son of Emperor Tenmu
Inagi 稲置	
ingai 員外	irregular official (extracodal)
Ingaijō 員外掾	Assistant Irregular Governor
Ingaisuke 員外佐	Irregular Assistant Official -- an extracodal office
Ise *Daijingū* 伊勢大神宮	
Ishi 医師	Medical Doctor
Issaikyō 一切經	the complete Buddhist canon
Itsukinomiya 斎宮	Abstinence Hall for Ise Princess

Izumo Kuni no Miyatsuko 出雲国造	Provincial Chieftain of Izumo
Jibu Kyō 治部卿	Head of the Ministry of Civil Administration
Jibushō 治部省	Ministry of Civil Administration.
Jijū 侍従	Chamberlain
Jiki Daiichi 直大壱	Greater Straight First Rank -- pre-*Ritsuryō* rank
Jingi Daifuku 神祇大副	Senior Assistant, Department of Deity Affairs
Jingi Haku 神祇伯	Head, Department of Deity Affairs
Jingi Shōfuku 神祇少副	Junior Assistant, Department of Deity Affairs
Jingikan 神祇官	Department of Deity Affairs
Jingo Keiun 神護景雲	767-770
jōgakuji 定額寺	temples established and supported by the provinces
jōheisō 常平倉	ever-normal granary
Junnin Haitei 淳仁廃帝	Deposed Emperor Junnin
Junsatsushi 巡察使	Regional Inspector
Jūsen Chōkan 鋳銭長官	Director of the Mint
Jutōe 授刀衛	Imperial Bodyguard
kabane 姓	
Kami 守	Governor of a province
kami 神	Shinto deity
Kaminoyatsuko 神奴	Shinto priest
Kamuiwai no Yogoto 神斎賀事	Liturgy read at court by Provincial Chieftain of Izumo
kanbyō zenshi 看病禅師	Healer Meditation Monk
kanfu 官符	*Daijōkan* order
Kannushi/ Kanzukasa 神主	Head Shinto Priest of a shrine
karimiya 行宮	temporary palace
Kasuga Sakadono 春日酒殿	
Kegon Kōshi 華厳講師	lecturer on the *Flower Ornament Sutra*
Kegonkyō 花嚴経/ 華嚴経	*Flower Ornament Sutra*
keka 悔過	repentance rituals
Kentōshi zōshikinin 遣唐使雑色人	lower level officials in the embassy to Tang
Kentōshi 遣唐使	Ambassador to Tang
ketsura 纈羅	dyed silk gauze
Kinai 京畿	
Kōfukuji 興福寺	
Kohone 虎賁衛	HQ of Left and Right Elite Tigers (*Hyōefu*)
Kōken/Shōtoku *Tennō* 孝謙/称徳天皇	
kokki omiogami 国忌御斎	national abstinence rite
koku 斛	bushel

Kokubunji 国分寺	Official Provincial Temples
Kokubun-Konkōmyōji 国分金光明經寺	Official Provincial Temples of the *Golden Light Sutra*
Koma 高麗	old term for Koguryō, used to mean Parhae
Kōmon 閤門	Side Gate -- a south gate of the Imperial Council Hall
Kōmyō Kōgō 光明皇后	
konden 墾田	new paddy
Kongōkyō 金剛般若経	*Diamond Sutra*
Kongūkan 坤宮官	Earthly Palace Council – *Shibi Chūdai*
Kōnin Tennō 光仁天皇	
Konkōji 建興寺	
Konkōmyōkyō 金光明経	*Golden Light Sutra*
Kōsen Yakushiji 香山藥師寺	
Koshi 高志	
Kotaigō 皇大后	Dowager Empress
kubunden 口分田	sustenance rice fields
Kufukuji 弘福寺	
kugetō 公廨稲	government loaned rice
*Kume Ma*i 久米舞	Everlasting Rice dance
Kūnai Kyō 宮内卿	Head of the Ministry of the Imperial Household
Kunaishō 宮内省	Ministry of the Imperial Household
Kuni no Miyatsuko 国造	Provincial Chieftain
Kuranotsukasa 尚蔵寮	Office of Palace Storehouse
Kusuinotsukasa 鼓吹寮	Office of Drums and Fifes
kyaku 格	ordinance -- amendment to *Ritsuryō*
Kyōshun 慶俊	
Kyūseidai In 糺政台尹	Head, Board of Investigation
Kyūseidai 糺政台	Board of Investigation (*Danjōdai*)
Mahito 真人	
Michinoshi 道師	
Mikado 帝	Junnin *Tennō*
Minbu Daifu 民部大輔	Senior Assistant, Ministry of Popular Affairs
Minbukyō 民部卿	Head of the *Minbushō*
Minbushō 民部省	Ministry of Popular Affairs
Misasagi 陵 /山陵	Imperial tomb
mitama 御霊	
mitegura/ nusa 幣	offerings of cloth, bark or paper made only to Shinto shrines
Miyosohi no Tsukasa 御装束司	temporary officials to prepare funerary clothing and supplies
Mokuku no Kami 木工頭	Head of the Carpentry Bureau

Mokuryō no Chōjō 木工寮長上	Head of the Carpentry Bureau
Monbushō 文部省	Ministry of Civil Affairs (*Shikibushō*)
Monminkushi 問民苦使	Special Inspector
Monmu *Tennō* 文武天皇	
Monoimi 物忌	lower level shrine officials at Ise *Daijingū*
Mubushō 武部省	Ministry of Military Affairs (*Hyōbushō*)
Muraji 連	
Myōbō Hakase 明法博士	Learned Scholars of the Law
Myōbu 命婦	Noblewoman of Fifth rank and up
Naidaijin 内大臣	Great Minister of the Middle
Naiin 内院	Inner Pavilion
Naiju 内豎	Imperial Page
Naikyōbō 内教坊	Palace Music School/Female Dancers and Musicians
Naishi Kami 内史頭	Head, Bureau of Books and Drawings
Naishi 内侍典侍	Inner Palace Assistant Head
Naishikyoku 内史局	Department of Palace Classics (*Zushōryō*)
Naiyakushi 内薬司	Palace Medical Office
Naizen Buzen 内膳奉膳	Master, Office of the Imperial Table
Naizenshi 内膳司	Office of the Imperial Table
Nakatsukasa Daifu 中務大輔	Senior Assistant, Ministry of Central Affairs
Nakatsukasa Kyō 中務卿	Head of Ministry of Central Affairs
Nakatsukasa Shō 中務省	Ministry of Central Affairs
Nan'in 南院	Southern Pavilion of Imperial Council Hall
Naniwa Murotsumi 難波館	Official guest house for foreign envoys at Naniwa
Nankaidō 南海道	
Nasihinnō 内親王	Imperial Princess
Negi 禰宜	Shinto shrine official
Ninbushō 仁部省	Ministry of Benevolence (*Minbushō*)
Ninnō-e 仁王会	Ritual for the *Sutra of Humane Kings*
Ninnōkyō 仁王經	*Sutra for Humane Kings*
Nintoku *Tennō* 仁徳天皇	
Nishi no Ichi no Kami 西市正	Head of the Western Market
nishiki 錦	brocade
Nuidonoshi 縫殿司	Wardrobe Office
nuno 布	hemp cloth
Nuribe 漆部司	Lacquer Office
Nyoju 女嬬	lower level female officials of the rear palace
Oharidachō 小治田朝	court of Suiko *Tennō*

Ōi Kami 大炊頭	Head, Bureau of Palace Kitchen
Ōkimi Kami 正親正	Head, Imperial Family Office
Okinagatarashihime Ōkisaki 気長足媛皇太后	Empress Jingū
Ōkōri no Miya 大郡宮	
Ōkura Kyō 大蔵卿	Head of Ministry of the Treasury
Ōkurashō 大蔵省	Ministry of the Treasury
okurina 諡	posthumous name
Omi 臣	
Ōmikaminomiya 大御神宮	*Ise Daijingū*
Ōname 大嘗	Great Thanksgiving Festival
onbotsuden 隠没田	developed land not entered on the registers
Onmyō Kami 陰陽頭	Head, Bureau of *Yin-Yang* Divination
Onmyōji 陰陽師	diviner
Onmyōryō 陰陽寮	Bureau of Yin-Yang Divination
Oribe 織部司	Office of Weaving
Ōtomo no Sukune 大伴宿禰	
Ōtoneri 大舎人	Imperial Attendant
Prince Fune 船王	a son of Imperial Prince Toneri
Prince Ikeda 池田王	a son of Imperial Prince Toneri
Prince Kusakabe 草壁皇子	a son of Emperor Tenmu, husband of Empress Genmei
Prince Minu 美努	father of Tachibana no Moroe
Prince Ōi 炊王	the later Emperor Junnin
Prince Shioyaki 塩焼王	a son of Imperial Prince Niitabe
Reibushō 礼部省	Ministry of Rites (*Jibushō*)
Risshi 律師	Master of Buddhist Precepts
roku 禄	stipend
Rokuefu 六衛府	Six Headquarters of the Guards
Rokuji 録事	Recording Officer
Rushana Buddha 盧舎那佛	Abbr of 毘盧舎那 *Vairocana*
ryō 両	unit of weight, especially for gold or silver -- an "ounce"
ryō 斗	unit of dry volume for grain -- a "peck"
Sabenkan 左弁官	Controlling Board of the Left
Sachūben 左中弁	Middle Controller of the Left
Sadaiben 左大弁	Major Controller of the Left
Sadaijin 左大臣	Great Minister of the Left
Sadaishi 左大史	Senior Recorder of the Left
Saeji Kami 左衛士督	Commander, Left Palace Guards
Saeji Suke 左衛士佐	Assistant Commander, Left Palace Guards

Saejifu 左衛士府	HQ, Left Palace Guards
Saeki no Sukune 佐伯宿禰	
Sahoyama Misasagi 佐保山陵	
Sahyōe Kami 左兵衛率	Head, Left Military Guards
Sahyōefu 左兵衛府	Headquarters, Left Military Guards
Sahyōgo Kami 左兵庫頭	Head of Military Storehouses, Left Division
Saigū Chōgan 斎宮長官	
Saigū Kami 斎宮頭	Head, Office of Ise Princess
Saigū Ōkanzukasa 斎宮大神司	Administrative Shinto Priest for the Ise Princess
saihaku **彩帛**	colored silk
Saiho 宰輔	Fujiwara no Nakamaro
Saikaidō 西海道	
Saiō/ Itsuki no Ōkimi 斎王	High Priestess of Ise Shrine
Sakan 主典	Clerk
Sakan 目	Special Assistant Governor
Sakanohimukashi / Bandō 坂東	Kantō (8 provinces)
Sakimori 防人	Frontier Guards (Coast Guards)
Sakyō Suke 左京亮	Assistant Commisioner, Left Capital
San'indō 山陰道	
San'yōdō 山陽道	
Sangi 参議	Imperial Advisor
Sashōben 左少弁	Minor Controller of the Left
Sauhyōefu 左右兵衛府	HQ, Left and Right Military Guards
Sayūeijifu 左右衛士府	Right and Left Palace Guards
Sayukyō In **左右京尹**	Head Commissioner, Left and Right Capital
senmyō 宣命	imperial edict in Old Japanese
Setsubushō 節部省 –	Ministry of Moderation (*Ōkurashō*)
Setsudoshi 節度使	Official Military Instructors
Settō 節刀	ambassadorial sword
Settsu Daibu 摂津大夫	Commissioner, Settsu Province
Settsu Suke 摂津亮	Settsu Assistant Governor
Seyakuin 施薬院	Medical Dispensary Pavilion at *Yamashinadera*
Shami 沙弥	Buddhist novice
Shamon Bodai 沙門菩提	Bodhisena
Sharamon Sō Bodaisena 沙羅門僧菩提僊那	Bodhisena
Shi 師	Buddhist Teacher
Shibi Chūdai 紫微中台	Office of the Dowager Empress' Household
Shibi Chūdai Shōchū 紫微中台少忠	

Shibi Daichu 紫微大忠	
Shibi Daihitsu 紫微大弼	Senior Assistant, Empress Dowager's Household
Shibi Daiho 紫微大保	Grand Guardian, Empress Dowager's Household
Shibi Naishō 紫微内相	Inner Minister, Empress Dowager's Household
Shibi Shōchū 紫微少忠	
Shibi Shōhitsu 紫微 少弼	
Shibi Shōsho 紫微 少疏	
Shibiryō 紫微令	Head of the *Shibi Chūdai*
Shiemonfu 使司門衛	HQ, Outer Palace Guards (*Emonfu*)
shiki 式	regulation/procedure -- amendment to *Ritsuryō*
Shikibu Daifu 式部大輔	Senior Assistant, Ministry of Ceremonial
Shikibu Kyō 式部卿	Head, Ministry of Ceremonial
Shikibu Shō 式部省	Ministry of Ceremonial
Shikibu Shōfu 式部少輔	Junior Assistant, Ministry of Ceremonial
Shikibushō 式部省	Ministry of Ceremonial
Shimone 司門衛	HQ of the Gatekeepers (*Emonfu*)
Shin Yakushiji 新薬師寺	
Shinbushō 信部省	Ministry of Fidelity (*Nakatsukasa Shō*)
shinobigoto 誄	eulogies
Shiragi 新羅	Silla
Shishō 史生	lower-level provincial headquarters clerk (below *Sakan*)
Shitennōji 四天王寺	
shizume no matsuri/ chinsai 鎮祭	pacification rites
shō 詔	imperial edict in classical Chinese
shō 升	unit of dry volume -- "a dry quart"
shobun 処分	pronouncement of the *Daijōkan*
Shōhanji 少判事	Minor Judge
Shōi 少尉	Lesser Defender
Shokinge 小錦 下	Smaller Brocade Lower -- pre-*Ritsuryō* rank
Shōkinjō 小錦上	Smaller Brocade Upper -- pre-*Ritsuryō* rank
Shōmu *Tennō* 聖武天皇	
Shōnagon 少納言	Minor Counsellor
Shōryō 小領	Assistant District Magistrate
Shōshi 少志	Lesser Recorder
Shōso 少初	pre-*Ritsuryō* rank
Shōsōzu 少僧都	Junior Assistant Abbott
Shotoku 小徳	Second in the 12-rank cap system at *Oharida no Miya*
shōzei 正税	stored tax rice

shōzui 祥瑞	auspicious omen
Shuchō 主帳	district officials of 4th level
Shukei no Kami 主計頭	Head, Bureau of Statistics
Shukeiryō 主計寮	Bureau of Statistics
Shuzai Kami 主税頭	Head, Bureau of Taxation
Shuzeiryō 主税寮	Bureau of Taxation
Sōgō 僧綱	Council of Buddhist Priestly Affairs
Sōjō 僧正	Chief Abbott
soku 束	sheaves
Soshi 小紫	Lesser Purple Cap -- pre-*Ritsuryō* rank
Sotoshimabō 外嶋坊	scriptorium of *Hokkeji*
Sūfukuji 崇福寺	
suguroku 双六	dice game, sometimes translated "backgammon"
suiko 出挙	loan rice
Suke 介 or 亮	Assistant Governor of a province
Suke 次官	Assistant head official
Sukune 宿禰	
Tachibana no Moroe 橘諸兄	
Tachibana no Naramaro 橘奈良麻呂	
Tachihaki Toneri 授刀舎人	Sword-bearing Retainers
Taishi 大使	Ambassador
Taishi 太子	Crown Prince
takamikura 高御座	
Takano Tennō	Empress Kōken/Shōtoku
takusen 託宣	oracle
Tamuratei 田村第	Fujiwara Nakamaro's mansion
tan 端	lengths of fabric
Tango 端五	festival, fifth day of fifth month
Tatefushi 楯伏	swords and shields dance
Ten'yaku Kami 典薬頭	Head of Bureau of Medicine
Ten'yakuryō 典薬寮	Bureau of Medicine
Tenji *Tennō* 天智天皇	
Tenpyō Hoji 天平宝字	757-765
Tenpyō Jingo 天平神護	765-767
Tenpyō Kanpō 天平感寶	749
Tenpyō Shōhō 天平勝宝	749-757
Tenpyō 天平	729-749
Tenzen 典膳	lower level official in the Imperial Table Office
Tō 唐	Tang dynasty China
Tōdaiji 東大寺	

Tofuka 踏歌	Stomping dance (*ararebashi*)
Tōgū Daibu 春宮大夫	Master, Spring Palace of the Crown Prince
Tōin 東院	Eastern Pavilion of the Heijō Palace
Tōkaidō 東海道	
ton 屯	hanks of fabric
Tōsandō 東山道	
Toyosakurahikono Sumera Mikoto 豊櫻彦天皇	Shōmu *Tennō*
Tōzen'in 唐禅院	Tang Meditation Hall at *Tōdaiji*
ubasoku 優婆塞	lay male Buddhist disciple
Uchihito 内人	lower level shrine officials at Ise *Daijingū*
Uchinoiya/ Nairaishi 内礼司	Palace Ceremonies Office
*Uchinokur*a 内蔵	Imperial Storehouse
Uchisomeshi 内染司	Office of Dyeing
Uchitakumi Kami 内匠頭	Head of Craft Industries
Udaiben 右大弁	Major Controller of the Right
Udaijin 右大臣	Great Minister of the Right
Ueji no Kami 右衛士督	Commander, Right Palace Guards
Uhyōe Kyō 右兵衛卿	Commander, Right Military Guards
Uhyōe Suke 右兵衛佐	Assistant Commander, Right Military Guards
Uhyōefu 右兵衛府	Headquarters, Right Military Guards
Uhyōjunryō 右平準令	Head, Right Ever-normal Granary
Ukarehito 浮浪人	vagrant – also furō 浮浪 or rōnin 浪人
Ukyō Daibu 右京大夫	Commissioner of the Right Capital
Ukyō Suke 右京亮	Assistant Commisioner, Right Capital
Uma Kami 右馬頭	Head of Bureau of Horses, Right Division
Uneme Kami. 采女正	Head, Office of Palace Women
Ushōben 右少弁	Minor Controller of the Right
Wajō 和上	Esteemed Monk -- Ganjin
Wajō 和尚	Preceptor -- Gyōki
wata 綿	floss silk
Yakuen no Miya 薬園宮/ 南薬園新宮	a hall in the Nara palace grounds.
Yakushiji 藥師寺	
Yakushikyō 薬師經	*Medicine Master Sutra*
Yamashinadera 山階寺	*Kōfukuji*
Yamato neko sumera ga mikoto 倭根子天皇	
Yamatsukuri no Tsukasa 造山司	temporary officials to oversee construction of the tomb
yashiro 社	Shinto shrines
Yawata Ōkami 八幡大神	Great God *Hachiman*
yō 庸	commuted tax in lieu of annual corvee
Yōmin Tsukasa 養民司	temporay officials to prepare funerary food and clothing

292

Yōyakubu no Tsukasa 養役夫司	temporary officials to provide food for the builders of the tomb
Yugayuishikiron 瑜伽唯識論	a text in the "Consciousness-Only" school
Yūshie 勇士衛	HQ of Brave Warriors (*Ejifu*)
Zengo Shidai Tsukasa 前後次第司	temporary officials to arrange the funeral procession
Zenshi 禅師	Meditation Monk
Zōgū Shōfu 造宮少輔	Junior Assistant for Palace Construction
Zōhōsō no Tsukasa 造方相司	temporary officials to prepare receptacles for funerary offerings
Zōshoku Kami 贓贖正	Head, office for the reclamation of stolen goods.
Zusho Kami 図書頭	Head, Bureau of Books and Drawings
Zushoryō 図書寮	Bureau of Books and Drawings

Bibliography

Primary Sources (Editions of *Shoku Nihongi* and *Senmyō*)

Kundoku Shoku Nihongi. 訓読續日本紀. Ed. Imaizumi Tadayoshi. 今泉忠義. 1933, 1986. Rinkawa Shoten.

Shoku Nihongi. 続日本紀. 1657. (School of) Tateno Harutoki 立野春節[校] . http://www.wul.waseda.ac.jp/kotenseki/html/ri05/ri05_02450_0016/index.html

Shoku Nihongi. 続日本紀.1897. *Kokushi Taikei.* Tokyo: Keizai Zasshisha.

Shoku Nihongi 続日本紀. 1989-1998. Ed. Aoki Kazuo 青木和夫 et al. 5 vols. *Shin Nihon Koten Bungaku Taikei* [SNKBT] 12-16. Iwanami Shoten.

Shoku Nihongi. 続日本紀. 1936, 2000. Ed. Kuroita Katsumi 黑板勝美. 2 vols. In *Shintei zōho Kokushi taikei* 新 訂増補・國史大系. Yoshikawa Kōbunkan.

Shoku Nihongi. 続日本紀. http://www.j-texts.com/jodai/shokuall.html

Shoku Nihongi: Hōsa Bunkobon 続日本紀蓬左文庫本. 1990-93. 5 vols. Yagi Shoten. [facsimile edition]

Shoku Nihongi 続日本紀.1999-2000. 5 vols. Kanzoku Shiryō Henshūkai. Rinkawa Shoten. [facsimile edition]

Shoku Nihongi Senmyō 続日本紀宣命. 1936, 2002. Ed. Kurano Kenji 倉野憲司. Iwanami Shoten.

Shoku Nihongi Senmyō 続日本紀宣命. 1982. Ed. Kitagawa Kazuhide 北川和秀. Yoshikawa Kōbunkan.

Primary Sources (Other)

Hōrei zensho-Meiji 3 (1870). 法令全書.明治３年. 内閣官報局 Naikaku Kanpōkyoku, 1912. Online http://kindai.ndl.go.jp/info:ndljp/pid/787950. National Diet Library, 2002.

Man'yōshū 万葉集. 1999-2003. Edited by Satake Akihiro 佐竹昭広 et al. *Shin Nihon Koten Bungaku Taikei* vols.1-4. Tokyo: Iwanami Shōten,

Nihon Kōki, Shoku Nihon Kōki, Nihon Montoku Tennō Jitsuroku 日本後紀、続日本後紀、日本文徳天皇実録. Ed. Kuroita Katsumi 黒板勝美. In *Kokushi Taikei Henshūkai*, vol 3. Tokyo: Yoshikawa Kobunkan, 1967 --.

Nihon Ryōiki 日本霊異記 1996. Ed. Izumoji Osamu. 出雲路修. Vol. 30 in Shin Nihon Bungaku Taikei. Iwanami Shoten.

Nihon Sandai Jitsuroku 日本三代実録. 1966. Ed. Kuroita Katsumi 黒板勝美. Vol. 4. In *Shintei Zohō Kokushi Taikei*. Yoshikawa Kōbunkan.

Nihon Shoki. 日本書紀. 1994-1995. Ed. Sakamoto Taro 坂本太郎 et al. 5 vols. Iwanami Shoten.

Rekidai shōchoku zenshū. 歴代詔勅全集. 1940-43. Ed. Miura Tōsaku 三浦 藤作 and Takeda Yūkichi 武田 祐吉. 8 vols. Kawade Shobō. Online http://kindai.ndl.go.jp/info:ndljp/pid/1041465. National Diet Library, 2002.

Ritsuryō 律令. 1976. Ed. Inoue Mitsusada 日本思想大系. Vol. 3. In *Nihon Shisō Taikei*. Iwanami Shoten.

Shinshaku Kanbun Taikei 新釈漢文大系, Tokyo: Meiji Shōin, 1972-.

Translations into modern Japanese

Kan'yaku-chūshaku Shoku Nihongi 完訳注釈続日本紀. Hayashi Rokurō 林陸郎. 1985-1989. Ed. and trans. 7 vols. Gendai Shichōsha.

Shoku Nihongi 続日本紀. 1986-1992. Ed. and trans, Naoki Kōjirō 直木孝二郎. 4 vols. Heibonsha.

Shoku Nihongi 続日本紀. 1992-1995. Ed. and trans, Ujitani Tsutomu 宇治谷孟. 3 vols. Kōdansha.

Yomikudashi Nihon Sandai Jitsuroku 読み下し日本三代実録. 1935, 2009. Ed. and trans. Takeda Yūkichi 武田祐吉 and Satō Kenzō 佐藤謙三. 2 vols. Fukkokuban.

Secondary Sources

Abe Takeshi 阿部 猛, ed. 1995. *Nihon Kodai Kanshoku Jiten* 日本 古代 官職 辞典. Takashina Shoten.

Aihara Seiji 相原精次. 2003. *Tenpyō no haha, Tenpyō no ko* 天平の母 天平の子. Sairyūsha.

Antoni, Klaus. 2012. *Kojiki: Aufzeichnung alter Begebenheiten*. Verlag der Weltreligionen.

Aoki Kazuo. 青木和夫. 1973. *Nara no Miyako*. 奈良の都. Chuōkōron.

Aston, W.G. 1896, 1956. *Nihongi: Chronicles of Japan from the Earliest Times to A.D. 697*. George Allen and Unwin, Ltd.

Augustine, Jonathan Morris. 2005. *Buddhist Hagiography in Early Japan: Images of Compassion in the Gyōki Tradition*. RoutledgeCurzon.

Batchelor, Martine, trans. *The Path of Compassion: The Brahma's Net Sutra*. Rowman and Littlefield.

Bauer, Mikael. 2011. The Yuima-e as Theatre of the State. *Japanese Journal of Religious Studies* 38:161-179.

Bender, Ross. 1979. The Hachiman Cult and the Dōkyō Incident. *Monumenta Nipponica* 34/2: 125-53.

Bender, Ross. 1980. The Political Meaning of the Hachiman Cult in Ancient and Early Medieval Japan. Dissertation, Columbia University.

Bender, Ross. 2009. Performative Loci of the Imperial Edicts in Nara Japan, 749-70. *Oral Tradition*, 24/1: 249-68.

Bender, Ross. 2010. Changing the Calendar: Royal Political Theology and the Suppression of the Tachibana Naramaro Conspiracy of 757. *Japanese Journal of Religious Studies*, 37/2: 223-45.

Bender, Ross. 2012. Emperor, Aristocracy, and the *Ritsuryō* State: Court Politics in Nara. In *Japan Emerging: Premodern History to 1850*, ed. Karl F. Friday, 111-121. Westview Press.

Bender, Ross. 2013. Auspicious Omens in the Reign of the Last Empress of Nara Japan, 749-770. *Japanese Journal of Religious Studies*, 40/1: 45-76.

Bender, Ross. 2015. *The Edicts of the Last Empress, 749-770: A Study and Translation of Senmyō 12-47 in Shoku Nihongi*. CreateSpace.

Bender, Ross. 2015. *Nara Japan, 749-770: A Study and Translation of Shoku Nihongi, Tenpyō Shōhō 1- Tenpyō Hōji 1*. CreateSpace.

Bender, Ross and Zhao Lu. 2010. Research Note – A Japanese Curriculum of 757. *PMJS Papers*.

Bentley, John R. 2001. *A Descriptive Grammar of Early Old Japanese Prose*. Brill.

Bentley, John R. 2002. *Historiographical Trends in Early Japan*. Edwin Mellen Press.

Birnbaum, Raoul. 1979. *The Healing Buddha*. Shambala.

Bock, Felicia. 1970, 1972. *Engi-Shiki: Procedures of the Engi Era [Books I-V],[Books VI-X]*. Sophia University.

Breen, John and Mark Teeuwen, ed. 2000. *Shinto in History: Ways of the Kami*. University of Hawai'i Press.

Breen, John and Mark Teeuwen. 2010. *A New History of Shinto*. Wiley-Blackwell.

Buswell, Robert E. and Donald S. Lopez, eds. 2014. *The Princeton Dictionary of Buddhism*. Princeton University Press.

Cleary, Thomas, trans. 1993. *The Flower Ornament Sutra: A Translation of the Avatamsaka Sutra*. Boston and London: Shambhala.

Coaldrake, William H. 1991. City Planning and Palace Architecture in the Creation of the Nara Political Order: The Accommodation of Place and Purpose at *Heijōkyō*." *East Asian History* 1:37-54.

Cranston, Edwin A. 1993. Ed. and trans. *A Waka Anthology, Vol. 1: The Gem-glistening Cup*. Stanford University Press.

Crump, James L. 1952. Borrowed T'ang Titles and Offices in the Yōrō Code. *Occasional Papers of the Michigan Center for Japanese Studies* 2: 35-58.

Crump, James L. 1953. T'ang Penal Law in Early Japan. *Occasional Papers of the Michigan Center for Japanese Studies* 4: 91-102.

de Bary, Wm. Theodore et al.,eds. 2001. *Sources of Japanese Tradition, Volume I: From Earliest Times to 1600*. New York: Columbia University Press.

Dettmer, Hans A. 2010. *Der Yōrō Kodex: Die Gebote. Übersetzung des Ryō no Gige. Teil 2: Bücher 2-10*. Harrassowitz Verlag.

De Visser, M. W. 2006. *Ancient Buddhism in Japan: Sutras and Ceremonies in Use in the Seventh and Eighth Centuries AD and Their History in Later Times*. Martino Publishing.

Dobashi Makoto 土橋誠. 2005. Junnin Tennō: Honrō sareta Kairai no Mikado 淳仁天皇−ほんろうされた傀儡の帝, in *Heijōkyō no Rakujitsu* 平城京の落日, ed. Sakaehara Towao 栄原永遠男, 44-65. Seibundō.

Duncan, John, trans. 2012. *A New History of Parhae*. (Northeast Asian History Foundation. 2005) *Parhae ui yoksa wa munwha*). Global Oriental.

Duthie, Torquil. 2014. *Man'yōshū and the Imperial Imagination in Early Japan*. Brill.

Elisséeff, Serge. 1936. The *Bonmōkyō* and the Great Buddha of the Tōdaiji. *Harvard Journal of Asian Studies* 1:84-95.

Ellwood, Robert S. 1973. *The Feast of Kingship: Accession Ceremonies in Ancient Japan*. Sophia University.

Emmerick, R.E. 1970, 2004. *The Sūtra of Golden Light: Being a translation of the Suvarṇabhāsottamasūtra*. Oxford: The Pali Text Society.

Encyclopedia of Shinto. Online: http://eos.kokugakuin.ac.jp/modules/xwords/

Enomoto Jun'ichi 榎本淳一. 2013. Fujiwara no Nakamaro seiken ni okeru Tōbunka no juyō 藤原仲麻呂政権における唐文化の受容. In *Fujiwara no Nakamaro Seiken to Sono Jidai* 藤原仲麻呂 政権とその時代, ed. Kimoto Yoshimoto 木本好信, 20-43. Iwata Shoin.

Farris, William Wayne. 1985. 1985. *Population, Disease and Land in early Japan, 645-900*. Harvard University Press.

Farris, William Wayne. 1998a. *Sacred Texts and Buried Treasures: Issues in the Historical Archaeology of Ancient Japan*. University of Hawaii Press.

Farris, William Wayne. 1998b. Trade, Money and Merchants in Nara Japan. *Monumenta Nipponica*, 53/3:303-334.

Farris, William Wayne. 2007. Pieces in a Puzzle: Changing Approaches to the *Shōsōin* Documents. *Monumenta Nipponica*, 62/4: 397-435.

Frellesvig, Bjarke. 2010. *A History of the Japanese Language*. Cambridge University Press.

Frellesvig, Bjarke; Horn, Stephen Wright; Russell, Kerri L; and Sells, Peter. *The Oxford Corpus of Old Japanese: Digital online text*. http://vsarpj.orinst.ox.ac.uk/corpus/

Friday, Karl F. 1992. *Hired Swords: The Rise of Private Warrior Power in Early Japan*. Stanford University Press.

Guisso, R. W. L. 1978. *Wu Tse-T'ien and the politics of legitimation in T'ang China.* Western Washington University.

Hayakawa Shōhachi 早川庄八.1993. *Shoku Nihongi* 続日本紀. Iwanami Shoten.

Hayakawa Shōhachi 早川庄八.1997. *Nihon Kodai Monjo to Tenseki* 日本古代の文書と典籍. Yoshikawa Kōbunkan.

Hayashi Rokurō 林陸郎. 1961. *Kōmyō Kōgō* 光明皇后. Yoshikawa Kōbunkan.

Heldt, Gustav, trans. 2014. *The Kojiki: An Account of Ancient Matters.* Columbia University Press.

Hirabayashi Akihito 平林章仁. 2015. *Tennō wa itsukara Tennō ni natta ka?* 天皇はいつから天皇になってか? Shōdensha.

Holcombe, Charles. 1999. The Confucian Monarchy of Nara Japan. In *Religions of Japan in Practice*, ed. Tanabe, George Jr., 293-98. Princeton: Princeton University Press.

Hon Sunchan 洪淳昶. 1981. Kan-Nichi kōshōshi kenkyū josetsu 韓日交渉史研究序說. In *Shiragi to Nihon Kodai Bunka* 新羅と日本古代文化, ed. Tamura Enchō 田村円澄, 301-327. Yoshikawa Kōbunkan.

Hosoi Hiroshi 細井浩志. 2002. Tenmondō to rekidō: Kodai ni okeru seiritsu no haikei to sono yakuwari. 天文道と暦道 ー 古代にお成立お背景とその役割. In *Onmyōdō no Kōgi* 陰陽道の講義, ed. Hayashi Makoto 林淳 and Koike Jun'ichi 小池淳一, 23-43. Sagano Shoin.

Hosoi Hiroshi 細井浩志. 2007. *Kodai no tenmon to shisho*. 古代の天文異変と史書.Yoshikawa Kōbunkan.

Hucker, Charles O. 1985. *A Dictionary of Official Titles in Imperial China.* Stanford University Press.

Inoue Hiroshi. 井上寛司. 2011. *"Shintō" no kyozō to jitsuzō.* 「神道」の虚像と実像. Kōdansha.

Inoue Hiroshi. 井上寛司. 2014. Trans. by Paul B. Watt. Japan's *Ritsuryō* System and Shintō Shrines Arose as Twins. *Journal of Religion in Japan*, 3/1: 36-46.

Jay, Jennifer W. 1996. Imagining Matriarchy. "Kingdoms of Women" in Tang China. *Journal of the American Oriental Society*, 116/2:220-29.

Johnson, Wallace Stephen. 1979. *The T`ang Code / Translated with an Introduction by Wallace Johnson*. Princeton University Press. (two volumes)

Katsuura, Noriko. 勝浦 令子. 2014. *Kōken shōtoku tennō: shukkeshitemo matsurigoto o okonau ni ani sawarazu* 孝謙・称徳天皇：出家しても政を行ふに豈障らず. Mineruva Shobō.

Kimoto Yoshinobu 木本好信. 1992. Tachibana Moroe to Naramaro Hen 橘諸兄と奈良麻呂の変. In *Nihon Shigaku Shuroku*, 14:1-5.

Kimoto Yoshinobu 木本好信. 2011. *Fujiwara no Nakamaro: sossei wa satoku kashikoku shite.* 藤原仲麻呂：率性は聡く敏くして. Mineruva Shobō.

Kimoto Yoshinobu 木本好信. 2012. *Nara Jidai no Seisō to Kōi Keishō.* 奈良時代の政争と皇位継承.Yoshikawa Kōbunkan.

Kimoto Yoshinobu 木本好信. 2013. *Fujiwara no Nakamaro Seiken to Sono Jidai.* 藤原仲麻呂政権とその時代. Iwata Shoin.

Kakehi Toshio. 2002. 筧敏生. *Kodai Ōken to Ritsuryō Kokka.* 古代王権と律令国家. Azekura Shobo.

Keene, Donald. 1999. *Seeds in the heart: Japanese literature from earliest times to the late sixteenth century*. Columbia University Press.

Kishi Toshio 岸俊男. 1969. *Fujiwara no Nakamaro* 藤原仲麻呂. Yoshikawa Kōbunkan.

Knechtges, David R. 2005. The Rhetoric of Imperial Abdication and Accession in a Third-Century Chinese Court: The Case of Cao Pi's Accession as Emperor of the Wei Dynasty. In *Rhetoric and the Discourses of Power in Court Culture*, ed. David Knechtges and Eugene Vance, 3-35. University of Washington Press.

Ko, Dorothy, JaHyun Kim Haboush, and Joan R. Piggott. 2003. *Women and Confucian cultures in premodern China, Korea, and Japan*. University of California Press.

Kōchi Haruhito 河内春人. 2013. Hendō no yochō: Fujiwara no Nakamaro seiken kangō kaieki no kokusaiteki hikaku 変動の予兆−藤原仲麻呂政権官号官号改易の国際的比較. In *Fujiwara no Nakamaro Seiken to Sono Jidai* 藤原仲麻呂　政権とその時代, ed. Kimoto Yoshimoto 木本好信, 89-110. Iwata Shoin.

Kuroda Toshio 黒田俊雄. 1981. Trans. by James C. Dobbins and Suzanne Gay. Shinto in the history of Japanese religion. *Journal of Japanese Studies*, 7/1: 1-21.

Lewin, Bruno and Horst Hammitzsch, ed. and trans. 1962. *Rikkokushi,die amtlichen Richsannalen japans.* Tokyo: Deutsche Gesellschaft fur Natur- und Voĺkerkunde Ostasiens. Kommissionsverlag O. Harrassowitz. [Die RegierungsannalenKammu-Tenno: Shoku-Nihongi 36-40 und Nihon-Koki 1- 13 (780-806)]

Linn, John Kenneth. 1950. "The Imperial Edicts of the Shoku-Nihongi: An Annotated Translation of Edicts ##30-62." Dissertation, Yale University.

Lowe, Bryan Daniel. 2012a. Rewriting Nara Buddhism: Sutra Transcription in Nara Japan. Dissertation. Princetion University.

Lowe, Bryan D. 2012b. The Discipline of Writing: Scribes and Purity in Eighth-Century Japan. *Japanese Journal of Religious Studies,* 39/2: 201–39.

Lowe, Bryan D. 2014a. Contingent and Contested: Preliminary Remarks on Buddhist Catalogs and Canons in Early Japan. *Japanese Journal of Religious Studies*, 42/1:221-253.

Lowe, Bryan D. 2014b. States of "State Buddhism": History, Religion, and Politics in Late Nineteenth and Twentieth-Century Scholarship. *Japanese Religions*, 39/1&2: 71-93.

Lurie, David B. 2011. *Realms of Literacy: Early Japan and the History of Writing.* Harvard University Press.

Martin, Samuel E. 1987. *The Japanese Language Through Time.* Yale University Press.

Meshcheryakov, A.N. 1983. Correspondence. *Monumenta Nipponica*, 38/1: 85-89.

Meshcheryakov, Alexander. 2008. Emperor Shōmu: Slave of Buddha or Faithful Servant of Shinto Gods? In *Symbolic Languages in Shinto Tradition*, ed. Shinto Kokusai Gakkai, 33-41. Tokyo: International Cultural Workshop.

Mescheryakov, Alexander. 2006, 2011, 2012. Ed. and trans. *Shoku Nihongi (Vols 1-3).* History and culture of ancient Japan. *Proceedings of the Institute of Oriental Cultures and Antiquity*. Russian State University for the Humanities.Сёку нихонги. / пер. и коммент. А.Н. Мещерякова // История и культура традиционной Японии (Orientalia et Classica: Труды Института восточных культур и античности). М: РГГУ.

Migliore, Maria Chiara. 2008."Un caso di mistificazione storiografica: Kōken-Shōtoku tennō", in Luisa Bienati & Matilde Mastrangelo, eds., *Un'isola in levante. Saggi sul Giappone in onore di Adriana Boscaro*, Napoli, Scriptaweb, 135-146.

Miller, Richard J. 1974. *Ancient Japanese Nobility: The Kabane Ranking System.* University of California Press.

Miller, Richard J. 1978. *Japan's First Bureaucracy*: *A Study of Eighth-Century Government.* Cornell University East Asian Program Monograph.

Miyake, Marc Hideo. 2003. *Old Japanese: A Phonetic Reconstruction.* Routledge.

Motoori Norinaga 本居宣長. 1971. *Motoori Norinaga Zenshū* 本居宣長全集 Ed. Ōno Susumu 大野晋. Chikuma Shobō, 1968-1993. *Shokki rekichō shōshikai* 続紀歴朝詔詞解 in Vol. 7, 189-478.

Muller, A. Charles. *Digital Dictionary of Buddhism/CKJV-English Dictionary.* http://www.buddhism-dict.net/ddb/

Nakamura Kyoko Motomachi, ed. and trans. 1973. *Miraculous stories from the Japanese Buddhist tradition; the Nihon ryoiki of the monk Kyokai.* 1973**.** Harvard University Press.

Nakanishi Yasuhiro. 中西康裕. 2000. "*Shoku Nihongi' to jitsuroku* 続日本紀と実録. *Shoku Nihongi Kenkyū* 328: 1-12.

Nakanishi Yasuhiro. 中西康裕. 2002. *Shoku Nihongi to Narachō no Seihen* 続日本紀と奈良朝の政変. Yoshikawa Kōbunkan.

Naoki Kōjirō 直木孝次郎. 2000. *Man'yōshū to Kodaishi* 万葉集と古代史. Yoshikawa Kōbunkan.

Naoki Kōjirō 直木孝次郎. 2009. *Nara no Miyako* 奈良の都. Yoshikawa Kōbunkan.

Nelson, Steven G. 2008. Court and Religious Music (1): History of *Gagaku* and *Shōmyō.* In *The Ashgate Research Companion to Japanese Music,* ed. Alison McQueen Tokita and David W. Hughes, 35-48. Ashgate.

Nemoto Seiji 根本誠二. 1999. *Nara Jidai no Sōryo to Shakai.* 奈良時代の僧侶と社会. Yūzankaku.

Nishimoto Yasuhiro 西本昌弘. 2004.Kōken/Shōtoku *Tennō* no Saigū to Hōtō Ikō 孝謙/称徳天皇の西宮と宝幢遺構, in *Shoku nihongi no shosō: Sōritsu gojisshūnen kinen* 続

303

日本紀の諸相:創立五十周年記念, ed. Shoku Nihongi Kenkyūkai, 273-293.Hanawa Shobō.

Omodaka Hisataka 澤瀉久孝 et al. 1967. *Jidaibetsu Kokugo Daijiten – Jōdaihen* 時代別国語大辞典一上代偏.Tokyo: Sanseidō.

On-line Glossary of Japanese Historical Terms. Historiographical Institute, University of Tokyo. http://wwwap.hi.u-tokyo.ac.jp/ships/db-e.html.

Orzech, Charles D. 1998. *Politics and Transcendent Wisdom: the Scripture for Humane Kings in the Creation of Chinese Buddhism*. Pennsylvania State Univesity Press.

Philippi, Donald L. 1969. *Kojiki: Translated with an Introduction and Notes*. Princeton University Press, University of Tokyo Press.

Philippi, Donald L.1990. *Norito: A Translation of the Ancient Japanese Ritual Prayers*. Princeton University Press. (originally published 1959)

Piggott, Joan. 1989. Sacral Kingship and Confederacy in Early Izumo. *Monumenta Nipponica* 44:1, 45-74.

Piggott, Joan R. 1997. *The Emergence of Japanese Kingship*. Stanford: Stanford University Press.

Piggott, Joan. 2003. The Last Classical Female Sovereign: Kōken-Shōtoku Tennō. In *Women and Confucian Cultures in China, Korea, and Japan*, ed. Dorothy Ko, JaHyun Kim Haboush, and Joan Piggott, 47-74. University of California Press.

Pulleyblank, Edwin G. 1995. *Outline of Classical Chinese Grammar*. University of British Columbia Press.

Reischauer, Jean and Robert Karl. 1937, 1967. *Early Japanese History, c. 40 BC – AD 1167*. 2 vols. Peter Smith.

Rothschild, Norman Harry. 2006. An Inquiry into Reign Era Changes Under Wu Zhao, China's Only Female Emperor." *Early Medieval China* 12: 123-49.

Ruch, Barbara, ed. 2002. *Engendering faith: women and Buddhism in premodern Japan*. University of Michigan.

Saeki Umetomo 佐伯うめとも. 1954. *Nara Jidai no Kokugo* 奈良時代の国語. Tokyo: Sanseido Shuppansha.

Saitō Tōru 斎藤融. 1995. Funado ō ritsutaishi ni tsuite no ichi kōsatsu: 道祖王立太子についての考察. In Toshiya Torao 虎尾俊哉, ed. *Ritsuryō Kokka no Seimu no Girei* 律令国家の政務と儀礼, 2-25. Yoshikawa Kōbunkan.

Sakaehara Towao 栄原永遠男. 1991. *Tenpyō no Jidai.* Shūeisha.

Sakaehara Towao 栄原永遠男. 2011. *Shōsōin monjo nyumon.* 正倉院文書入門. Kadokawa Gakugei Shuppan.

Sakamoto Tarō 坂本太郎. 1970. *Rikkokushi* 六国史. Yoshikawa Kōbunkan.

Sakamoto Tarō 坂本太郎. 1991. *The Six National Histories of Japan.* Trans. John Brownlee 1991, University of British Columbia Press.

Sasayama Haruo 笹山晴生 and Yoshimura Takehiko 吉村武彦. 2000. *Shoku Nihongi Sakuin Nenpyo.* 続日本紀索引年表. Shin Nihon Koten Bungaku Taikei [*bekkan*]. Iwanami Shoten.

Sansom, George. 1924. The Imperial Edicts in the *Shoku Nihongi. Transactions of the Asiatic Society of Japan,* (2nd series, Issue 1), 5-40.

Scheid, Bernhard. 2014a. Wer Schūtz Wen? Hachimanismus, Buddhismus, und Tennōismus im Altertum. *Asiatische Studien/ Etudes Asiatiques* 68/1: 263–284.

Scheid, Bernhard. 2014b. Shōmu Tennō and the Deity from Kyushu: Hachiman's Initial Rise to Prominence. *Japan Review* 27:31-51.

Schemm, Matthias. *Nengo-Calc.* http://www.yukikurete.de/nengo_calc.htm.

Schultz, Edward J. and Hugh H.W. Kang 2012, trans. *The Silla Annals of the Samguk Sagi,* by Kim Pusik. Academy of Korean Studies Press.

Snellen, J. B. 1934, 1937. *Shoku Nihongi*: Chronicles of Japan, continued, from 697-791 A.D.: Translated and annotated by J. B.Snellen. *Transactions of the Asiatic Society of Japan, Second Series* 11, (1934), 151-239; 14 (1937), 209-28.

Taira Ayumi 平あゆみ. 1990. Kibumi Ō Tei'i Keishō Kibō to Tachibana Naramaro no Hen 黄文王帝位継承企謀と橘奈良麻呂の変. *Seiji Keizaishigaku* 政治経済史学 287: 1-12.

Takashima Masato 高島正人. 1997. *Fujiwara no Fuhito* 藤原不比等. Yoshikawa Kōbunkan.

Takinami Sadako 瀧浪貞子.1998. *Saigo no jotei: Kōken Tennō*.
最後の女帝孝謙天皇. Yoshikawa Kōbunkan.

Takinami Sadako 瀧浪貞子. 2004. *Josei tennō* 女性天皇. Shūeisha.

Takinami Sadako 瀧浪貞子. 2013. *Narachō no seihen to Dōkyō* 奈良朝の政変と道鏡.
Yoshikawa Kōbunkan.

Tamura Enchō 田村円澄 and Chin, Hong-sap 秦弘燮. 1981. *Shiragi to Nihon Kodai Bunka*. 新羅と日本古代文化. Yoshikawa Kōbunkan.

Teeuwen, Mark. 2002. From Jindō to Shinto: A concept takes shape. *Japanese Journal of Religious Studies*, 29/3-4, 233-63.

Teeuwen, Mark and Bernhard Scheid. 2002. Tracing Shinto in the history of kami worship: Editors' Introduction. *Japanese Journal of Religious Studies*, 29/3-4, 195-207.

Teeuwen, Mark. 2012. What Used to be Called Shinto: The Question of Japan's Indigenous Religion. In Karl F. Friday, ed. *Japan Emerging: Premodern History to 1850*, 66-76.

Tokoro Isao 所巧. 1996. *Nengō no Rekishi: Gengō Seido no Shiteki Kenkyū* 年号の歴史: 元号制度の 史的研究. Yūzankaku Shuppan.

Tōno Haruyuki 東野治之.1999. *Kentōshisen: Higashi Ajia no naka de* 遣唐使船: 東アジアのなかで. Asahi Shinbunsha.

Tōno Haruyuki東野治之. 2007. *Kentōshi* 遣唐使. Iwanami Shoten.

Tonomura Hitomi, Anne Walthall, and Wakita Haruko, eds. 1999. *Women and Class in Japanese History*. University of Michigan Press.

Tsumura, Susan. 2012. Adjusting Calculations to Ideals in the Chinese and Japanese Calendars. In Ben-Dov, Jonathan., Wayne Horowitz and John M.Steele (eds), *Living the Lunar Calendar*, 349-72. Oxbow Books.

Ueda Masaaki 上田正昭. 1973, 2006. *Kodai Nihon no Jotei*.古代日本の女帝.
Kōdansha.

Ueda Masaaki 上田正昭 et al., ed. 2006. *Nihon Kodaishi Daijiten*. 日本古代史大辞典.
Tokyo: Daiwashobō.

Ueda Takeshi 上田雄. 2004. *Bokkaikoku* 渤海国. Kodansha.

von Verschuer, Charlotte. 2006. *Across the Perilous Sea: Japanese Trade with China and Korea from the Seventh to the Sixteenth Centuries*. Trans. Kristen Lee Hunter. Cornell East Asia Series.

Vovin, Alexander. 2005. *The Descriptive and Comparative Grammar of Old Japanese. Part 1: Sources, Script and Phonology, Lexicon, Nominals*. Global Oriental.

Vovin, Alexander. 2009. *The Descriptive and Comparative Grammar of Old Japanese. Part2: Adjectives, Verbs, Adverbs, Conjunctions, Particles, Postpositions*. Global Oriental.

Vovin, Alexander. 2009-2016. *Man'yōshū: A New English Translation containing the Original Text, Kana Transliteration, Romanization, Glossing and Commentary*. (Books 5, 14, 15, 17, 20.) Global Oriental/Brill.

Wang Zhenping. 2013. *Tang China in Multi-Polar Asia: A History of Diplomacy and War*. University of Hawai'i Press.

Waterhouse, David. 1991. Where did *Toragaku* come from? In Marett, Allan, ed. *Musica Asiatica* 6:73-94. Cambridge University Press.

Watson, Burton, ed. and trans. 2013. *Record of miraculous events in Japan: the Nihon ryoiki*. Columbia University Press.

Watanabe Ikuko 渡部育子. 2010. *Genmei Tennō, Genshō Tennō: masani ima, toyū o tatsubeshi*. 元明天皇・元正天皇 ： まさに今，都邑を建つべし. Mineruva Shobō.

Yermakova, L.M. 2006. Imperial edicts as a genre of ancient Japanese literature: The political culture of ancient Japan. *Orientalia et Classica. Proceedings of the Institute of Oriental Cultures and Antiquity*. Moscow: Russian State University for the Humanities, 2006, Issue VII, p.66-80. Unpublished translation by Ekaterina Komova, 2013.

Yoshie Akiko. 義江明子. 2009. *Agata no Inukai no Tachibana no Michiyo*. 県犬養橘三千代.Yoshikawa Kōbunkan.

Yoshie Takashi 吉江崇. 2010. Kōi to shite no *Senmyō* to *Kushikiryō Shōshoshiki* 行為としての宣命と公式令詔書式. In *Ritsuryō kokka shironshū* 律令国家史論集. ed Sakaehara Towao 栄原永遠男 et al. Tokyo: Hanawa Shobō.

Yokota Ken'ichi 横田健一. 1967.Tachibana Moroe to Naramaro 橘諸兄と奈良麻呂. *Rekishi Kyōiku* 歴史教育 15/4: 34-43.

Watt, Paul B. 2012. Review of Inoue Hiroshi *'Shinto' no kyozō to jitsuzō*. *Journal of Religion in Japan*, 1:247-76.

Wilkinson, Endymion Porter. 2000. *Chinese History: a Manual* . Harvard University Press.

Zachert, Herbert. 1950. *Senmyō: Die kaiserlichen Erlasse des Shoku-Nihongi.* Akademie-Verlag.

Photos by the author

Cover – *Daigokuden*, Nara 2012

Back Cover – *Tōdaiji*, Nara 2013

CPSIA information can be obtained at www.ICGtesting.com
Printed in the USA
BVOW09s0615240616

453318BV00018B/59/P